The Year the RED SOX Won the Series

The Year the RED SOX Won the Series

A Chronicle of the 1918 Championship Season

Ty Waterman and Mel Springer

Northeastern University Press

Library of Congress Cataloging-in-Publication Data
Waterman, Ty, 1948–
    The year the Red Sox won the Series / Ty Waterman and Mel Springer
       p. cm.
    A compilation of newspaper columns and cartoons from 1918, with commentary.
    Includes bibliographical references and index.
    ISBN 1-55553-381-7 (alk. paper)
    1. Boston Red Sox (Baseball team)—History. 2. Newspapers—Sections, columns, etc.—Sports. I. Springer, Mel. II. Title.
GV875.B62W36   1999
796.357'64'0974461—dc21   98-47871

Designed and composed by Sherry Fatla

Printed and bound by Quebecor Printing, Kingsport, Tennessee.
The paper is Fox River Evergreen Matte, an acid-free sheet.

MANUFACTURED IN THE UNITED STATES OF AMERICA
03 02 01 00 99   5 4 3 2 1

TO HARRY AND JOHN HOOPER

They Followed Their Quest

ACKNOWLEDGMENTS

We are grateful to the many people who have assisted us during the five years we have written and researched this book. Our thanks to:

the staff of the Microtext, Humanities, and Social Science Research departments, and the Research Library Office, all of the Boston Public Library (especially Henry Scannell, for his research expertise, and John Dorsey, for photographing the cartoons);

the staff of Harvard University's Lamont Library and the Sharon Public Library;

John Hooper and Harry Frazee III for their historical perspective and enthusiasm for our project;

Alice Springer for her assistance and support throughout this five-year project, editing our manuscripts and critiquing our drafts;

Ed Bacon, a Virginia sportswriter, for his helpful suggestions in the early stages of the writing of our book;

Dan Shaughnessy, a prominent sportswriter with the *Boston Globe*, who wrote the foreword;

Andrew Rock for his guidance and support;

the researchers and librarians at the National Baseball Library at the Hall of Fame at Cooperstown, New York—they were the last word when we encountered discrepancies in our statistical sources;

the many sportswriters whose contributions are included in our book (for the most part, we have printed their words without modification; on occasion we have edited or abridged their articles for the sake of clarity)—they told the real story of the 1918 Boston Red Sox;

and, finally, John Weingartner, Allison Morse, and Ann Twombly of Northeastern University Press for believing in our book.

We wish to extend thanks to the following sources:

the Boston Red Sox for photographs of Sam Agnew, Ed Barrow, Dutch Leonard, Stuffy McInnis, and Dave Shean from the Charles Conlin collection, and for allowing us to use the August 26, 1993, press release;

Harry Frazee III for a photograph of Harry Frazee;

John Hooper for the photographs of Harry Hooper and Walter Johnson, and Harry Hooper's 1918 World Series emblem, and for allowing us to reprint his father's May 10, 1973, letter to Bowie Kuhn;

the National Baseball Hall of Fame Library, Cooperstown, New York, for photographs of Ban Johnson, Sam Jones, Carl Mays, Everett Scott, Hippo Vaughn, and George Whiteman;

the Society for American Baseball Research for photographs of Wally Schang and Dutch Leonard from the Ottoson Photo Archive;

Transcendental Graphics for a photograph of Ty Cobb;

the Trustees of the Boston Public Library for photographs of Johnny Evers, Connie Mack, and Lefty Tyler;

and Bob Wood for photographs of Babe Ruth, Tris Speaker, Smoky Joe Wood, and the 1918 Boston Red Sox.

CONTENTS

PHOTOGRAPHS

FOREWORD

Sports libraries are stocked with a tonnage of tomes relating to the Boston Red Sox. Everyone from Ken Burns to John Updike has spun his or her version of Red Sox lore. More has been written—and written well—about this team than about any other. Not even the championship-glutted New York Yankees have inspired the proliferation of prose that's been showered on Boston's long-suffering American League franchise.

All of the above makes one skeptical about any new book on the Red Sox, but it turns out that Massachusetts natives Mel Springer and Ty Waterman have found something old and new to say about the old Boston Red Sox. *The Year the Red Sox Won the Series* explains so much about where the Red Sox have been and why they are still important to us today.

All good New England sports fans know the sad saga of the Sox as well as they know "The Midnight Ride of Paul Revere." Boston was a charter member of the upstart American League in 1901 and dominated major league baseball for a decade and a half, winning five of the first fifteen World Series. When Babe Ruth pitched the Sox to a six-game World Series victory over the Cubs in 1918, there was every expectation that the Red Sox would remain a perennial power in America's favorite professional sport. But Boston owner Harry Frazee—a native New Yorker with his heart on Broadway—sold Ruth to the New York Yankees, unleashing a curse that appears certain to carry into the next millennium.

The Curse of the Bambino is a handy explanation for all the woes endured by the Sox and their fans over the last three-quarters of a century. The Curse helps us to explain the unexplainable. It's superstition over science, a tidy excuse for Johnny Pesky holding the ball in '46, and Luis Aparicio falling down in '72, and Jim Burton in '75, and Bucky Dent in '78, and Bill Buckner in '86. The Curse is part of Boston baseball folklore and serves to soothe citizens of the Red Sox Nation when bad things happen to good teams.

But now we have a first-ever look at the last time the Red Sox actually ruled the baseball world. On these pages, you will relive the 1918 season as told by the colorful baseball scribes of 1918. It's a trip to a time when our nation was at war and baseball was king and the Red Sox were regarded as a powerhouse bully, most likely to kick sand in the faces of the opposition. Between these covers there is none of the cynicism and dissent that plagues the Red Sox at the end of the century.

It is a fascinating journey, one that provides surprises and harbingers of future woes.

The characterizations of a young Babe Ruth are priceless. On the day before the first game of the 1918 Series, Burt Whitman, a *Boston Herald and Journal* writer and a loud voice in this Greek chorus of Sox scribes, wrote, "Ruth absolutely lacks the nervousness which has hampered so many great pitchers on the eve of this title series." Whitman then quotes Ruth saying, "I'd pitch the whole series, every game, if they'd let me."

Ruth went on to beat the Cubs 1–0 in Game 1, and eventually won two games with a 1.06 ERA in Boston's six-game victory.

His words were confident and prophetic. And I was delighted to note that they appeared in the newspaper on September 4, 1918.

Numerology is a large part of the Sox story and every Fenway fan knows that the numerals 9–4–1–8 are displayed in large, circular signs on the facade over the right field grandstand. In fact, the numbers commemorate the retired digits of four Sox Hall of Famers—Ted Williams, Bobby Doerr, Joe Cronin, and Carl Yastrzemski. But in Fenway folklore, it has been noted that 9–4–1–8 is also a date—September 4, 1918. It is the date of the eve of the Red Sox' last World Series victory. And to read Ruth's words in a newspaper on this day of destiny is truly eerie. Thanks to this book, we know exactly what Ruth was doing and saying on 9–4–1–8.

There's more, of course. Readers get a true sense of how important baseball was to the local culture in 1918. The war is raging in France and the World Series has to be played early, but baseball is America's true pastime and the newspapers' best writers are assigned to cover the hometown team. And the cartoons are priceless.

Here we find out when and why "The Star-Spangled Banner" (before it was our national anthem) was played before the start of a baseball game. We are informed that Carl Mays—who later threw a pitch that killed a batter—was as important as Ruth in the Sox' quest for the grail. And we will be reminded that this World Series was played one year before the Chicago White Sox took money to throw a World Series against the Cincinnati Reds.

Perhaps most fascinating is the detail surrounding the near–player strike over World Series shares that threatened the 1918 Fall Classic and left hard feelings that still exist today. Harry Hooper's 1973 letter to then-Commissioner Bowie Kuhn is fascinating; it portrays the chaotic, drunken environment that permeated baseball leadership in the early part of the century. When we see how the players were mistreated by ownership and league officials, it is easier to understand why baseball was ripe for scandal one year later.

We also get a taste of the deep involvement of the baseball writers of that time. Reporters were far from neutral and often had a hand in brokering deals between management and players.

Springer and Waterman are baseball fans in the purest sense. It would be impossible to effectively collect and edit this much material unless one truly knows and loves the game. They have managed to take us back to an earlier time and teach us old-new lessons, without cluttering our minds with excess detail and description. It must have been a daunting task, but they've gathered well and presented it well.

Red Sox fans recite "1918" whenever they moan about the plight of their current team, but not many of them really know anything about the 1918 championship season. They might know that Ruth had something to do with it, but on these pages they can truly relive Boston's last golden autumn, and maybe find some hints as to why the Sox have never been able to get back to the promised land.

Dan Shaughnessy

Newton, Massachusetts

PREFACE

On September 4, 1993, I was among 31,223 fans who packed Fenway Park before a meaningless, rain-delayed, late-season game. Most of us sat through the deluge in order to watch a very unusual ceremony. We witnessed the official recognition of the 1918 World Champion Boston Red Sox, the raising of the 1918 flag, and the honoring of men and women like John Hooper and Julia Ruth Stevens with their fathers' world championship pins.

Tears flowed freely on that nostalgic occasion while forgotten heroes such as Dave Shean, Joe Bush, Everett Scott, and the rest of the 1918 Red Sox team were memorialized. It was a day I'll never forget. Seventy-five years after their glorious triumph, the last Red Sox team to win a World Series was finally crowned as the champions!

This book will transport you back to an era when the First World War was raging in France, dozens of baseball players were enlisting in the service or jumping their teams to play for shipyard ball clubs, and the government was threatening to close down the season early to draft all eligible players.

Babe Ruth's magnetic personality and enormous talents dominated the entire American League. The great southpaw pitcher became a sensational slugging left fielder; and when the Red Sox needed pitching help, Ruth returned to the mound, leading the Sox to the title.

These newspaper accounts describe many of the Babe's monumental home runs, including a spring training blast that stirred up an alligator farm in Arkansas, and another blow that knocked the back off a bleacher seat. Ruth quickly became a legend while leading the league in home runs for the first time.

Harry Frazee, one of the most despised men in Red Sox history, was a key part of the Red Sox success in 1918. The colorful Red Sox owner orchestrated several wonderful trades to offset the loss of a dozen players to the armed forces, refused offers by the Yankees to buy Ruth, and sparred with Ban Johnson, the president of the American League.

Harry Hooper, Walter Johnson, Tris Speaker, Ty Cobb, and Carl Mays epitomized the tough, crafty, hard-fought baseball of the dead ball era. Cobb and Mays had a private beanball war; Hooper fielded brilliantly and was a superb leadoff hitter for the Red Sox; Johnson mowed down the opposition with amazing regularity while pitching for the Washington Senators; and Speaker led the Indians' charge for the pennant with his fabulous fielding and clutch hitting.

Shoeless Joe Jackson left baseball early in the season to work for a shipyard; the Washington owner organized a bat-and-ball fund to send baseball equipment to soldiers overseas; proceeds of games were given to the Red Cross; and Mary Pickford, the great silent-screen actress, raised money at games for Liberty Bonds.

Although horse racing, boxing, rowing, golf, tennis, and schoolboy football were popular sports of the day, baseball was clearly the national pastime in 1918. Sports stars like Jack Dempsey and Jess Willard (boxing), Bill Tilden (tennis) and Francis Ouimet (golf) were overshadowed by heroes such as Cobb, Speaker, Johnson, and Ruth.

Travel back to 1918 while viewing baseball through the colorful, partisan writing of the sportswriters of this bygone era. Experience this amazing season, which had a World Series controversy that still reverberates today. Revel in a young Babe Ruth's heroics and antics both on and off the field. Come and share the excitement of *The Year the Red Sox Won the Series*.

Let the games begin!

Ty Waterman

The Year the RED SOX Won the Series

Part 1 The Hot Stove Season

Babe Ruth has been doing his bit for the auto repairers this fall. Two or three repair shops would have been closed up long ago but for persons who insist in running into the machine that Babe is navigating.

Edward F. Martin, *Boston Globe*

Red Sox Team Is Shot to Pieces

President Frazee of the Red Sox has a monumental task to restore order out of chaos, putting in the field an aggregation that will bear some resemblance to a major league team. The Red Sox outfit has been shot to pieces, and of the long list of regulars and substitutes on the Boston payroll last season, less than 50 per cent are left because of enlistments and the draft.

Frazee has a really disheartening job in front of him when he decides to begin assembling a team.

Paul H. Shannon, *Boston Post*

[The United States had been fighting in World War I since April 1917. Jack Barry, Boston's manager and second baseman, had joined the navy after leading the Red Sox to a second-place finish in 1917, nine games behind the World Champion Chicago White Sox. In addition, the Red Sox had also lost to the armed forces their star left fielder, Duffy Lewis, three reserve infielders, and three pitchers.]

PRESIDENT FRAZEE OF THE RED SOX, HAS A TOUGH PROPOSITION ON HIS HANDS FOR A 1918 BASEBALL TEAM

AS THE BOSTON FAN SEES IT.

Scott, *Boston Post*

Before bounding back to Broadway, Pres. Harry Frazee, the cherubic impresario of the Red Sox, told business manager Dan Considine to get estimates on the cost of replacing all of the wooden bleachers at Fenway Park with the concrete stuff. The wooden stands at the Fenway, unhappily, do not harmonize with esthetic tastes of the president. He says that with concrete in place of the wood he will be able to get lower insurance rates and then, again, they will be more pleasing to the eye.

Edward F. Martin, *Boston Globe*

[Fenway Park was new, having opened in 1912 with a seating capacity about 27,000—one of the larger ballparks of that era. There was a single-deck grandstand with a right field pavilion and large wooden bleachers in right and center fields.

The left field fence was 321 feet from home plate, the center field 488 feet away, and the right field fence only 313 feet. During this dead ball era, it was extremely rare for anyone to hit the ball over the fence. Only fourteen home runs were hit by the Red Sox in 1917, a typical year.

One of the more interesting features of the park was Duffy's Cliff, named after the popular left fielder Duffy Lewis. It was a steep, ten-foot embankment that warned the fielder of an impending crash into the left field fence. Fans also sat on top of the cliff whenever there was an overflow crowd. It wasn't until 1934 that owner Tom Yawkey removed Duffy's Cliff and erected a thirty-seven-foot-high concrete wall that eventually became known as the Green Monster.]

Red Sox Owner Makes Big Deal

Dwarfing by comparison the famous sale of Tris Speaker two years ago, President Harry Frazee put through the most sensational deal in the history of baseball yesterday when he purchased pitcher "Bullet" Joe Bush, catcher Wallie Schang, and outfielder Amos Strunk from the Philadelphia Athletics, surrendering in exchange $60,000 in cash and handing over catcher Chester Thomas, pitcher Vean Gregg and outfielder Merlin Kopp.

Paul H. Shannon, *Boston Post*

Deal Expels Weakness That Cost Sox Pennant

Harry Frazee has come through with his promised big deal and the enormity of it startles us no more than it pleases us. He has strengthened his team in its vital positions, catcher, pitcher and centre fielder.

Schang is a natural ball player and his hitting is of a clean-up variety. He is a great thrower and is one of the few receivers who successfully block off the plate against men trying to score on close plays. [Schang had batted .285 with 3 home runs and 36 runs batted in during 1917.]

Bush, the Bullet Boy, has one of the fastest balls at the command of any big league pitcher. His curve is good and, in the last two years, Joe has developed a wonderful slow ball. [Bush had won 11 and lost 17, with 121

Frazee's deal puts the team back on its feet and the baseball world is willing to admit that the Boston Sox need have no fear of Chicago.

strikeouts and a 2.47 earned run average during 1917. He had been the ace on a pitiful Athletics team that finished last, 44.5 games behind the White Sox.]

Strunk is one of the best "go and get 'em" outfielders in the game. He comes closer to Tris Speaker than any other mid-fielder in the junior league. He is fast, and like Schang, is a fine batter, naturally entitled to the .300 class. [Strunk had batted .281 with 83 runs scored and 16 steals in 1917.]

Great defensive strength has been added to the Red Sox, but above everything else the club's punch has been increased. Lack of good catching and good centre-fielding, together with a team weakness in hitting, kept the Hub Hose from winning the pennant in 1917. Frazee's deal puts the team back on its feet and the baseball world is willing to admit that the Boston Sox need have no fear of Chicago.

Burt Whitman, Boston Herald and Journal

Monday, December 17

A TOUCH OF WAR SPIRIT IN BASEBALL

Scott, Boston Post

Between Connie Mack [the manager of the Athletics] and Pres. W. F. Baker [the owner of the Phillies] nothing is safe in Philly. Don't be surprised if the Liberty Bell bobs up in a Red Sox uniform.

Bugs Baer, Boston Globe

Eleven Red Sox Now in the Service

Another Red Sox player has enlisted. Harold Janvrin is the 11th member of the Boston team to enter the service. [He had batted .197 as a backup second baseman and shortstop in 1917.]

Janvrin's enlistment will leave another gap that Pres. Harry Frazee will have to hustle to fill. Gardner and Scott are now the only infielders that are left to the club.

No club in either major league has been so depleted by the war as have the Red Sox, but Pres. Frazee will shortly put over another trade, getting some infield material that will be needed badly.

Boston Globe

"Barrow is a good clever baseball man, and a close friend of mine, but he never had any chance to come to the Red Sox as manager. In fact, he is not coming here at all. You can set it down as absolutely certain that he will not be the next Red Sox manager."

Paul H. Shannon, quoting Harry Frazee, *Boston Post*

[Edward Barrow, who recently had quit as president of the International League, was rumored to become either the next Red Sox president or their next manager.]

Frazee Bets That War Will Be Over by April

Harry Frazee, president of the Red Sox, shortly after his arrival from New York yesterday, said that he had wagered $2,000 against $12,000 that the war would be over by April 15. He insists that Jack Barry will be able to manage the Sox in 1918, but qualified this optimistic outlook by saying that he may have something definite to announce in the manager situation by Feb. 15.

Burt Whitman, *Boston Herald and Journal*

Trio of Macks Means '18 Flag, States Frazee

President H. H. Frazee of the Red Sox is confident that the acquisition of Bush, Strunk and Schang means the 1918 American League flag will come to Boston.

"An hour after I gave Connie Mack $60,000 for the three players— and that was the price—Comiskey [White Sox owner] offered me $50,000 for Joe Bush alone," said Frazee.

Harry Frazee, Red Sox president

"The way to get a ball player, to my way of thinking, is to buy him. Money talks louder than newspaper chatter."

Boston American

[Frazee believed in the power of money. The theatrical magnate owned the Longacre Theater in New York, had produced the hit Broadway show "Nothing But the Truth," promoted a heavyweight championship fight in 1915 between Jack Johnson and Jess Willard, and bought the Boston Red Sox in late 1916 with two other investors for $675,000.]

Tuesday, January 1, 1918

New Year's Resolution

Scott, Boston Post

All First Division Clubs in on Spoils

Eight Teams to Get Part of World's Series Money

CHICAGO, Dec. 31—Teams finishing in the first division in the National and American League pennant races hereafter will share in the players' receipts of the World's Series. This decision was reached at a conference today between August Herrmann, representing the National League, and Pres. Ban Johnson of the American League.

"After awarding the winning players $2,000 each and the losers $1,400 each, we will divide the remainder of the prize money among the players on the teams which finished second, third and fourth," Chairman Herrmann said.

"I think the new division will be satisfactory. It will stimulate interest in the races. I do not believe there will be any lagging of clubs hopelessly out of the championship race. I am sorry to say that has been the case in previous years."

Boston Globe

[In 1917 members of the champion White Sox were paid about $3,600 each, with the defeated Giants receiving a thousand dollars less. The new rule would reduce the payoff for the pennant winners by 45 percent in 1918; this would become a source of conflict during the World Series.]

The way to get a ball player is to buy him.

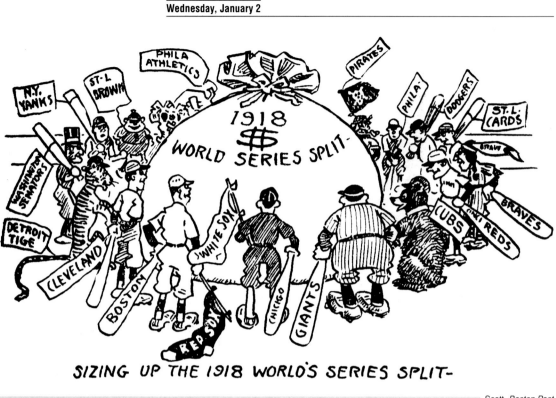

SIZING UP THE 1918 WORLD'S SERIES SPLIT-

Scott, *Boston Post*

So the World Series coin will go eight ways hereafter. Such an idea should prove a good thing for the little fellows, but hardly for the leaders. To the victor belong the spoils. Two teams that have proven their calibre in a long season's race deserve the lion's share of the rewards.

Arthur Duffey, *Boston Post*

Friday, January 4

Sox Regulars Will Be Exchanged for New Recruits

"The big deal I am about to put across involves players and not money," declared Harry H. Frazee, president of the Red Sox, yesterday at the downtown office of the club.

"When I obtained Schang, Bush and Strunk, the big consideration was money, $60,000 of the real stuff," he continued. "But I cannot get these new players for money.

"It is a swap which will be of great benefit to the Red Sox and to the other team. It will be equivalent to clinching the pennant for us, I am positive. It will be a big boon for the other team, giving them strength where most needed.

"No. There is not a chance of it falling through. I tell you everything is fixed. No use of trying to pump me. I can't let it out yet and all you can do is guess."

Burt Whitman, *Boston Herald and Journal*

PRESIDENT FRAZEE OF THE RED SOX PREDICTS THE PULLING THROUGH OF ANOTHER SENSATIONAL BASEBALL DEAL

Scott, *Boston Post*

If the players of the American League follow the good example of President Ban Johnson, everything will be smooth sailing next season. At the recent Chicago meeting Ban decided that he was getting too much money for war times and demanded that his salary be sliced from $30,000 to $10,000.

Eddie Hurley, *Boston Record*

Red Sox Land Stuffy McInnis

Athletics Yield Another Star to Strengthen Hub Outfit

John (Stuffy) McInnis of Gloucester, last of the great Athletics of a few seasons ago, and for years a Boston idol, yesterday was sold to the Boston Red Sox by Manager Connie Mack of the Philadelphia Athletics.

The deal is incomplete. Mack has two courses open. He may take Stuffy's equivalent in Red Sox players or money.

It is the big deal which Frazee promised as a thrilling follow-up to his purchase of Bush, Schang and Strunk. It makes the Hub Hose appear the strongest club "on paper" in either league.

The newest Red Sox star is a .300 hitter. He has batted for a grand average of .313 in the nine years he has been with the Athletics, the only big league club with which he has played. He is small of stature as first basemen go, only 5 feet 8 inches in height, and weighs 155 or 160, but is of the tough unbreakable type, like Ty Cobb.

Burt Whitman, *Boston Herald and Journal*

Stuffy McInnis, latest Red Sox addition

The Year the Red Sox Won the Series

Babe Ruth Signs Up with Sox

Yesterday afternoon, following a conference of three hours, George (Babe) Ruth, the burly southpaw of the Red Sox, finally came to terms with the management, and before leaving the office signed up for the season of 1918.

Babe was not unreasonable, but it took a long time before owner and player came to terms. He is one of the few men in the majors whose work last season was really deserving of an increase. Consequently, President Frazee was disposed to grant him a substantial raise, but the club owner was not inclined to hand him Bunker Hill Monument, a fact that Babe eventually was brought to realize.

Babe went into the office clad in a coonskin coat and minus a rubber. He had walked out of the one on his left foot on the way down to the office, but had never noticed the absence of the golosh until someone at headquarters tried to figure out whether the shoes the big left-hander wore were black or tan.

Paul H. Shannon, *Boston Post*

[Ruth pitched spectacularly during 1917, winning 24 games and losing 13, with a 2.02 earned run average. He also batted .325, with 2 home runs in 123 at bats.]

Scott, *Boston Post*

The only thing left of the champion Athletics of 1914 is Connie Mack's watch fob, emblematic of the American League championship. He's lucky to have it. Evidently, Frazee didn't see it.

Eddie Hurley, *Boston Record*

Manager Connie Mack,
Philadelphia Athletics

McInnis Near-Gift to Sox, Says Mack

Traded Out of Gratitude

PHILADELPHIA, Jan. 13—In speaking of the McInnis deal, Connie Mack said:

"My reasons for letting McInnis go to Boston are purely personal. I know I could have received a good big price for Stuffy had I wanted to sell him, but I owe a debt of gratitude to McInnis. When he did not want to play on the terms I offered him, I let him go to Boston, where he wanted to go and where he will have the opportunity of being with a pennant contender."

Boston Globe

[Mack managed the Philadelphia A's for fifty years. His teams finished first nine times and last sixteen times, with some of the greatest and worst ball clubs in the history of baseball.

A tall, thin man dressed in a boater and stiff collar, he was known to everyone as Mr. Mack. He was loved by his players but was never able to pay them adequately. Mack continually sold off his top stars to stay within a limited budget, destroying some very good teams in the process.

Connie Mack was elected to the Hall of Fame in 1937 but continued managing until 1950. When he finally retired at the age of eighty-seven, New York City gave him the ultimate sign of respect—a ticker-tape parade.]

"Stuffy" No Gift, Declared Frazee

"It's ridiculous," said owner Harry Frazee of the Red Sox last night when told that Connie Mack had presented Stuffy McInnis to the Boston club. "You can bet Mack will get what he is after. He is not in baseball for love."

Boston Herald and Journal

Babe Ruth Needs One More Hit to Be Select Class Member

Babe Ruth of the Red Sox is the nearest approach to a .300 hitting pitcher there is in major league captivity. The Boston southpaw has a batting average of .299 for the time he has been on the junior circuit. If Ruth makes a hit the first time he bats next season he will have a .300 average to sport.

In 1915 Ruth hit .315; in 1916 he hit .272, and last year his average was .325. During his entire American League career he has been in 166 games, batted 361 times, scored 49 runs, made 108 hits and sacrificed 13 times. Ruth still has to steal a base.

Babe's long hit collection includes 22 doubles, seven triples and nine home runs. His four bagger off Bill James of the Tigers on Aug. 10 last season, was the longest hit made in the American League, the ball going into the centre field bleachers at the Fenway.

Ernest Lanigan, *Boston Record*

Babe Ruth was in town again yesterday and for an hour was in charge of the Red Sox offices. He was instructed, however, not to sign up any players and not to let any advance money slip out of the safe.

Boston Globe

Tuesday, February 12

Barrow Is New Manager of Sox

NEW YORK, Feb. 11—President Frazee of the Boston Red Sox gave the baseball world the third sensation of the winter when he named as manager, Edward G. Barrow, lately President of the International League.

The appointment of Barrow will cause profound satisfaction in baseball circles and especially in American League ranks, where his worth as a leader had long been acknowledged. No sooner had the news been tipped off to the big gathering at the Hotel Imperial than Barrow was surrounded by a mob eager to extend their congratulations.

Barrow is delighted to return to Boston and the big league. He feels that the club which he will find partly assembled for him should come pretty near to landing the American League pennant.

Paul H. Shannon, *Boston Post*

[The former bare-knuckle fighter was a pioneer in the game of baseball. He set up the first minor league night game in 1896, promoted the only woman ever to pitch in organized baseball (Lizzie Arlington, in 1897), was the first man to paint distances on outfield fences, discovered Honus Wagner, switched Babe Ruth to the outfield, and served as general manager and president of the Yankees from 1921 to 1945, masterminding them to fourteen flags and ten world championships.

Barrow is memorialized by a plaque beyond the left center field fence at Yankee Stadium. He was elected to the Hall of Fame in 1953.]

Wednesday, February 13

THE RED SOX "DARK HORSE" MANAGER, WHOSE INDENTITY HAD THE FANS GUESSING, HAS NOW MATERIALIZED AS E. G. BARROW, BASEBALL EXPERT–

Scott, *Boston Post*

Johnny Evers Signs with Sox

NEW YORK, Feb. 13—Johnny Evers signed a contract tonight to act as coach for the Boston Red Sox. Although signed up for but one year, he is expected to get a good tryout at second base, and may shine at that berth.

"I love Boston and have always wanted to be a member of the Red Sox team," said Johnny tonight. "I have told Frazee and Barrow that I would play at a much lower figure than the Cardinals have offered me."

Barrow feels that Evers can still jump in and play at least part of the season at second base, and with McInnis and Scott on either side would show his old wonderful game.

Paul H. Shannon, *Boston Post*

[The thirty-six-year-old second baseman played on three world championship teams with the Chicago Cubs and Boston Braves. Although his lifetime average was a modest .270, he had been part of the most famous double play combination in the history of baseball, Tinker to Evers to Chance.

The 140-pound Evers was nicknamed "The Crab" because of his grouchy personality. He slid into runners with his spikes high, feuded with umpires and teammates, and rarely spoke with Joe Tinker, the Cubs' star shortstop.

A brilliant fielder and noted sign stealer, Johnny's most memorable season was in 1914, when he was selected the National League's Most Valuable Player, sparking the Boston Braves miracle drive from last to first place. He batted .438 in the World Series, driving in the winning run in the fourth and final game.

Evers was elected to the Hall of Fame in 1946.]

Another coup for the newest of A.L. managers was the purchase from the Toronto Internationals of outfielder George Whiteman. Whiteman is no kid. He came up to the Red Sox back in the last decade, along with Tris Speaker. But despite a brilliant start, which caused many of the folk to label him the superior of Speaker, he was sent back.

Whiteman batted .342 last year [in the minors]. He is ambitious, believes fully that he is of big league material and will give a delightful run for one of the outfield berths, or for the job of first utility outfielder.

Burt Whitman, *Boston Herald and Journal*

[The thirty-five-year-old veteran came up with the Red Sox in 1907 but batted only eleven times that year. He surfaced again as a major leaguer in 1913 with the Yankees, batting .344 in just eleven games. Owing to the war and the shortage of quality players, this was probably Whiteman's last opportunity to play in the big leagues.]

It's a funny story how Frazee picked me to manage the Red Sox. I had been signed to act as sort of assistant president and called upon Harry at his office one afternoon.

"Well, Ed, I guess it's about time I began looking around for a manager," said Frazee. "I know that Barry won't be able to play this year."

Ed Barrow, new Red Sox manager

I didn't pay much attention to the remark and kept on reading the war news in a local paper. Frazee was going through his mail at the time and didn't even look up as he addressed me.

About a minute later I caught Frazee giving me the "up and down." He looked at me like one would size up an automobile he was about to buy.

"Say, Ed, I have just selected you as manager of the 1918 Red Sox," he suddenly flung at me. "Want the job?"

Did I want the job? I was so happy that I could hardly answer.

"Well, Harry," I finally replied, "I wanted that job ever since I knew Jack Barry couldn't return, but I was afraid if I asked for it you might say, 'Get out of this opera house.'"

And that's how I was selected as manager.

Ed Barrow, *Boston American*

Frazee Tried to Land Cobb

Now that it is all over, dead and buried, it is altogether fitting to let Boston fans know that Harry Frazee, owner of the Red Sox, seriously contemplated a desperate attempt to buy Ty Cobb from Detroit. He prepared a figure for President Frank Navin of the Michigander Tigers which was far in excess of the multiple-figured checks juggled in the instances of Eddie Collins and Tris Speaker.

But Navin has given the thumbs down to any and every effort to woo Tyrus Raymond from Detroit. In his years in the Jungle, Ty has made many close and dear friends. His going from a prosperous baseball centre like the Michigan metropolis would raise the dickens, the deuce and, probably, the devil.

Burt Whitman, *Boston Herald and Journal*

ONLY A FEW DAYS MORE TILL THE
BASEBALL TRAINING DOWN SOUTH~

Scott, *Boston Post*

Gardner, Walker and Cady Traded

Sent to Athletics in Exchange for Stuffy McInnis

The Red Sox team lost three more veterans yesterday when Connie Mack, insisting upon his pound of flesh, forced the Boston club to hand over Larry Gardner, Tillie Walker and Forrest Cady to the Philadelphia outfit in exchange for Stuffy McInnis.

The passing of at least one of this trio will be sadly lamented by Boston fans. While the loss of Walker and Cady might be accepted with cheerful resignation, the going of Gardner, one of the most powerful batters on the team for years, one of its most dependable members and a model player in every way, will be severely felt. The Vermont lad's loss can be considered almost irreparable. With Gardner gone, and no player of anywhere near his calibre to replace him [at third base], the Red Sox are in a very ticklish position.

Paul H. Shannon, *Boston Post*

[The thirty-two-year-old veteran went on to play seventeen seasons with a lifetime batting average of .289, retiring in 1924. Gardner had been a World Series hero for the Red Sox in 1912 and 1916, with three Series home runs.]

Babe Ruth is dusting off his niblicks, midirons, and drivers. Babe has had all his golf equipment brought in from Melrose and it will go South with him. If out along the fresh water jumping-off places the natives see a bareheaded giant hop off a train, take a terrible smash at a little white pill and watch 'er sail they will know it is only the Babe. He says he is going to win 30 games this year, too.

Edward F. Martin, *Boston Globe*

Sox Pilot to Try McInnis at Third

Manager Ed Barrow of the Red Sox plans to play Stuffy McInnis at third base. "With Stuffy's natural ability it should be a cinch for him to play that third corner," said Barrow. "He can come in for those bunts and you will appreciate his ability in being able to gaffle a hard hit ball. He is good at going for balls hit either to the right or left of him, and that baby can throw. I believe he will make another Jimmy Collins." [Collins was the great third baseman of the 1903 World Champion Red Sox and a member of the Hall of Fame.]

Edward F. Martin, *Boston Globe*

"STUFFY" MCINNIS, WILL PLAY 3RD BASE FOR THE BOSTON RED SOX, THIS SEASON~

Scott, *Boston Post*

Saturday, March 9

Just what the Hub Hose will do this year under their new manager is a problem which only time can solve. The team is experimental to a large degree. There is nothing sure about who will play any of the infield positions with the exception of shortstop, where Deacon Everett Scott appears a sure-enough fixture.

The team has enough pitching material of the highest grade to make it a pennant contender, but reports from the Ozarks will make doubly interesting reading for the super-fans this spring. Everyone is wondering who will play third, who will tackle the second base situation, where Stuffy McInnis will play and how well, how the left field assignment will be handled and by whom, and what sort of a catcher Wallie Schang will make.

Bob Dunbar, *Boston Herald and Journal*

Just what the Hub Hose will do this year under their new manager is a problem which only time can solve.

MANY BOSTON BASEBALL FANS WILL BE ON HAND AT SOUTH STATION TO GIVE
THE ADVANCE SQUAD OF THE RED SOX A GOOD SEND·OFF ~

TOOT! TOOT!! DING! DING!! AND AWAY THE RED SOX GO

Scott, *Boston Post*

The Hot Stove Season

Part 2 Spring Training

Red Sox Arrive at Hot Springs

HOT SPRINGS, ARK., March 11—A little late and plenty tired from excessive train riding, the Boston Red Sox advance squad arrived in Hot Springs today shortly after noon, glad to get back to the heart of the Ozarks. The spring training of the Sox for 1918 was officially started when the boys stepped off the train, and it will be a serious piece of business from now until April 15.

Manager Barrow outlined his training plans about like this: "The players arise at 8:30 A.M.; be out of the dining room before 9 A.M.; leave the hotel for the ball park an hour later and walk to the ball yard, a matter of a couple of miles.

"Three hours' work on the diamond will start them home about 1:30 o'clock, and they will take the course over the mountains on the return trip. Then the famous Hot Springs baths will follow and, after the usual hour of rest, the boys will be ready to descend full strength upon the dining room."

Boston Herald and Journal

[Hot Springs was a thriving resort town set in the foothills of the Ozark Mountains, amid forty-six hot springs. Approximately 150,000 tourists went there each year to soak up the healing waters and relax in the famous bathhouses.

The Red Sox had trained in Hot Springs since 1909, with tourist delights such as the ostrich and alligator farms, the "Dolly Dimples" opera house, the notorious Black Orchid dance hall, the Happy Hollow Saloon, and several race tracks. It wasn't always easy for players to keep their minds on baseball surrounded by these diversions!]

The bookmakers may get some of their roll before they get away, but Barrow is determined that no money of any consequence will be lost by men over the card table. He will insist that poker be confined strictly to the 10-cent variety and all games must end promptly each night at 11 o'clock. This rule goes for scribes, rooters and every one of the Boston party with whom the Sox are thrown in daily contact.

Paul H. Shannon, *Boston Post*

Reports from Hot Springs indicate that Johnny Evers has regained his old-time form. Troy John is said to be shooting the ball around with a snap that has been lacking the past few seasons. His right arm seems to have regained its normal strength and Johnny is confident he will win a regular berth with the Sox this season. Come on Johnny, we're pulling for you and hope to see you covering that second sack this season.

Boston Record

Babe Ruth is certainly a physical marvel. Almost any other player who followed the pace that Ruth set yesterday would have been hobbling about in crutches this noon, but Babe suffered neither ache nor pain, and no one at the Hot Springs will dispute his claim to the title of "Iron Man." While Trainer Lawlor was rubbing some of his charges down, Babe was shooting them across the diamond, batting fungoes to the outfield and hurrying along the infield practice, so that he might wrest permission from his manager to sneak out to the race track and get down a couple of bets on the ponies.

Paul H. Shannon, *Boston Post*

Friday, March 15

The practice took on a sluggish feeling at one stage, only to be livened up when Manager Barrow yelled out: "A little more pep, boys, or over the mountains on the way home; take your choice."

The boys would rather do anything else in the world than return to the hotel over the Ozark Hills route. It is a tough grind and they know it.

Henry L. Daily, *Boston American*

Saturday, March 16

Tennessee Boy Pays Way to Hose Camp

Mimos Ellenburg, an eighteen-year-old high school boy, traveled all the way from Moshern, Tenn., to get a tryout with the Red Sox.

Ellenburg's arrival at the Spa was unheralded. No one met him at the station and he just walked into the Majestic Hotel, quietly announced himself, put on a uniform, went out to the park and began to play in Scott's place at short.

After practice Ellenburg did not wait for his bath, but went scouting around the town, looking for a place to sleep. When Manager Barrow heard of this he sent a posse out to hunt him up and bring him back to the hotel saying, "I would rather pay his expenses myself than have the kid away from the team."

Frazee has agreed to let Ellenburg go through with the spring training course. He was turned over to Johnny Evers. So the youngest member of the team and the oldest became "bunkies" right away.

Henry L. Daily, *Boston American*

When there is nothing else to do, the boys walk down the street to the De Soto Cabaret, where they do nothing but drink water and eat popcorn. This is a minor league cabaret in action, but you don't mind this when everybody is licking up the spring water. And you ought to see some of the people around the tables. If it ever occurred in some of Boston's cafés, the floor-walker would take them outside and hand them over to a jolly gendarme. The water here has a worse effect than a tank of wine.

Eddie Hurley, Boston Evening Record

Johnny Evers, veteran second baseman

Evers of Old in the Red Sox Practice

Trojan Seems Destined to Stage a Great Comeback

HOT SPRINGS, ARK., March 16—Dashing over behind the keystone hassock and making sensational one-hand stops, getting his throws away with that old-time skill and accuracy and constantly chattering, Johnnie Evers demonstrated very clearly that he may yet conquer all obstacles and force us to acknowledge that he is "the man who came back."

Such an exhibition he gave today. There was that old Evers technique in every move. The magnetic, hustling Trojan is rejuvenating the noiseless Red Sox.

Edward F. Martin, Boston Globe

Red Sox Open with a Great Bombardment

Beat Robins, 11–1, Driving the Ball to All Corners

HOT SPRINGS, ARK., March 17—What a wallop when the lid was pried off the 1918 baseball season here this afternoon! What a cannonading those Brooklyn pill servers received. It was Red Sox all the way, the score being 11 to 1. The Barrow troupe looked to be as fast as the movies. Rotunder Robby's crew were as harmless as a flock of soft drinks.

Allow me to introduce our new first sacker, "Hal Chase" Ruth. It was not only the way the big Oriole boy played the first sack that brought the fans to their feet, but also two home run crashes. One landed in a pile of lumber in extreme left center. The other scaled the rightfield barrier and continued on to the alligator farm, the intrusion kicking up no end of commotion among the "Gators."

Edward F. Martin, Boston Globe

[The Dodgers were sometimes called the Brooklyn Robins in honor of their beloved manager, Wilbert Robinson, who was affectionately nicknamed "Uncle Robby."

Ruth was being compared to the slick-fielding Hal Chase, the first baseman of the Cincinnati Reds.]

Lucky for Red Sox that Hooper Was Unlucky with Raisin Crop

HOT SPRINGS, ARK., March 18—You have doubtless heard that quotation about "an ill wind that blows no good to anybody." The ball players along the Ozark Trail today are applying it to the situation in which Harry Hooper, the peerless right fielder of the Red Sox, found himself this winter.

"Hoop" had decided to retire. As every fan knows, Harry is just in his prime, but he was contented, had gathered what he deemed a sufficient bank roll from the grand old pastime, and was about to fold up his old baseball tent. Then along came Jack Frost and when he completed his visit to Capitola, Calif., the Hooper raisin crop was practically destroyed.

So Harry decided to give the game a little more of his time, and he is on the job here today, willing to do his best just as soon as he completes a little interview with Pres. Frazee. Harry is not actually a "holdout." One might describe him as a "conscientious objector." Whatever slight financial differences exist between the two Harrys should be adjusted easily. It was hard on Harry to lose that raisin crop, but through his misfortune the club is a gainer.

Edward F. Martin, *Boston Globe*

[A ten-year veteran who had slumped to .256 in 1917, Hooper was an excellent right fielder with a legendary throwing arm. He was a clutch performer with a knack for playing his best ball in the crucial games.

In the final game of the 1912 World Series against the Giants, Harry went back for a deep fly ball, leaped high, and speared the ball barehanded, falling backward into the stands. This remarkable play saved the series, allowing the Sox to win in the tenth inning.

In 1915, after hitting only two home runs all season, he slugged two round-trippers in the final game of the World Series against the Phillies, to provide the ultimate margin of victory. Then, in the 1916 Series against the Dodgers, Harry batted .333 and scored 6 runs in 5 games.

A crafty leadoff batter, Harry concluded his career with a modest lifetime batting average of .281, but he drew a lot of walks, allowing him to score 1,429 runs. A charter member of a great Red Sox outfield with Duffy Lewis and Tris Speaker, Hooper was elected to the Hall of Fame in 1971.]

THE RED SOX PLAYERS HIKE TO AND FROM THE MORNING PRACTISE -

Scott, *Boston Post*

Kid Ellenburg has been sent back to his home at Moshern, Tenn. It will be some time before he will be able to deliver in fast company.

Henry L. Daily, Boston American

Tuesday, March 19

HOT SPRINGS, ARK., March 18—Manager Barrow does not believe in mountain climbing for training purposes, and this long, hard grind has been cut out. The players cheered when they heard the edict, for the mountain climbs never made any hit with the players.

The first day they were cut out, Johnny Evers left the park five minutes ahead of the other players. All were ordered to run back to the hotel, a distance of about a mile and a half. Evers had not heard that the mountain climbs had been cut out, and he raced all over the Ozarks on his way back to the hotel and arrived 10 minutes after the others. Johnny was in fine humor when he was told that he was the only one who made the long trip. "I'll be in on that short cut in the future," said Evers.

Eddie Hurley, Boston Evening Record

Wednesday, March 20

The boys visited the race track again this afternoon and had quite a good day, Evers, Ruth and Harry Hooper enjoying a profitable afternoon. President Frazee stepped on several live ones that netted him a little better than $500.

Boston Herald and Journal

Thursday, March 21

Barrow's Men Flirt with Death in Wild Automobile Ride

HOT SPRINGS, ARK., March 20—Five of the Red Sox had a narrow escape from serious injury this afternoon while returning from the race track. They were Harry Hooper, Babe Ruth, Everett Scott, Joe Bush and Wally Schang.

The boys engaged a big touring car to take them back to the hotel from the race track. The driver put the machine in high and when the centre of the city was reached he stopped the car and demanded that they pay him and that he would take them no further.

He apparently wanted to hike back to the track after more fares. An appeal was taken by the ball players and a policeman called in, who ordered the driver to take them where they wanted to go. After much argument he consented, saying that he would tip them all out before they got to the hotel.

In order to make his threat good, he opened the machine up, tearing through the centre of the city on high. He banged a jitney [a small bus] aside, knocked down a horse, smashed a wagon and was getting ready to "bust" things up generally, when Hooper reached over the seat and threatened to beat him up.

Scott leaped from the car into the reservation near the public bathhouse. The entire party was much upset, but all were thankful that nothing serious took place.

Boston Herald and Journal

Hobby Takes Up His Old Job on First

HOT SPRINGS, ARK., March 20—Capt. Richard C. Hoblitzell, who would prefer to, and may yet be, Lieut. Hoblitzell of the United States Dental Reserve Corps, donned the spangles today.

The dentist looks good, and he is the same shrewd old scholar. Every time that he takes the floor he generally utters something worth remembering. Hoblitzell ranks with the smartest men of baseball, and the day when he will be banished to the minor league is never going to arrive.

"If they call me [in the draft]," said Hobby, "I am going to make myself efficient at handling the bayonet. You can do great things with one. I will not only practice all day, but after taps I will go to it. You can just tell the world that."

Edward F. Martin, *Boston Globe*

[Doc Hoblitzell was at the end of a ten-year career with Cincinnati and Boston, during which he batted .278. He had played first base for the 1915 and 1916 World Champion Red Sox.]

Friday, March 22

Babe Ruth Is a Hard Worker and a Considerable Hitter

"BABE" RUTH'S MORNING WASH-UP, IS ALWAYS A VERY VIGOROUS AFFAIR-

"BABE" RUTH OFTEN LEADS THE BUNCH TO THE MORNING TRAINING GROUNDS-

Scott, *Boston Post*

The Year the Red Sox Won the Series

"BABE" RUTH –
THE RED SOX STAR SOUTHPAW
PITCHER AND FENCE BREAKER
AT THE BAT—

"BABE" RUTH IS APT TO PULL OFF MOST
ANYTHING IN HIS BATTING PRACTISE –

Scott, *Boston Post*

Sunday, March 24

It is Captain Dick Hoblitzell now. This afternoon Manager Barrow called Hobby under the grandstand and offered him the captaincy. It took but a few minutes to convince Dick that he was the logical man for the job, and so hereafter the infielders and outfielders will take their playing orders on the field from the surgeon dentist.

Paul H. Shannon, *Boston Post*

When the new uniforms reach the team this spring the players will all be required to make a deposit, for the Boston management has decided to put a stop to the mysterious disappearance of sweaters and uniforms each fall. Barrow thinks that the deposit system will remedy this.

Paul H. Shannon, *Boston Post*

Monday, March 25

Ruth's Crash Good for Four Sox Runs

Boston Heavy Artillery Routs the Robins, 7–1

HOT SPRINGS, ARK., March 24—Barrow's heavy artillery shelled Camp Robinson again today, routing the entire Flatbush army and ringing up a 7 to 1 victory in which G. "Babe" Ruth took a very conspicuous part.

In the third frame, with the sacks crushed, Ruth hammered out a circuit smash which every ball player in the park said was the longest drive they had ever seen. The ball not only cleared the right field wall, but stayed up, soaring over the street and a wide duck pond, finally finding a resting place for itself in a nook of the Ozark hills.

Had Ruth made the drive in Boston it might have cleared the bleachers in right center. As he was rounding first he said: "I would liked to have got a better hold on that one."

Edward F. Martin, Boston Globe

Babe Ruth a Star of First Magnitude

HOT SPRINGS, ARK., March 25—"I know how to write a ticket on that fellow now," said Ed Barrow this morning. "He may say that he is Babe Ruth, but I have another name for him. He is John J. Production or I miss my guess."

It is the opinion of baseball veterans like Barrow, Johnny Evers and others that no man in the history of the game ever hit the ball any harder than the Oriole sharp-shooter.

"Just pipe [notice] that swing he takes," said Evers. "I will admit that there are many of those old boys who performed before my time who could whale them, but I never saw a player that could send it on the journey that Babe does, and never did I see any student smash at them so hard."

It is the belief of many that at an early date Ruth will win a place among the greatest attractions of the game. They will go out to see Babe Ruth just as they now flock to Cobb, Speaker, Walter Johnson and Grover Alexander.

Edward F. Martin, Boston Globe

[Babe had started playing in the minors in 1914 with his hometown Baltimore Orioles, who were named after the famous National League champions of the 1890s. Today's A.L. version of the Orioles is not related to either of its previous namesakes.]

Thursday, March 28

STEAM

ZZZT

WHACK!

AGNEW
THE RED SOX'
HUSKY CATCHER

Scott, Boston Post

[A good-fielding but weak-hitting catcher, Sam Agnew had batted only .208 in 1917. The thirty-one-year-old veteran had played five seasons with the St. Louis Browns and the Red Sox.]

Saturday, March 30

HOT SPRINGS, ARK., March 29—Owner Frazee, sporting a pair of beautiful black eyes hidden by tortoise shell glasses, arrived here this morning congratulating himself that he had not lost his eyesight. Last Monday morning while standing on the station platform beside the golf course at French Lick Springs, a friend of his tried to show Harry how to get a drive off, and using Frazee's cane hooked a good size rock straight into the magnate's face.

Paul H. Shannon, Boston Post

Sam Jones is expected to reach the Springs tonight and he will get a cordial welcome from Frazee and Barrow. Sam will certainly find the chance he failed to secure during the past two seasons, and, if he has the goods, Barrow will make frequent use of him.

Paul H. Shannon, Boston Post

[Jones, a twenty-six-year-old journeyman pitcher with a lifetime record of only 4 victories and 11 defeats, was acquired by the Red Sox in 1916 in a trade for the great Tris Speaker, the Cleveland Indians' center fielder. Sam pitched a mere 43 innings during the preceding two seasons and had yet to win his first game in a Boston uniform.

He was dubbed "Sad Sam" by Bill McGeehan of the *New York Herald Tribune* because of his melancholy demeanor on the mound.]

Sunday, March 31

Red Sox Rally in 9th and Beat Dodgers, 4–3

Babe Ruth Crashes Home Run, and Drives in Winning Run in Final Frame

LITTLE ROCK, ARK., March 30—The Boston Red Sox made one of their old-fashioned killings today, pulling a game out of the fire in the ninth inning and once more sending Brooklyn down in defeat. It certainly looked dark for the Red Sox today, but before the boys gathered up their war clubs and made a hasty retreat to the dining room, they uncorked a shower of wallops that nearly drove Wilbert Robinson out of the park.

With the score 3 to 0 against the Sox in the last of the eighth it certainly looked dark and dreary. But things began to happen. Sam Agnew, the old warhorse, celebrated his return to the game by pasting the pill over the wall and scoring Boston's first run. Then Babe Ruth planted the pill over the right field wall a mile away, but it was foul by inches. On the next pitch Ruth slashed out another mighty drive that cleared the fence for the circuit.

Hobby opened the festivities in the ninth with a drive to left and George Whiteman tried to sacrifice. His efforts were futile, however, and the best he could do was a two base knock against the right field wall. With two on and none out, Bob Fisher dropped a Texas leaguer to right which scored Hobby [to tie the score]. Sam Agnew then forced Fisher at second.

As Babe Ruth strutted to the plate, Robinson sent in "Lefty" Mitchell. The Babe is supposed to be weak against left handed pitching, but the first ball served up by Mitchell was sent far away over Myer's head in centre field and Whiteman trotted in with the winning run.

It was a grand finish by the Boston club after being seemingly out-pointed, and it was a fine game of ball for this time of year.

Boston Herald and Journal

HOT SPRINGS, ARK., March 30—If Evers can play through the remainder of the summer as he has since he came South, the Red Sox will not cast longing eyes at any second sacker in the league. Johnny has been out almost every day, has shown speed of leg and arm and the same old judgment at batting, and has not given any indications of being done as a live wire in the big leagues.

But the fear is that when the heat of the summer and the nervous strain of the season comes on, Johnny's condition will not remain as robust. It is feared that he may not stand the pace once the bell rings in the American League, and that along about July the Sox will need another second baseman.

Boston Herald and Journal

Monday, April 1

Fighting Red Sox Again Wallop Dodgers, 7 to 4

LITTLE ROCK, ARK., March 31—Another of those sparkling ninth inning finishes, which are becoming so popular with the Red Sox, was responsible for a 7 to 4 triumph over Brooklyn today.

The Red Sox are proving a game ball club this spring and they exhibited their fighting qualities today. With one gone in the last frame, the Red Sox failed to give up and finally pummelled Burleigh Grimes all over the lot, scoring five runs before the curtain fell.

Boston Herald and Journal

[Grimes was a twenty-four-year-old spitballer who would go on to win 19 games during his first season with the Dodgers, and wind up with 270 victories in his Hall of Fame career.]

Red Sox Trade George Foster to Cincinnati for Dave Shean

LITTLE ROCK—Manager Ed Barrow announced that he put through a deal whereby Dave Shean becomes the property of the Red Sox and George Foster goes to the Cincinnati club.

Foster is a holdout, having refused to sign the contract which the club presented him some time ago. Foster received a big cut in his salary and the veteran declined to sign, stating that he would devote his time to his farm. [He had won 8 and lost 7 during 1917 for the Red Sox.]

Shean is a former Boston [Braves] infielder and is a resident of Arlington, Mass. [He batted only .210 during 1917 as the Reds' regular second baseman.]

Eddie Hurley, *Boston Record*

Tuesday, April 2

JOHNNY EVERS, SPEEDY SECOND SACKER OF THE RED SOX. WHOSE 1918 SLOGAN IS "MORE OF THE OLD "PEP".

Scott, *Boston Post*

Sox Do It Again in Ninth Inning

Whiteman's Drive Beats Striving Robins, 3–2

LITTLE ROCK, ARK., April 1—Shooting across that ninth inning finish by the Red Sox is getting to be just as common as the beans on Saturday night. Today, for the third consecutive time, they nosed out the Robins in the final chapter.

George Whiteman, otherwise known as "Bandit Pete," the mighty hunter from Houston, slashed out the bingle that drove Strunk home with the deciding tally. The score was 3 to 2.

Edward F. Martin, *Boston Globe*

Shean's Run Wins for Sox in 16th

DALLAS, TEX., April 2—It took 16 long innings beneath the blazing Texas sun for the Red Sox and Dodgers to settle the daily argument this afternoon, but the result was just the same as usual. The Boston team showed the punch at the critical time and the big tally made in the 16th inning gave Barrow's team the verdict by the score of 7 to 6.

A Boston lad was the hero of the game. Dave Shean rushed to the fore at the eleventh hour to fill the shoes of Johnny Evers, who is now sick abed, and drove out the longest wallop of the battle, a hit that struck the top of the left field fence in the 16th. He then scored the winning run on a long sacrifice fly by Amos Strunk to centre.

Paul H. Shannon, *Boston Post*

[The Sox had broken camp and were barnstorming with the Dodgers through southern towns before heading north to open the season. In 1918 it was common for two professional baseball teams to play one another throughout spring training.]

[Bullet Joe] Bush is a fun-maker. He finds it hard work to keep quiet, and his antics have caused many of the players to lose considerable sleep during the night trips of the club. Joe is always one of the last players in the party to hit the pillow and is one of the first to arise in the morning.

Joe cannot understand how John McCormack inherited such a wonderful voice while he has to be satisfied with the vocal cords of a hawkster. Although Bush is no Caruso, his songs are a source of great pleasure on the trip.

Eddie Hurley, *Boston Record*

[John McCormack and Enrico Caruso were famous tenors of the era.]

Scott, *Boston Post*

The Year the Red Sox Won the Series

Red Sox Slam Ball Hard and Win, 10–4

AUSTIN, TEX., April 4—Spitball pitching proved to be just the tonic that the Old Family Physician prescribed for the Red Sox today. They laced the Robins 10–4, whacking moist ball chuckers Dan Grimer and Larry Cheney for 20 blows. Joe Bush pitched the first six innings for the Sox and was extremely effective.

Edward F. Martin, *Boston Globe*

Shean, the newcomer obtained from Cincinnati, was the hero of the day. He was all over the field, mixed up in several double plays, had four assists and four putouts, and at the plate he had a regular old home week with the willow. Five times Davie stepped to the swatting station and five times he cracked out safe wallops. The Sox are all jubilant this evening over the acquisition of the Arlington boy. He has put a punch in the line-up that makes it even more dangerous than it has been.

Boston Herald and Journal

[Dave Shean, thirty-four years old, had played with five teams since 1906 and had a lifetime batting average of .228. The Red Sox hoped he would cover second base until the war was over.]

Late reports from the Red Sox camp indicate that Johnny Evers is through as an infielder. The famous Trojan has practically admitted that his attempted comeback has been a failure. Johnny worked too hard at the Springs, and soon after the team left there he was taken ill. The Red Sox will retain Johnny as a coach and he may get into a game now and then, but it looks as though his fight to be a regular has been a losing one. He was one of the gamest and nerviest players that ever donned an infielder's mitt.

Harry J. Casey, *Boston Record*

CENTER-FIELDER AMOS STRUNK- ONE OF THE RED SOX' LIVE WIRES FOR THE 1918 SEASON -

OH GLADYS! ISN'T HE STUNNINGLY HANDSOME?

STRUNK IS A CLASSY DRESSER IN STREET CLOTHES -

Scott, *Boston Post*

NEW ORLEANS, April 6—There was a lot of rain today. It ceased just long enough to let the residents view a great Liberty Loan parade. "Buy, buy Liberty Bonds, or bye bye Liberty" was the message flashed from every banner.

Edward F. Martin, *Boston Globe*

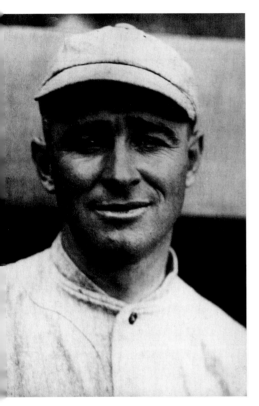

Dave Shean, Boston's new second baseman

Tuesday, April 9

"There were few second basemen in the National League last year any better than Shean. Not only is Shean a fine fielder but he is also a wicked hitter. He is what is known as a hard luck hitter. He drives the ball hard, but last year he always seemed to hit directly at some waiting fielder. He is a fighter, too. He knows the game thoroughly, and if he gets the chance to get in there every day he will be a hard man to keep out of the lineup."

Eddie Hurley, *Boston Record*

[These comments were made by Bill Klem, a National League umpire.]

Wednesday, April 10

Dodgers Edge Red Sox 3 to 1 in Listless Game

Players Are Chilled by Frigid Blasts and Rush Through Seven Innings in 30 Minutes

BIRMINGHAM, ALA., April 9—It was so cold at the park today that neither club cared who won. McCabe, pitching for the Sox, tossed the ball over without a thing on it, to get the seven innings played.

The score meant nothing to either team, but the warm rooms in the hotel certainly did. The seven innings were played in about half an hour, which shows how fast the boys were hitting the first ball and not waiting for good ones.

Boston Herald and Journal

Seven innings were played with Babe Ruth as umpire. In the last inning, with the bases filled and two out, the newspapermen made a motion that Ruth be commandeered as a pinch hitter. The motion went through. Babe pulled off his sweater and knocked the first one over the fence, foul by a foot. Then he fanned. He said his hands were cold.

Edward F. Martin, *Boston Globe*

When the players arrive in the Hub, they will be a worn out lot. They've been hitting and running through the South, and the one-day stands have not done the club much good. They have had little rest on the sleepers, and the boys will be mighty glad to get back to Boston. These southern trips are not all they are cracked up to be.

The players will need a couple of nights' rest in anchored beds before they open the season. They have been rolling around in berths so long that they will be glad of a chance to get a night's rest in real comfortable beds.

Eddie Hurley, *Boston Record*

Friday, April 12

BOSTON, MASS., "You can say that I am well pleased with the club's prospects for the coming season," said owner Harry Frazee of the Red Sox, who arrived in this city last night. "The men all looked good in the South. I promise they will show the same spirit that has given the Hub so many championships in recent years."

Boston Herald and Journal

[The Red Sox were World Champions in 1903, 1912, 1915, and 1916. They were the most successful franchise in baseball through the first two decades of the twentieth century.]

Sunday, April 14

Red Sox Primed for League Race

There is every reason to believe the Red Sox will be in the hunt for the American League honors. We have a good ball club that has the ability to sail along once it strikes its stride. They are seasoned and many have been on championship clubs, but I find with all this high-class material that there is an absence of emergency players. Once we get this department bolstered up all the other teams will have to watch out.

The race will not be an easy one. The White Sox, with their championship team intact, is the club all will go after. You can wager none will be after them any stronger than the Boston club.

I look for a stronger batting team than the Sox were last year, and I think the catching department is a big improvement. The leading pitchers, Ruth, Leonard, Mays and Bush, form the best quartet in the league.

The infield is strong, with Hoblitzell at first, Shean and Evers alternating at second, Scott at short, and McInnis at third. McInnis is sure to be a wonderful third sacker. He's a natural ball player, and when you have a man like him you feel secure no matter where you place him.

Strunk and Hooper will be good, and I look for either Whiteman or Smith to play the other position [left field] acceptably.

Ed Barrow, *Boston Herald and Journal*

There is every reason to believe the Red Sox will be in the hunt for the American League honors.

Part 3 The Pennant Race

Sox Play A's Today in Opener

This afternoon the championship race in the American League begins. Throughout the entire east, defying snow, weather conditions, the activities of the Hun and the countless changes that the war situation has evolved, the hardy athletes will begin the battle.

Many old-time favorites will be missing from the lineup that Boston puts in the field for this opening game. Barry, Lewis, Shore, Janvrin and others will be badly missed. But in the places of these acknowledged stars are others whose reputations will surely bear comparison. Nearly $100,000 worth of newly purchased stars fill up the gaps in the ranks that drafts and enlistments have created.

In Bullet Joe Bush, Stuffy McInnis, Amos Strunk and Wallie Schang the Sox have procured a quartet of the finest players in the American League. A splendid pitcher, a peer among infielders, a grand outfielder and a hard hitting, fleet-footed catcher are included in the quartet.

Duffy Lewis and his famous bat will be missed, but in the capable left fielder's place will be the veteran Whiteman, whom Barrow confidently expects to fill the bill.

At the middle sack, pending the disposition of the once great Johnnie Evers, will be found a popular Greater Boston lad, Dave Shean. Critics believe Shean will make good.

For today's opening clash, Manager Barrow will undoubtedly select as his mainstay on the rubber Big Babe Ruth, whose sterling work with the bat and all around behavior has had the whole South talking for the past few weeks. Ruth is in grand shape and crazy to twirl the opening contest. Old reliable Sam Agnew will do the catching.

Paul Shannon, *Boston Post*

OVERTURE BATTING ORDER

RED SOX	ATHLETICS
Hooper, rf	lf, Kopp
Shean, 2b	rf, Jamieson
Strunk, cf	3b, Gardner
Hoblitzell, 1b	1b, Burns
McInnis, 3b	cf, Walker
Whiteman, lf	c, McAvoy
Scott, ss	2b, Shannon
Agnew, c	ss, Dugan
Ruth, p	p, Myers

Gates open at 1:30. Game starts at 3:15.

The Pennant Race

[Below are some managers' statements at the opening of the season.]

Clarence Rowland: Chicago White Sox

Judging by the way the "bushers" whaled us about in the South, it looks as if we are going to break to a slow start. However, I think we'll go on about our business when the flag falls.

You know, a world's championship ball club is the hardest of all to get going down in the South in the Spring. The boys know that it doesn't make a lick of difference what happens then. The manager just cannot make them hit it up.

But we're ready for the bell, and I am sure we will stay up above the .500 notch all the way. Repeat? Sure we will! I know we will!

[Chicago had won the 1917 American League pennant, with 100 victories and 54 losses, 9 games ahead of the Red Sox.]

Hugh Jennings: Detroit Tigers

In view of the coming draft it is difficult to form any opinion about the outlook for the coming season. The Tigers look good right now, and with the added strength in the box, we ought to be up in the running all through the season.

We will still have the punch, with Cobb, Veach and Heilmann in the outfield, and our infield ought to be just as strong, if not stronger, than last year.

[The Tigers had finished fourth in 1917, with 78 wins and 76 losses.]

Lee Fohl: Cleveland Indians

There is no reason why Cleveland should not finish in the first division, providing the present makeup is not disturbed by the government. We have some valuable players eligible for the service, and should they be taken, it will be a serious blow.

I do not believe Boston is as strong as last year, while it is doubtful if Chicago will be as lucky as in '17. Detroit will be dangerous.

[The Indians had finished third in the 1917 race, with 88 wins and 66 losses, 12 games behind Chicago.]

Miller Huggins: New York Yankees

Apart from the pitching, the Yankees appear to be just the kind of a team I want. I have a dandy infield, both on offence and defence, a good outfield and a fine catching department.

As far as can be told beforehand, there's a hot race coming in the American League, and I expect to be right in it.

[The Yankees had a disapointing sixth-place finish in 1917, with 71 wins and 82 losses.]

Boston American

Red Sox Open with Victory

BOSTON, April 15—Colossal Babe Ruth of the Sox sideswiped the ambitious Athletics of Philadelphia, 7 to 1, in the opening game at Fenway Park yesterday afternoon. It is Babe's delight to take the joy out of things for ambitious ball clubs in the first game of the season, and this is the third straight April in which the giant southpaw has whistled his way through to a win in the "They're off" game.

Before the game the newly tailored athletes of both teams swung into line and, with the band in the middle, marched to the flagpole, where Capts. Dick Hoblitzell of the Sox and Rube Oldring of the A's hoisted a new and more significant Old Glory to the masthead. Back they came, each athlete carrying a plea for subscriptions to the third Liberty Bond issue. At the plate they were met by Mayor Peters, who, in behalf of the Royal Rooters and other Hose fans, gave President Frazee and Capt. Hoblitzell several floral pieces.

Amos Strunk appeared in centre field for the domestics. Both afield and at bat, Amos looked like a big part of the odd million or so that Harry Frazee gave Connie Mack for Messrs. Bush, Schang, and Strunk.

This new centre-fielder of ours made a catch off the bat of Joe Dugan in the second inning which was a gem. The bases were full at the time and but one man had been retired. Babe had been showing an unaccountable streak of wildness. The game was on the edge of one of those well known breaks.

When Dugan spanked the ball, it seemed ticketed for the fence, for two bases, maybe three; for two runs, maybe three. But in came Strunkie like a flash. He caught the ball near the close-cropped tops of last summer's grass, was rolled over by the force of the ball, but held it and straightened up in time to throw to third base.

One run did score after the catch of this sacrifice fly; but if Amos had not caught the ball it would have been a bevy of tallies coming over for the A's.

You can never tell where a young remade team like the A's would have stopped if they had been lucky or good enough to have amassed three or four runs off the great Ruth in the second frame. So, here's to Strunkie and his fleetness. He is a great outfielder and fits into the Hoseman's centre garden.

• [Winning pitcher, Ruth (1–0); losing pitcher, Myers.]

Burt Whitman, *Boston Herald and Journal*

It is Babe's delight to take the joy out of things for ambitious ball clubs in the first game of the season . . .

Babe Ruth in Mid-Season Form in First Game

Scott, *Boston Post*

Johnny Evers has passed out of Boston baseball. As was to have been expected, the Trojan made his exit in a somewhat exciting fashion. All Boston expected him to be out in uniform yesterday at the Fenway, but he wasn't. Instead, he appeared in the rear of the grandstand.

He had come over, he declared, ready to play in the opening game. He said he was in great shape and had been going good. But, he was told that he was not to play. He claims to have been used rather roughly all round.

The Red Sox had just about decided to get rid of the fiery Trojan anyway. Waivers were asked on him recently shortly after he had indulged in an argument with Huburt (Dutch) Leonard, who is also inclined to be temperamental.

The famous second baseman has a contract with the Sox, but said contract, of course, contains the ten-day clause, so he'll have to go willy-nilly.

Nick Flatley, Boston American

[The hard-driving, intense Evers infuriated his teammates and upset the morale of the team, forcing Barrow to get rid of him. The future Hall of Famer didn't play in the majors again until 1922, when he batted three times with the White Sox.]

Wednesday, April 17

Mays Pitches a One-Hit Game

Scott Drives McInnis Home with the Only Tally of the Contest

BOSTON, April 16—This came within an ace of being the most thrilling triumph ever registered by the submarine delivery. A base hit by Joe Dugan, a solid smack toward right with one out in the eighth frame, which Dave Shean valiantly endeavored to get in front of, spoiled the story and kept Blonde Carl Mays from putting over a no-hit game and horning into baseball's hall of fame.

However, the Sox grabbed the ball game in the ninth, Scotty driving Stuffy McInnis home with the one big marker of the contest, the score being 1 to 0.

It was a great day for the uplift delivery. The sturdy Oregonian, who serves a grunt with every underhand fling, never pitched a better game in his life. Just three of the Mackmen got to first, two of them walking. They went down in order from the third to the eighth stanzas. Mays fanned eight of them and demonstrated cleverly just how a pitcher should field his job.

* [Winning pitcher, Mays (1–0); losing pitcher, Perry. Red Sox' standing: 2 wins, 0 losses; in first place.]

Edward F. Martin, Boston Globe

[Carl Mays, twenty-six years old, was one of the young aces in baseball, winning 18 games in 1916 and 22 in 1917. He went on to win 207 against only 126 losses in his career with the Red Sox, Yankees, and Cincinnati Reds. However, Mays was remembered primarily as the pitcher who killed Ray Chapman with a beanball in 1920.

A morose loner, Mays was unpopular with many of his own teammates and the fans. All that mattered to him was his success, which was considerable. Mays played on six pennant winners in Boston and New York.]

Van Ulm, *Boston Record*

Red Sox Snatch Victory in Thrilling Climax, 5–4

BOSTON, April 17—An Athletics alumnus, Wallie Schang, busted up a ball game which Connie Mack thought he had tucked away at Fenway Park yesterday afternoon. Wallie slapped a most timely single to right field in the last of the ninth, with the bases full and none out. The two Red Sox runs needed to win were chased across in the persons of George Whiteman and Everett Scott.

The score of the feverishly ending game was 5 to 4. It was the third straight win for Barrow's Crimson Hosemen, who still lead the world in victories, with three wins and no defeats. Best of all, it was a winning, uphill fight.

[Winning pitcher, Leonard (1–0); losing pitcher, Adams. Red Sox' standing: 3 wins, 0 losses; in first place.]

Burt Whitman, *Boston Herald and Journal*

Last year the Sox could not win unless their pitchers, Ruth, Mays, Shore, Leonard and Foster, were at the top of their game. This year it is different. Leonard, as yesterday, can spend the day at the seashore or take a trip to the White Mountains and the heavy artillery, bought for a big price this winter, will get down to expert target practice and knock over enough runs to win the game.

Bob Dunbar, *Boston Herald and Journal*

Ex-Mayor John F. Fitzgerald spoke for the Camp Devens baseball plant fund and the Navy Yard band played the national anthem. Pretty misses passed around bright shining dishes for the collection and the response was generous.

Boston Herald and Journal

[John (Honey Fitz) Fitzgerald, one of the most loyal fans in Boston and a longstanding member of the Royal Rooters, was the grandfather of President John F. Kennedy, who had been born the previous year.]

Friday, April 19

NOTHING DOING YESTERDAY, OLD JUPE PLUVIUS PUT THE KIBOSH ON THE PROGRAM

Scott, *Boston Post*

Miller Huggins and his gang of rejuvenated Yanks are here and although the 1918 season is only a few days old, they have two scalps, secured from Walter Johnson, dangling from their belts. This is almost unheard of but nevertheless it's true. Both victories scored by the Yankees were at the great Walter's expense.

Eddie Hurley, *Boston Record*

Saturday, April 20

Red Sox Win Two from Yankees

Take Morning Game 2–1 with Bush, Repeat with Ruth by 9–5 Score

BOSTON, April 19—By winning both games from the strongest aggregation that has represented the New York American League club in years, the

Boston Red Sox yesterday annexed their fifth successive victory and added to a rapidly increasing lead over their American League rivals.

In the forenoon engagement, essentially a pitchers' battle, another of the great quartet of stars that Frazee purchased last winter came through in gallant style. This game, which was won by Boston, 2 to 1, gave a splendid exemplification of the wonderful effectiveness of Bullet Joe Bush, who allowed his rivals but three scattered hits and was really entitled to a shutout.

The afternoon contest, much more exciting and full of loose play and free hitting, ended in a second triumph for the Barrow organization, the Red Sox winning out to the tune of 9 to 5. The bitter cold was undoubtedly accountable for New York's many fielding slumps in this battle. The disastrous errors of Pratt, Pipp and Baker enabled Babe Ruth to reel through to a comfortable win.

- [Game one: winning pitcher, Bush (1–0); losing pitcher, Russell. Game two: winning pitcher, Ruth (2–0); losing pitcher, Thormahlen. Red Sox' standing: 5 wins, 0 losses; in first place.]

Paul H. Shannon, *Boston Post*

[The Boston Marathon was held in the morning. But unlike previous races, 1918's marathon was a twenty-five-mile relay by armed service teams. Camp Devens, with ten runners, won the race in two hours, 24 minutes, 53 seconds.]

G. Babe is still the same old attraction. While his serving was far from hit-proof yesterday he still can sting them. Once he hit a ball so high that when it finally came down Pratt [the Yankee's second baseman] dropped it. Bill Slocum [a sportswriter] of New York said it came in contact with snow in the upper realms.

Edward F. Martin, *Boston Globe*

Scott's Improvement with Stick a Pleasant Surprise

One of the features of the attack of the Red Sox is the hitting of Everett Scott. The latter, never considered a heavy hitter, is now clouting the ball. Of course, we do not expect Scott to maintain his present clip. Although Scotty is one of the best fielding shortstops in the league, his one weakness has been his stick work.

In 1916 he managed to hit for .232 and last season he boosted this nine points, finishing with an average of .241. If he can add another five points to his average this year Manager Barrow will be satisfied. In the series against the Athletics he hit for an average of .400.

Harry J. Casey, *Boston Record*

Hub Hose Make Yanks Sixth Victim in Row

Barrow's Men Give Carl Mays Sensational Support with Harry Hooper Starring at Bat and Afield

BOSTON, April 21—Ed Barrow's Boston tank crushed the New York Yankees, 4 to 3, at the Fens yesterday afternoon, making it six wins in a row for the Red Sox, a continued perfect percentage and another argument that these 1918 Hub Hose form about the greatest ball club any of our managers has had.

Blonde Carl Mays fired for the Red Sox and went the distance, but was pummelled rather briskly by Huggins' men, who made 11 hits. But behind the white-haired pitcher, the Hose played sensational baseball. It was their third straight errorless game, and four times they staged double plays, cutting off incipient Yankee riots.

Harry Hooper was the pilot of the modern juggernaut, the god in the machine. His far double to the right field corner in the last of the eighth inning, with the score knotted at 3 to 3, eventually worked into the winning run.

Just to stamp his modest name a little deeper into the story, Harry had to go and save the game for the Sox in the last frame. With two outs and eager Yanks on first and second base, Ping Bodie, who already had whacked out a double and a single, caught the ball with the fat part of his bat, lining it to right field, far enough away from Hooper to get a double, maybe a triple.

Hooper had to travel on the wings of light to get the poke, but his speed is just equal to that sort of traveling and he grabbed the ball, writing "finis" to the yarn of the sixth straight.

- [Winning pitcher, Mays (2–0); losing pitcher, Love. Red Sox' standing: 6 wins, 0 losses; in first place.]

Burt Whitman, *Boston Herald and Journal*

Sam Agnew, Red Sox catcher

Whence the assumption that Sam Agnew cannot throw? He picked off the Yankees repeatedly yesterday. No medals will be given to them for baserunning. They were not taking chances and getting caught; they were merely wandering away from the sacks, and hesitating in a dreamy sort of way until Agnew burned the ball to Hoblitzell or to Stuffy. Three of them Sam threw out, and when he caught Gilhooley napping it was for the third time in the Yankee series.

Francis Eaton, *Boston American*

Sox Get Away to Best Start Ever

With three straight victories over the rejuvenated Mackmen and as many more from the New York Yankees to their credit, the rushing Red Sox may well be satisfied with the result of the first week of the championship campaign.

The sensation of the team is undoubtedly Amos Strunk, who gives promise of filling a breach left in the team ever since the great Tris Speaker was sold to Cleveland. The change from Philadelphia to a team of winners is bound to prove a great inspiration to the lad. Many believe that this is going to be Strunk's greatest year in baseball.

Paul H. Shannon, *Boston Post*

[The Red Sox had not played on Sunday, the 21st, because Sunday baseball was then banned in Boston. Eleven years later, in 1929, the Red Sox and Braves were permitted to play on the Sabbath; but the Red Sox had to schedule Sunday home games at Braves' Field because of Fenway Park's proximity to a church. It wasn't until July 3, 1932, after further legislation and much brouhaha, that the Red Sox finally played their first Sunday game at Fenway Park.]

AMERICAN LEAGUE STANDINGS

	Won	Lost	PCT.	GB
Boston 6		0	1.000	—
Cleveland 2		1	.667	2.5
Chicago 1		1	.500	3
Washington 2		2	.500	3
St. Louis 2		2	.500	3
New York 2		4	.333	4
Detroit 0		1	.000	3.5
Philadelphia 0		4	.000	5

Red Sox Are Halted by Baker's Batting

New York Wins by 11 to 4

BOSTON, April 22—Miller Huggins' heavy artillery continued its bombardment today against another of Ed Barrow's pitching stars, and the winning streak of the Red Sox came to an end after six successive victories had been chalked up. The Yanks mauled the offerings of Dutch Leonard and Sam Jones mercilessly and, helped along by some Boston errors, won in easy fashion by the score of 11 to 4.

They hit anything and everything, went through the game without being charged with a strikeout, and only sharp fielding prevented the Yanks from running their total of hits far above thirteen.

Frank [Home Run] Baker led the attack with two long doubles, two clean singles, and a sacrifice fly in five trips to the plate. The New York third baseman came up in the third inning with the score 2 to 0 against the Yanks and the bases filled, and his double to the left-field fence chased three runners home. His sacrifice fly in the fourth sent another run home, and his singles in the seventh and ninth innings started the Yanks on more scoring sessions.

- [Winning pitcher, Mogridge; losing pitcher, Leonard (1–1). Red Sox' standing: 6 wins, 1 loss; in first place.]

New York Times

[Baker was the American League home run champion from 1911 to 1914 while playing with the Philadelphia Athletics. As the king of the dead ball era, he swung an enormous fifty-two ounce bat, producing a single-season high of twelve homers in 1913.

After playing in four World Series with the Athletics, he sat out the 1915 season in a salary dispute. As a result, Connie Mack sold him to the Yankees in 1916 for the gigantic sum of $37,500. Baker proceeded to become New York's biggest star and concluded his career with the Yankees in 1922. His lifetime batting average was .307 and he hit 96 home runs during thirteen seasons. "Home Run" Baker was elected to the Hall of Fame in 1955.]

In the two games Dutch Leonard has twirled, he has shown poor form. He has been wild and has not been able to get his ball working. Leonard did not do much work in the South, and it will be some time before he is right.

Boston Record

Dick Hoblitzell continues in a rut. Dick has made but one hit in 25 times to the bat. His inability to hit has been felt, as he is still batting in the cleanup position.

Boston Record

Wednesday, April 24

Sox Go Hitless until Ninth, Then Win 1–0

Red-Hot Game Ends When Ping Bodie Drops Easy Fly

BOSTON, April 23—What Amos Strunk and Babe Ruth did to the youthful and ambitious Herbert Thormahlen of New York in the last of the ninth yesterday at the Fens was absolutely atrocious and unprecedented. They dented into a performance of Herbie's which had been hitless for eight full innings, and furnished the big guns in the manufacture of the only run scored in the game, enough to win for Barrow's Sox 1 to 0.

Amos rapped the first Sox hit of the game to left field, with one out in the ninth. Babe Ruth, interposed as a pinch hitter for Dick Hoblitzell, pounced on the very first pitch and sent it to centre field, the fleet Strunk going all the way to third base.

Here was a pretty howdye. McInnis, the hard hitting Stuffy, was the next batter, and he has the reputation of being able to do quite wicked things to young left-handers. So a conference of war among the Yanks resulted in the intentional passing of Stuffy, filling the bases.

George Whiteman rapped a fly to left field, not so very deep. Bodie was all set for the catch, and apparently was too darned eager to start his throw to the plate. For the routine fly dropped from his hands and Strunk scored, and the game was over.

Against Thormahlen the Sox used Joe Bush. He pitched a fine article of ball, allowing but three hits.

[Winning pitcher, Bush (2–0); losing pitcher, Thormahlen. Red Sox' standing: 7 wins, 1 loss; in first place.]

Burt Whitman, Boston Herald and Journal

Thormahlen fouled into the stands in the third inning and the ball hit a spectator and broke his cigar. The fan, not to be outdone, lighted another one.

Boston Record

IT WAS ALL OFF WITH THE N.Y. YANKS IN THE 9TH WHEN WITH BASES FILLED, "PING" BODIE MUFFED WHITEMAN'S FLY—

Scott, Boston Post

The Red Sox

When Boston comes to town to play
  Its line-up seems familiar.
You think you'll call the turn that day —
  You say it well—but will yer?
To see our favorites once again
  On our hearts leaves a scar.
Since Connie Mack started trading off his men
  We dunno where we are.

With Strunk and Schang and old Joe Bush
  Not to mention Stuff McInnis
They make a team that's in the push
  To old times they write "Finis."
The saddest words of tongue and pen
  Are "Traded is each star."
Since Connie Mack started trading off his men
  We dunno where we are.

Philadelphia Evening Bulletin

[The Philadelphia Athletics were one of the great teams in the early twentieth century, with six American League pennants and three world championship teams between 1901 and 1914.

Beginning in 1915, Connie Mack began selling off his stars, and the A's immediately plummeted from first to last place. They finished last consistently over the next decade, fielding some of the worst teams in the history of baseball. For instance, the 1916 Athletics finished with a record of 36 wins and 117 losses, 58.5 games out of first. Needless to say, their fans felt betrayed by Mack's deals.]

Thursday, April 25

Burns's Homer Beats Red Sox

Shean's Error Paves Way for Athletics' 3–0 Triumph

PHILADELPHIA, April 24—A glaring error on an easy grounder and a carelessly pitched ball cost the Red Sox a ball game at Shibe Park this afternoon. Dave Shean perpetrated the foozle, and Babe Ruth put the ball in the groove with nothing on it but Ban Johnson's signature. George Burns walloped it into the left-field stands for a homer, and the Athletics captured the first home conflict of the season, 3 to 0.

The former Athletics now playing with the Red Sox were remembered by their friends before the game. Joe Bush was presented with a diamond Elks badge, Stuffy McInnis got a chest of silver, Wally Schang drew a basket of flowers and a cane, and Amos Strunk was handed a set of golf clubs. That's all they got during the afternoon, but it was enough.

[Winning pitcher, Gregg; losing pitcher, Ruth (2–1). Red Sox' standing: 7 wins, 2 losses; in first place.]

Boston Herald and Journal

They sold $111,300 worth of Liberty Bonds at the New York American League opener. Owner Jacob Ruppert of the Yankees purchased $63,000 worth.

H. W. Lanigan, *Boston American*

Friday, April 26

Red Sox Square Up Count with Macks

Mays and Strunk Shine in Boston's 6–1 Victory

PHILADELPHIA, April 25—The Red Sox defeated the Athletics 6 to 1 today. Carl Mays, with his underslung slants, had the Mackmen eating out of his hand. It was not until the eighth when they made three hits, two of them scratches, that the home talent was able to score.

- [Winning pitcher, Mays (3–0); losing pitcher, Adams. Red Sox' standing: 8 wins, 2 losses; in first place.]

Boston Globe

2,000 Fans Watch Athletics Play First Twilight Game

The first day of twilight baseball in Philadelphia cannot be put down as a success.

About 2,000 fans came out for the late start at Shibe Park yesterday. They sat and shivered through more than two hours of rather spotty baseball. The game did not start until 4 o'clock, the supposition being that people who work late would have a better opportunity to see the games. Not many availed themselves of the privilege yesterday, and nearly half of those who came out hurried home to dinner before the contest ended.

Philadelphia Evening Bulletin

[The first night game in the major leagues would not be played until May 20, 1935, in Cincinnati.]

Saturday, April 27

Red Sox Snatch 2 to 1 Game from Athletics

PHILADELPHIA, April 26—The Philadelphia 4 o'clocks were spotted 10 bases on balls, seven husky hits and one perfectly good score in the twilight baseball game today. But despite this handicap, they easily lost to the Red Sox by the score of 2 to 1. It's pretty hard to go down in defeat with odds like that, but it must be remembered that the Athletics are past masters in the art of losing ball games.

Dutch Leonard, who labored for the Barrows, had everything but speed, curves, and control. Toward the end of the game the heroic audience

There's nothing a ball player likes so much as to come back and whip the ball club that let him go.

believed that someone had mislaid the home plate, for the portsider couldn't find it without a microscope.

- [Winning pitcher, Leonard (2–1); losing pitcher, Perry. Red Sox' standing: 9 wins, 2 losses; in first place.]

Boston Herald and Journal

Sunday, April 28

Ex-Athletics Rout Present Mack Team, 4 to 1

Sweet Revenge for Men Traded to Boston

PHILADELPHIA, April 27—Those ex-Athletic ball players slipped the Mackmen another trimming today, when the Red Sox won the fourth and final engagement of the series, 4 to 1, making it three triumphs out of four games.

There's nothing a ball player likes so much as to come back and whip the ball club that let him go. There is nothing charitable or magnanimous about the callous soul of the average ball player, and past friendships hold no ties for him.

The Red Sox amassed just four runs while engaged in the pleasant job of handing out the third consecutive trimming. "Stuffy" McInnis batted in two of them, while the other two were whaled home by Amos Strunk and Wally Schang. Bullet Joe Bush kept the Mackmen away from home plate, making these four tallies an ample sufficiency to win the ball game.

- [Winning pitcher, Bush (3–0); losing pitcher, Myers. Red Sox' standing: 10 wins, 2 losses; in first place.]

Boston Globe

Monday, April 29

AMERICAN LEAGUE STANDINGS			
	Won	Lost	PCT.	GB
Boston 10		2	.833	—
Cleveland 6		2	.750	2
Chicago 3		2	.600	3.5
New York 5		7	.417	5
Detroit 2		3	.400	4.5
Washington 4		6	.400	5
Philadelphia 3		7	.300	6
St. Louis 2		6	.250	6

RED SOX BATTING

	AB	R	BH	2B	3B	HR	SB	AVG
Strunk, cf 35		7	16	1	1	0	5	.457
Ruth, p 10		1	4	0	0	0	0	.400
Hooper, rf 36		8	12	4	1	0	4	.333
Shean, 2b 38		4	12	3	0	0	1	.316
Schang, c, lf 14		4	4	1	0	0	0	.288
McInnis, 3b 43		6	12	2	0	0	0	.279
Scott, ss 41		5	10	0	0	0	1	.244
Whiteman, lf 31		4	6	1	0	0	3	.194
Hoblitzell, 1b 42		3	4	1	0	0	2	.095
Agnew, c 38		3	3	2	0	0	0	.079

Stuffy's Fielding Errorless So Far

Any fears the Red Sox manager and supporters may have felt that "Stuffy" McInnis might not be able to play the third base position are rapidly being dispelled. In an even dozen games, he has yet to have an error recorded against him in 44 chances, which is a highly encouraging record for a first season at the hot corner.

Boston Post

Scott, *Boston Post*

Tuesday, April 30

Frazee Rejects $100,000 Offer for Pitcher Ruth

Red Sox Owner Declares He Sooner Would Think of Selling Franchise Than Parting with Big Ace

Since the start of the championship season owner Harry Frazee of the Red Sox has been offered more than $100,000 for one ball player. His name is George H. "Babe" Ruth, colossal southpaw pitcher and hitter most extraordinary. The magnate turned down the offer, saying:

"I might as well sell the franchise and the whole club as sell Ruth. The sum named was three times as much as was paid for Tris Speaker, and is far and away bigger than any figure that has been used in baseball. But it is ridiculous to talk about it. Ruth is our Big Ace. He's the most talked of, most sought for, most colorful ball player in the game."

It is a certainty the offer came from New York or Chicago.

Burt Whitman, *Boston Herald and Journal*

Wednesday, May 1

Babe Ruth Looks Like One Million Iron Men

Performance of Diamond-Studded Colossus Contagious and Red Sox Canter Through to 8–1 Victory

BOSTON, April 30—"Yes, sir, I was offered $150,000 for that Baby and I would not think of selling him," quoth owner Harry H. Frazee of the Red Sox just before Babe Ruth unfurled his southpaw wares yesterday afternoon. Babe, the colossus, thereupon proceeded to look like a million dollars, rather than a picayune $150,000. He dosed the Washington Senators with an 8 to 1 set-back, winning so easily that there never was any question of the outcome.

Only five hits the Senators made, and only four men did they have left on base, which gives a fairly good idea of just how dangerous they were not.

- [Winning pitcher, Ruth (3–1); losing pitcher, Harper. Red Sox' standing: 11 wins, 2 losses; in first place.]

Burt Whitman, *Boston Herald and Journal*

They're still talking about that catch Amos Strunk made in the fourth inning off Clyde Milan. There did not seem to be a chance that Amos would spear the ball, but he dived head first and came up with it. It was one of the best catches ever pulled off at Fenway Park, and the fans gave him a big hand for it. Amos is proving to be a wonderful all-round man for the Sox. His fielding has been brilliant, while his sticking has been timely.

Boston Record

STRUNK MADE A WONDERFUL DIVING CATCH OF MILAN'S FLY IN THE 4TH INNING AND THE FANS WILDLY CHEERED—

Scott, *Boston Post*

More Than One Dream

Early yesterday morning big Babe Ruth awakened suddenly from a dream that he had been sold by the Red Sox. Later he read all about such a plan in the paper. I told Harry Frazee about Ruth's dream at the ball game yesterday afternoon, and he laughed and said that Babe was not the only dreamer. Harry would sell Babe, along with his right eye.

Boston Globe

[On January 5, 1920, Babe's dream came true. After Ruth set a major league record with 29 home runs in 1919, Frazee sold him to the New York Yankees for $110,000 in cash, notes, and interest, plus a $300,000 loan. Frazee was losing money on several Broadway shows, and he was being pressured to pay at least $300,000 for his 1916 purchase of the Red Sox. In addition, Ruth was demanding a $20,000 salary for 1920.

At the time of the sale, Frazee called Ruth one of the most selfish and inconsiderate men ever to put on a baseball uniform. He felt that Babe was out of control and the Boston club could no longer tolerate his bizarre behavior.

The Red Sox suffered through fifteen straight losing seasons following Ruth's sale. Meanwhile, Babe became the greatest hitter in baseball, finishing with 714 home runs and a lifetime batting average of .342. He led the Yankees to seven American League pennants and four world championships during Boston's dismal years.

Some people still believe that Ruth's sale laid a curse on the Red Sox, who haven't won a World Series since the Babe left them.]

Thursday, May 2

Johnson's Pitching Wins, 5–0

BOSTON, May 1—While Walter Johnson was standing the Red Sox on their heads this afternoon, the Senators gathered an armful of runs for him off Carl Mays. Walter splattered the Sox with a nice coat of whitewash and the Griffs finished the day on the heavy end of a 5 to 0 score.

It was the real Walter Johnson who was facing the Barrow clan today, and he kept the hits as scarce as fur coats in Washington in August. Four were all the Sox could gather off him, and two of these were of the infield variety. Harry Hooper was credited with three of the blows off Johnson. The Washington pitcher was never in danger of being beaten.

- [Winning pitcher, Johnson, losing pitcher, Mays (3–1). Red Sox' standing: 11 wins, 3 losses; in first place.]

J. V. Fitzgerald, *Washington Post*

[Johnson, with 416 lifetime victories, was one of the great pitchers in baseball history. Pitching for a Washington team that finished in the second division during ten of his twenty-one seasons, he set the major league record with 110 shutouts and compiled a brilliant 2.17 earned run average, the seventh best career mark of any pitcher.

He won more than 30 games in each of two seasons, more than 20 in ten other years. Johnson was also the premier strikeout artist of his day, leading the league twelve times, with a high of 313 in 1910. This was accomplished in an era when most batters choked up and rarely struck out.

Nicknamed the "Big Train" for the sound of his fastball, he was one of the most popular men in baseball. A shy, modest, and honest man, Johnson was among the first five players elected to the Hall of Fame in 1936.]

Walter Johnson and Harry Hooper

Walter Johnson is a tough bird to beat when he starts from scratch. But when you spot him five runs to work with it is just like handing Bennie Leonard, the lightweight champion, a loaded revolver and a blackjack when he steps into the ring to fight.

Edward F. Martin, *Boston Globe*

Clark Griffith [the Senators' manager] suggested to the umpires that the two men who were painting a sign on the left field fence at Fenway suspend their labors until after the game. "Let 'em stay there, they won't get hurt," said Nick Altrock, "it's a safety razor sign."

Bob Dunbar, *Boston Herald and Journal*

[Altrock, a forty-one-year-old pitcher/coach for the Senators, was one of baseball's funniest men. He performed baseball comedy acts, in pantomime, between games of doubleheaders.]

Fast Flying Sox Give Senators 8–1 Drubbing

Hooper and McInnis Hit Everything in Sight
Leonard Has One of His Good Days

BOSTON, May 2—Those two modest, ever-young athletes, Harry Hooper and John Stuffy McInnis, conducted a joint tour of vengeance yesterday afternoon at the Fens. They swiped the offerings of several Washington pitchers to the 32 points of the compass, wiped out the taint of Walter Johnson's browbeating performance of Wednesday, and proved the big cogs in the undoing of the Senators by the score of 8 to 1.

Harry Hooper was as fast as thought yesterday afternoon. He made three doubles, all rousing blows, but over and above that was his demonstration of great speed. In the second inning he stole second base in a most outrageous fashion, against the defense of pitcher Jim Shaw's pitch-out and catcher Eddie Ainsmith's fine, true throw. Then he beat out a bounder to the pitcher, which the flinger recovered in almost no time at all, throwing rapidly to first.

Hooper is putting up the grandest game of his career. He hits everything and hits to all fields. As a lead-off man, he is the charter member of the 100 percent efficiency club.

Stuffy continued playing his flawless fielding game. He has not made an error so far this season. He also made three hits in as many official appearances at bat. One of these blows was a regular whack to left field in the sixth inning with the bases jammed. All three runs scored before the Senators got through throwing the ball around the lot.

Hubert Dutch Leonard, that latter-day fashion plate for big league pitchers, worked one of his fine warm weather games. He repressed the usually free-hitting Senators to five hits. Dutch's half side-arm southpaw curve was swishing up to specifications.

[Winning pitcher, Leonard (3–1); losing pitcher, Shaw. Red Sox' standing: 12 wins, 3 losses; in first place.]

Burt Whitman, *Boston Herald and Journal*

Hank Shanks [Washington's left fielder] lammed the ball against the shoe sign in left in the second inning. That means Hank will appear Sunday morning with a new pair of shoes.

Edward F. Martin, *Boston Globe*

The Boston fans have been delighted with Harry Hooper's hitting. Harry, who always has been a prime favorite, has been stinging the ball better than at any time since he joined the club. His work in the field has also been consistent.

Harry starts with .396 as his batting average. In his 15 games he has been at bat 48 times and has made 19 hits, including eight two-baggers. He has scored 11 runs.

Melville E. Webb, Jr., Boston Globe

George Whiteman did not accompany the Red Sox to New York. The little outfielder is ill and was left at home. Whitey has not been in good health since he left Hot Springs. He had a serious attack of [grippe] there, and has not been able to get into good shape. Babe Ruth will do outfield duty for the Sox should anything happen to the regular trio while Whiteman is absent.

Boston Record

[The Red Sox had a critical shortage of outfielders because of Whiteman's health problems. Hooper suggested that Babe Ruth could move into left field, improving both the offense and the attendance.

However, Barrow felt he would become the laughingstock of baseball if he changed his ace left-hander into an outfielder. Wally Schang was tried in left field instead.]

Saturday, May 4

Miller's Heave Saves Yankees

Beat Sox 3–2 in 11th

NEW YORK, May 3—Successive singles by Frank Baker, Derrill Pratt and Wally Pipp gave the Yankees a 3 to 2 decision this afternoon in a grilling 11-inning battle. It was Bullet Joe Bush's first defeat of the season, although he pitched well enough to win an ordinary ball game.

A sensational heave home by Elmer Miller in the eighth inning prevented a Yankee humiliation. Bush started the trouble with a sharp single. Harry Hooper followed with a stinging bounder to right, which sent the pitcher to third. Dave Shean took a healthy swing and slammed a high fly to deep centrefield. It was dollars to doughnuts that the Bullet would score on the catch. Not one in a hundred fans expected otherwise.

Bush was off as the ball landed in Miller's hands. Without any apparent effort the centrefielder took aim and let the ball fly. It came in with the speed of a French 75 [an artillery weapon], and straight as a die for Hannah's big mitt. The catcher caught Bush as he was sliding in, and the Red Sox chance had flown.

* [Winning pitcher, Caldwell; losing pitcher, Bush (3–1). Red Sox' standing: 12 wins, 4 losses; in first place.]

Boston Herald and Journal

Babe Ruth Is Hero, Wields a Vicious Cudgel

Bangs Out a Double and a Home Run but Huggins' Clan Is Victor 5 to 4

NEW YORK, May 4—It was Babe Ruth's busy day at the Polo Grounds yesterday. The Yankees kept the big Boston lefthander hustling along through eight and one-half innings of highly exciting baseball. At the end, Ruth was one lap behind in the race and the New York contingent had taken its second straight game from the Boston rivals. The score was 5 to 4.

• [Winning pitcher, Russell; losing pitcher, Ruth (3–2). Home run: Ruth (1). Red Sox' standing: 12 wins, 5 losses; in first place.]

New York Times

[Ruth handled thirteen fielding chances as the Yankees bunted repeatedly on him. Babe made two errors, including a wild throw that allowed two runs to score.]

When Babe came to bat for the second time, Boston was trailing 4 to 1, with a runner on and two out. Mr. Ruth then decided to give a demonstration of why opposing pitchers consider him the king of the swatting clan. He eased one of Allan Russell's best into the upper right hand tier of the grandstand that lit foul by inches. It was a swat that shot out in a white streak and put the fear of the Lord into Huggins' clan.

Russell then fiddled around with Babe till he carried him to a count of 1 and 2. He put everything he had on a spitter and trusted to the god of battles. Ruth took him out and slammed the spitball fair on the trade mark. It hurtled into the upper deck of the right field stand just about twice as fast as the preceding foul and fair by as far as you could throw a stone.

W. J. MacBeth, *New York Tribune*

AMERICAN LEAGUE STANDINGS				
	Won	Lost	PCT.	GB
Boston 12		5	.706	—
Cleveland 9		6	.600	2
New York 8		8	.500	3.5
Chicago 6		6	.500	3.5
Detroit 5		6	.455	4
Philadelphia 6		8	.429	4.5
St. Louis 6		8	.429	4.5
Washington 5		10	.333	6

AND PERHAPS A SPECIAL SUNDAY "SKULL" PRACTICE WAS CALLED FOR THE RED SOX·

Scott, *Boston Post*

Tuesday, May 7

Yankees, Aided by Ping Bodie's Cudgel, Defeat Red Sox 10 to 3

NEW YORK, May 6—Ping Bodie personally conducted an uprising against the Boston Red Sox at the Polo Grounds yesterday. Bodie curled his trusty bat around the ball hard and often. He drove in five runs, scored another himself and was galloping the bases with wild abandon. There was only one run in which Ping did not have a hand or foot.

This was the third straight shock which the Yanks have handed the Boston club. The Yanks riddled Carl Mays, one of Barrow's best flingers, and drove him from the box in the fifth inning. Mays is the last of the old-fashioned flingers who delivers the ball with an underhand swing. He lets the ball go when the hand is down near the carpet and it gradually rises up to the batter. The Yanks encouraged the rising movement of the ball and sent it still higher.

Mays is also the only pitcher in baseball who grunts every time he throws the ball. Spectators not only can see him pitch, but they can hear him pitch. With every toss of the ball he makes a noise as if he were getting a tooth pulled.

* [Winning pitcher, Mogridge; losing pitcher, Mays (3–2). Home run: Ruth (2). Red Sox' standing: 12 wins, 6 losses; in first place.]

New York Times

The Pennant Race

The dastardly Ruth got in his back-biting slam. He lined one into the upper right tier some fifty feet fair, that shot on a line like a rifle bullet and knocked the back out of the seat.

W. J. Macbeth, *New York Tribune*

[Babe batted sixth and played first base, replacing the slumping Doc Hoblitzell. May 6, 1918, marked the first time Ruth played at any position other than pitcher.]

Babe Ruth continues to thrill the New Yorkers with his potential batting strength. They scoffed along Broadway when we sent them the story that there had been a $150,000 offer for Ruth. Now they will appreciate his worth. He'd be a better investment for the Yankees than would Ty Cobb. How the Babe would maltreat that right field stand, the upper tier, and the none too distant barriers.

Bob Dunbar, *Boston Herald and Journal*

[Five of Ruth's first eleven home runs were hit in New York's Polo Grounds. When he was sold to the Yankees in 1920, while playing half his games in the Polo Grounds, Babe blasted fifty-four home runs. Babe hit more round-trippers than any other team in the American League that year!]

Wednesday, May 8

Griffs Hit Leonard Hard and Rout Red Sox, 7 to 2

Babe Ruth Does His Best to Help Out Mates, His Homer Making Two Runs

WASHINGTON, May 7—Base hits were as plentiful again yesterday for the Nationals as straw hats in August. They made the pitching delivery of Dutch Leonard look like a target on which a squad of sharpshooters had been working at short range, gathering fourteen hits. Once they got their batting artillery in action the Sox never had a chance.

Babe Ruth, who swings a wicked bat, did his best to check Washington. He performed at first base instead of in the box, taking Hoblitzell's place. The regular first sacker has an injured finger. From the manner in which the buxom Babe performed yesterday, it wouldn't be such a blow to the Sox if Hobby is on the hospital list for some time.

All Babe did was to field his position faultlessly, almost gracefully, and rap out a home run, his third in as many successive games. His long swipe sailed over the right field wall, and he thereby won a suit of clothes for himself. The tailor is going to use a lot of cloth to rig out Babe.

- [Winning pitcher, Johnson; losing pitcher, Leonard (3–2). Home run: Ruth (3). Red Sox' standing: 12 wins, 7 losses; in first place.]

J. V. Fitzgerald, *Washington Post*

Walter Johnson, in addition to pitching in his best form, turned in a 1.000 batting average for the afternoon. He got three singles and a walk, drove in two runs and made possible the scoring of another.

Washington Post

Babe Ruth's stellar slam came in the sixth. Ruth got hold of a fast one and gave it wings. It sailed on and on and over the wall, messing up a war garden, and scaring a mongrel pup half to death. It was the first homer over that distant fence this season. As he trotted around behind Strunk, the big pitcher was given an ovation.

Boston Herald and Journal

Ruth Ties a Record

While the Red Sox have not had much occasion to smile lately, the club has had the satisfaction of seeing one of its members tie a baseball record that has stood several years. Babe Ruth now shares with Ray Caldwell of New York the American League distinction of having whacked out a home run in three successive ball games. Ruth did this trick with a homer in each of the last two games against the Yankees, followed by yesterday's base clearing clip against Walter Johnson in Washington.

Melville E. Webb, Jr., *Boston Globe*

[Caldwell hit a grand total of 8 home runs from 1910 to 1921; Ruth finished his career with 714 home runs.]

Thursday, May 9

Nationals, Off on Another Clubbing Spree, Rout Sox to Win, 14 to 4

WASHINGTON, May 8—Clark Griffith must be feeding his athletes raw meat these warm days. They ran mad on the bases for the third consecutive day, going on another of their wild batting orgies and driving Joe Bush and Carl Mays to the bracing patter of the showers. They made themselves dizzy whirling around the bases, and had the Red Sox infielders stepping on their tongues chasing the base clouts that rattled off their bats with the regularity of machine gun fire.

* [Winning pitcher, Shaw; losing pitcher, Bush (3–2). Red Sox' standing: 12 wins, 8 losses; in first place.]

J. V. Fitzgerald, *Washington Post*

The Nationals made the Sox look foolish when they got on the path, stealing five bases. The visitors threw the ball around like a lot of collegians once the Griffs got their rally underway. The Sox didn't look like a pennant winning club at all.

Washington Post

It's too early to perform an autopsy on the Red Sox. They'll prove a very lively corpse here at the Fens.

Friday, May 10

Nationals Rally Three Times to Take Ten-Inning Game from Red Sox, 4–3

WASHINGTON, May 9—Showing the same fighting spirit which has marked their play over a good part of the season, the Nationals turned in three batting rallies yesterday that enabled them to come from behind and take another game from the Red Sox. It was their third victory over Boston's pennant hopefuls, and gave them a clean sweep for the series.

Babe Ruth, who pitches and plays first base alternately, but hits almost always, was on the hill for the Sox. If it hadn't been for Babe playing his usual heavy role with the willow, the game would not have gone into extra innings. His double started the Beaneaters toward the run that tied the score in the eighth. He got a triple, three doubles and a single for a perfect day at bat. Babe can't hit any more than a bird can fly.

• [Winning pitcher, Johnson; losing pitcher, Ruth (3–3). Red Sox' standing: 12 wins, 9 losses; in second place.]

J. V. Fitzgerald, *Washington Post*

[While the Red Sox were losing their sixth game in a row, the Indians, with a 6–3 win over the Tigers, moved into first place .005 percentage points ahead of Boston.]

It's too early to perform an autopsy on the Red Sox. They'll prove a very lively corpse here at the Fens. There's altogether too much inherent strength to permit a collapse at this stage of the game. Just a little expert doctoring of pitchers and Ed Barrow's boys will come back as sturdily as they campaigned in the first few weeks of the season.

Bob Dunbar, *Boston Herald and Journal*

Saturday, May 11

Red Sox Defeat the Browns, 4–1

Carl Mays Is in Form Again, Allows But Five Hits

BOSTON, May 10—The Red Sox returned to their own camping ground yesterday and celebrated their arrival, as well as Manager Barrow's birthday, by downing the Browns in the first meeting of the season between the two teams.

Mays was himself again. Not a single pass did he give, and he was nearly as stingy with his base hits, allowing only five. The fielding behind Mays was better than usual, too. The snappy work of Shean, Scott, and Hooper aided Carl to get out of one or two threatening situations.

Another shakeup occurred in the Red Sox yesterday. While it may not prove to be permanent, Ruth was played in left field where his good ground-covering ability and a mighty whip might bolster up an outfield defense that has proven pretty weak of late. Strangely enough, Babe had not a single chance, and he failed in three trips to get a hit.

[Winning pitcher, Mays (4–2); losing pitcher, Davenport. Red Sox' standing: 13 wins, 9 losses; in second place.]

Paul H. Shannon, *Boston Post*

[This was Ruth's first game as an outfielder in the major leagues.]

"Gee, it's lonesome out there," lamented Babe Ruth, as he came back to the bench in the eighth inning yesterday afternoon. "Why, it's hard to keep awake. There's nothing to do."

The huge fellow made a fine impression as a left fielder, even if he did not have a putout or an assist. He handled three base hits which went to his district, playing them in the infield style which recalls Tris Speaker. He drove home the impression that he is a natural born ball player. Before the end of the season he may be playing shortstop or catching.

Bob Dunbar, *Boston Herald and Journal*

There is a world of speculation as to what regular playing will do to the $150,000 Babe Ruth arm. Hurling them in from the outfield is not conducive to helping a flinging wing.

The big Babe cut a couple back from left yesterday with a lot on them. If he keeps at it, he's likely to toss about a hundred thousand dollars' worth of pitching wing along with the ball someday soon.

Nick Flatley, *Boston American*

Babe Ruth Leads Batters

CHICAGO, May 11—Babe Ruth, Boston pitcher, leads the American League in batting, having displaced Tris Speaker of Cleveland. Ruth has an average of .407.

Speaker and Strunk are contending for the lead in base stealing, with seven each. Shean of Boston continues to top the sacrifice hitters with eight.

Ty Cobb is up to his old form, with an average of .362 for 11 games, having made 17 hits, five of them doubles. He has stolen five bases and registered 12 runs.

Boston Globe

Sox Blunder in Eighth and Let Browns Win, 4–2

Wally Schang Drops Throw at Plate

BOSTON, May 11—It would have been a lovely game at the Fens yesterday afternoon if it had not been for the eighth inning, in which the St. Louis visitors to our far eastern metropolis made three runs on some irregular play by the Sox.

It was a delightfully brilliant game for six innings, with players of each team performing wonders afield, and with Bert Gallia of Missouri and Dutch Leonard of the Sox pitching tight, clever ball.

But catcher Wally Schang went on a long excursion to some far country in that unfortunate frame. He dropped a thrown ball from Dave Shean,

Wally Schang, Red Sox catcher

which paved the way to three runs for Fielder Jones' [the Browns' manager] cohorts. Wally is a hard and far whacker, but if his work behind the bat in this series is a fair criterion, he stands a better chance of being used as a pinch hitter or a utility outfielder than behind the plate.

- [Winning pitcher, Gallia; losing pitcher, Leonard (3–3). Red Sox' standing: 13 wins, 10 losses; in second place.]

Burt Whitman, *Boston Herald and Journal*

Babe Ruth made some neat plays at first, the classic being a stop of a hard hit ball off Tobin in the sixth, which he knocked down with one hand and smothered before tossing the agate to Leonard at first for an out. He dug them out of the dirt and plucked them from the ozone.

Edward F. Martin, *Boston Globe*

Monday, May 13

Red Sox in First Place Again, Thanks to Chicago Champs

The Red Sox are leading the American League again! Walter Johnson defeated Cleveland Saturday and the White Sox hung another defeat on the Indians yesterday, which was enough to knock Lee Fohl's club off the top.

Boston Record

AMERICAN LEAGUE STANDINGS			
	Won	**Lost**	**PCT.**	**GB**
Boston 13		10	.565	—
Chicago 10		8	.556	0.5
Cleveland 12		10	.545	0.5
New York 12		10	.545	0.5
Washington 10		11	.476	2
St. Louis 9		10	.474	2
Detroit 7		10	.412	3
Philadelphia 8		12	.400	3.5

Most Valuable Player in the Game

Babe Ruth is the most valuable player in the American or National League. The big fellow can cover the initial sack with the best of them, and when it comes to pitching he does not have to take his hat off to any lefthander in the game.

Several of the best baseball men in the country have predicted that Ruth would outhit Cobb, Speaker or Jackson if he played regularly. The

Babe, at present, is doing that little thing. Furthermore, the Babe is learning to chop them instead of taking a good, healthy swing.

The Babe pulled this stunt twice in the game against the Browns on Saturday. The first time up he took his customary swing and dropped the ball over Hendryx's head in right field for a double. On his next trip to the plate he went out by the Gerber to Sisler route [short to first]. When he came up again, the St. Louis outfield went so far back that a pair of field glasses were needed to distinguish the players' features. Instead of taking a full swing, Babe chopped one over second for a single. He repeated this performance on his fourth and last trip to the plate.

A few days ago Stuffy McInnis said: "If Babe ever learns to chop them he will set a new record for hitting." The Babe is learning to chop them and is now on his way to the record.

Harry J. Casey, *Boston Record*

RED SOX BATTING

	AB	R	BH	2B	3B	HR	SB	AVG
Ruth, p	39	9	19	7	1	3	1	.487
Hooper, rf	80	14	28	10	2	0	5	.350
Strunk, cf	79	10	25	3	1	0	7	.316
McInnis, 3b	81	9	23	2	1	0	2	.284
Shean, 2b	79	10	20	4	1	0	3	.253
Whiteman, lf	40	2	9	1	0	0	4	.225
Scott, ss	82	9	18	1	1	0	4	.220
Schang, lf, c	43	9	9	2	1	0	0	.209
Agnew, c	70	6	9	4	0	0	1	.129
Hoblitzell, 1b	65	3	8	1	0	0	3	.123

Tuesday, May 14

Scotty Is Big Factor in 7–5 Triumph of Sox

Shortstop Knocks in Winning Runs and Saves Game by Marvellous Stop

BOSTON, May 13—Everett Scott was the big hero in the 7 to 5 victory of the Red Sox over the St. Louis Browns at Fenway Park yesterday afternoon. He knocked in two of the runs, and a wonderful one-handed stop saved at least two, possibly three, St. Louis hirelings from crossing the plate.

Mister Bush worked the entire distance. Bush wasn't particularly invincible. There were times, however, that he whizzed that fast ball of his through the groove. It looked as much like a pea as the smoke ball of Walter Johnson or Ruth. But the Browns spanked his delivery irreverently, piling up 10 hits.

Manager Ed Barrow pulled his big shift yesterday, Stuffy McInnis going back to his dearly beloved first base assignment, with Fred Thomas trying out his luck at third. Both did nicely under the new scheme, even if Stuffy did make an excusable error on a fly ball in back of the bag. Babe Ruth, huge batsmith, was benched, presumably because he will pitch today's game and needs all the rest he can get.

[Winning pitcher, Bush (4–2); losing pitcher, Sothoron. Red Sox' standing: 14 wins, 10 losses; in first place.]

Burt Whitman, Boston Herald and Journal

WHITEMAN CLEANED THE BASES IN THE 1ST INNING WITH A DOUBLE TO CENTER SCORING HOOPER, SHEAN AND STRUNK.

Scott, Boston Post

Scott Hero of Combat

Scotty first stepped into the picture in the fourth inning, after the Browns had scored one run, had the pillows loaded, and a three-run lead looking like a dollar bill in a cabaret safe.

Mister Tobin of St. Louis cracked a hot grounder through the box. Scotty came over back of second, stuck down his glove as the onion glanced off the bag, came up with it (the onion, not the bag) and threw to first retiring the side.

In his own half of the same chapter, Scotty pounded out a one-shot that rescued two of his brothers and made Joe Bush feel more comfortable.

Then Everett ended the pastime in the early dusk. A fine stop and a long throw retired the Browns when the bases were full, as they were practically all afternoon. The game was a great argument for prohibition.

Nick Flatley, Boston American

Hoblitzell Gets Commission

Dick Hoblitzell, captain and first baseman of the Red Sox, has been called for the Big Game. President Wilson has sent Hoblitzell's name to the Senate for appointment as a first lieutenant in the dental corps of the army.

The news means that Hobby will soon exchange his Red Sox uniform for the khaki of Uncle Sam's fighting men. The loss of Hobby will put McInnis on first base, where he played in yesterday's game against the Browns.

Boston American

[Hoblitzell had had a horrible start for Boston, batting .123 with only one extra-base hit. His army induction date was still unknown.]

Jackson to Help in Building Ships

Slugger Lost to White Sox for Balance of Season

PHILADELPHIA, May 13—Joe Jackson, star outfielder of the Chicago White Sox, notified Manager Rowland that he had accepted a position with the Hollingsworth Shipbuilding Company at Wilmington, Delaware, and that he would not play with the White Sox any more this season.

Jackson said that he would start work at the shipbuilding plant tomorrow, but declined to say whether he would seek exemption from the draft on the grounds that he is employed in a war industry. He played his last game with Chicago on Saturday.

Boston Globe

[Jackson's departure was a critical blow to the White Sox efforts to repeat as world champions. One of the top hitters in baseball, Joe was batting .354 when he left Chicago.

Jackson returned to play in 1919 and became involved in the Chicago Black Sox scandal to throw the World Series. A simple country boy from South Carolina, he was thrown out of baseball at the end of the 1920 season. Joe was finished at thirty-one, despite his lifetime batting average of .356, the third highest of all time.

Although he had Hall of Fame credentials, Jackson has never been elected.]

Fans, meet two of the greatest batters baseball has seen, Tyrus Raymond Cobb of the Tigers and George Babe Ruth of the Red Sox.

Detroit Appears at Fenway Park

Scott, *Boston Post*

Ty Cobb Leads Tiger Attack at Fens Today

Ruth and Cobb, Kings of Swat, Will Add Color to Fray

Fans, meet two of the greatest batters baseball has seen, Tyrus Raymond Cobb of the Tigers and George Babe Ruth of the Red Sox. They'll both be at the Fens this afternoon, Ty leading the offense of the Jungaleers, and Babe lefthanding for the Sox, swinging that mighty black flail of his.

We'll have a chance to compare their widely different styles of hitting. The slim Tyrus is a speed merchant, beating out many an infield bounder by his remarkable fleetness of foot. He is not a slugger, holding his bat with hands apart, some distance from the small end.

Babe is the slugger extraordinary. He handles a long, heavy bat that would break the back of the average ball player. It takes a man with Babe's great strength to get that flail up and around in time to meet the ball, but he swings it as if it were as light as a toothpick. He hits the ball hard, takes a healthy, lusty, full swing, and HITS everything.

Tyrus is a left field hitter, as a result of the way pitchers pitch to him. I once heard a big league manager say he could put up a stick in left field and the Georgian would hit the ball within 10 yards of the stick.

Just now the Georgian has not hopped to the top of the batters in the A.L. But he has started, and will come through, just as surely as they play out the 154 game schedule.

Burt Whitman, *Boston Herald and Journal*

[Cobb, thirty-one years old, had won the batting championship of the American League nine of the eleven previous years. He went on to achieve the highest lifetime batting average in the history of baseball, .366, ranked second in hits with 4,190, first in runs scored with 2,245, and fourth in steals with 892. Although he seldom hit home runs, managing only 118 during his

Ty Cobb, Detroit Tigers outfielder

twenty-four seasons, Cobb was no powder-puff singles hitter. He led the league in slugging average eight times in the dead ball era. In 1925, at thirty eight, he blasted three home runs in one game.

Cobb was one of the toughest men in baseball, willing to do whatever it took to succeed. Nicknamed "The Georgia Peach," Cobb was mean, selfish, cruel, and hot-tempered. He spiked many an infielder and fought anybody who stood in his way.

The biggest star and one of the most disliked players of his day, Ty was the first man elected to the Hall of Fame in 1936. When he died, only three baseball people showed up at his funeral.

"We may never see his like again," Connie Mack once said of Cobb.]

Fighting Red Sox Snare Snarling Tigers in Ninth, 5–4

BOSTON, May 15—Take nothing for granted with these astonishing Sox of 1918. At the start of the last half of the ninth inning the Michiganders had the affair sewed up tight, 4 to 3. When the big Boston wind stopped blowing the Barrowmen had won the game 5 to 4, sending home a happy crowd of fans, happy to see their hero Big Babe Ruth pitch another victory, and happy to see the home boys sidetrack Ty Cobb and the rest of that tough Bengal bunch.

In the last of the ninth Manager Ed Barrow made judicious and crafty use of what reserves he has on his reservation. McInnis had been tossed out on a close play. Then Wallie Schang walked. Quiet, dangerous Everett Scott smote the ball languidly, but safely to left field, Schang taking second.

Lt. Dick Hoblitzell of the U.S. Reserve Medical Corps batted for Sam Agnew. Hobby singled sweetly to short left field and Schang tore on from second base.

Coach Heinie Wagner at third waved for Schang to stop at that station, but Schang never saw the signal; possibly he saw it and didn't give a dern. At any rate, he kept sprinting. Walker's throw from left was wide and not strong enough, Schang crossing with the tieing run. Scott had moved to third and Hobby had reached second when all this throwing was over.

Babe Ruth never had a chance to bat with first base open. Dauss did the only sensible thing, passing the Colossus, filling the bases. The Detroit outfielders played close and the infield was in tight to the plate. The outfielders feared a long sacrifice fly and the infielders dreaded the squeeze play.

Hooper settled all arguments, however, by whacking the ball far over Bobby Veach's head in right field, Scott scoring with the winning run.

- [Winning pitcher, Ruth (4–3); losing pitcher, Dauss. Red Sox' standing: 15 wins, 10 losses; in first place.]

Burt Whitman, *Boston Herald and Journal*

The consensus of opinion regarding Ty Cobb is that he is not yet in form. The Peach had a chance to drive in runs three out of the four times that he came to bat and never once delivered.

Detroit News

IN THE 9TH INNING—HOBBY" BATTING FOR THOMAS SCORED SCHANG TYING THE SCORE, DAUSS TOOK NO CHANCES WITH RUTH AND WALKED HIM FILLING THE BASES, THEN HOOPER CLOUTED WINNING THE GAME -

Scott, *Boston Post*

Walter Johnson Wins in 18 Innings

WASHINGTON, May 15—Walter Johnson and "Cy" [Lefty] Williams battled 18 innings here today before Washington got a 1 to 0 decision over Chicago. Johnson helped win his victory with a long single.

The game was the longest of the season in the American League and one of the longest on record, each team using only nine players. The actual playing time was 2 hours and 47 minutes.

Boston Globe

Friday, May 17

Hooper Hits for Circuit as Tigers Are Whipped, 7–2

BOSTON, May 16—Carl Mays did the chucking for the Sox and it was a good day for the uplift delivery, as he held the Junglemen to four scattered blows, Tyrus getting two of them.

Babe Ruth worked in the left garden and got through the game without breaking any bones. He hit safely once, drew a pass and even had the infielders playing deep.

- [Winning pitcher, Mays (5–2); losing pitcher, James. Home run: Hooper (1). Red Sox' standing: 16 wins, 10 losses; in first place.]

Edward F. Martin, *Boston Globe*

Ban Johnson Hits at Draft Dodgers

CHICAGO, May 16—Baseball players who have sought employment in shipyards and other war industries in an attempt to evade military service "should be yanked into the Army by the coat collar," Pres. Ban Johnson of the American League said tonight.

"The American League has lost more than 70 players in the draft and through enlistment, and expects to lose more, but it does not approve of players trying to evade military service," Pres. Johnson said. "Some of them apparently have been badly advised."

Boston Globe

[Johnson's tirade was probably directed at Shoeless Joe Jackson, the White Sox' star outfielder, who had escaped the draft by working at a shipyard.]

Saturday, May 18

Red Sox Scrape Hide Off Ferocious Tiger Cat, 11–8

BOSTON, May 17—There wasn't any finesse to Boston's 11 to 8 victory over the Detroit Tigers at the Fens yesterday afternoon, but Dutch Leonard managed to stay on the mound for the full nine innings.

It was the third straight victory over the Tigers, making the Barrows' claim to first place all the more secure. Boston hit almost at will, getting 13 safeties. Dutch Leonard hit better than he pitched, getting three hits. His receiver, Wallie Schang, in addition to catching a very neat game, hammered out three hits in as many times at bat.

Cobb made two hits out of three official at bats, but the Georgian had a rough time of it in centrefield. Ty almost made a wonderful diving catch of McInnis' short drive to left centre in the sixth, sliding along on his knees for yards after his unsuccessful try. After his error, he had a vitriolic chat with one of the occupants of a front box in the grandstand, telling that person "a few things."

[Winning pitcher, Leonard (4–3); losing pitcher, Finneran. Red Sox' standing: 17 wins, 10 losses; in first place.]

Burt Whitman, *Boston Herald and Journal*

Sunday, May 19

Strunk's Swat Puts End to Tiger Hopes, 3–1

BOSTON, May 19—Yesterday afternoon, the Sox won their fourth consecutive game from the Tigers, 3 to 1. They have now won five games in a row and closed the week with a clean slate.

Bullet Joe Bush pitched for the Sox and had a good day, barring the third inning when one Tiger tallied on a wild pitch. The Minnesota speed boy improved as he went along, just blazing the agate over in the ninth after Heilmann opened with a double.

The Sox kept smashing Erickson safely, but could not get the men around until the sixth when Babe Ruth started with a double. The hit was a beauty. It struck the advertising sign in extreme left center and ordinarily would have been a home run. Cobb was playing very deep for the big Oriole boy and made a futile stab for the ball.

That was Babe's only hit, but the other times he stung the ball hard, giving Veach [the Tigers' left fielder] a couple of long runs, and hitting a wicked one back at Erickson, who turned it into a force play. In left field Ruth looked like ready money, accepting two chances with astonishing nonchalance.

[Winning pitcher, Bush (5–2); losing pitcher, Erickson. Red Sox' standing: 18 wins, 10 losses; in first place.]

Edward F. Martin, *Boston Globe*

The crowd which witnessed the downfall of the Tigers today was the largest of the season, 10,230 being the official count. There would have been at least another thousand but the Red Cross parade kept them away.

Detroit News

Babe Ruth worked in the left garden and got through the game without breaking any bones.

SATURDAY WAS GET AWAY DAY FOR
THE DETROIT TIGERS — CLEVELAND TEAM NEXT.

Scott, *Boston Post*

Monday, May 20

AMERICAN LEAGUE STANDINGS

	Won	Lost	PCT.	GB
Boston 18		10	.643	—
New York 15		12	.556	2.5
Chicago 13		11	.542	3
Cleveland 15		13	.536	3
Washington 13		14	.481	4.5
St. Louis 11		13	.458	5
Philadelphia 11		15	.423	6
Detroit 7		15	.318	8

The Babe has been kicking around the outfield so long that he is just pining to get back in the box where he is within speaking distance of the game. Ruth is not strong for being anchored near Duffy's Cliff. He claims he's too far away and also says that he does not get any action out there. "They refuse to hit any to me, and all I do is run in and out," he says.

Eddie Hurley, *Boston Record*

Tuesday, May 21

Red Sox Land on Indians, 11 to 1

BOSTON, May 20—Carl Mays pitched magnificent ball, held his opponents to five hits and fanned eight. Mays was a power on the offence as well. Taking the place of Babe Ruth, who had been suddenly taken to the hospital, Carl batted out a triple and two singles in four times at bat, scored twice and started the assault which led to Bagby's undoing in the fifth.

- [Winning pitcher, Mays (6–2); losing pitcher Bagby. Red Sox' standing: 19 wins, 10 losses; in first place.]

Paul H. Shannon, Boston Post

Beaning of Spoke Riles Whole Tribe

BOSTON, May 21—The whole Tribe is riled over the beaning of Tris Speaker by Carl Mays. The incident threatens to put a lot of extra pepper into the remaining three games of this series.

The Tribe was hopelessly swamped by the Red Sox fusillade, when Mays caromed a shot off Spoke's head so hard it bounded into the grandstand. It only glanced off the top of the head or the result might have been serious. Spoke charged that Mays did it intentionally but Mays denied this.

"I worked on the same team with you long enough to know your methods," shouted Spoke at Mays.

Every Indian on the squad is good and sore over the affair. They are going into these remaining three games thirsting for revenge.

Cleveland Press

MAYS WILD PITCH IN THE 8TH INNING TO SPEAKER'S HEAD WOULD HAVE STUNNED AN OX BUT "TRIS" GAMELY RESUMED PLAY—

Scott, Boston Post

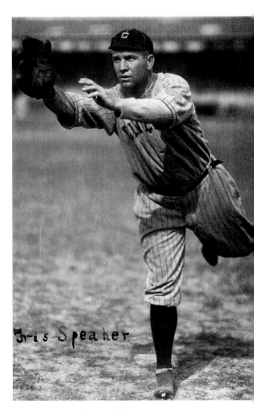

Tris Speaker, Indians' center fielder

[Playing an extremely shallow center field, Tris Speaker sometimes made unassisted double plays on short flies, was an occasional pivot man on 4–8–3 double plays, and even took pickoff throws at second. Yet he could still catch flies over his head with the best of them.

Tris was also a terrific hitter with a lifetime mark of .344. His 792 doubles rank first on the all-time list, and his 223 triples rank sixth. He finished his career with 3,514 hits, the fifth best record in major league history.

The Red Sox made a monumental blunder when they traded "Spoke" in 1916. Tris became the Indians' star and led them to their first pennant in 1920, when he batted .388. He was elected into the Hall of Fame in 1937.]

Ruth Collapses in Tonsilitis Attack

Babe Ruth is at the Massachusetts Eye and Ear Infirmary suffering from a severe attack of tonsilitis and will not be able to play for at least a week. He collapsed while having a prescription filled in a drugstore yesterday afternoon.

The big Oriole boy has not been feeling well for several days, but in spite of this continued to play every day, insisting that he was just suffering from a little cold and would work it off.

Boston Globe

Wednesday, May 22

Red Sox Beaten by Indians, 6–5

BOSTON, May 21—Every time the Red Sox have an opportunity to win seven consecutive games, along comes Dutch Leonard, who gives the leg to the party that is carrying the beans. After winning six in a row, the Red Sox were beaten 6 to 5 yesterday by the Fohlmen, principally because Leonard did not have the goods.

Manager Fohl and the Cleveland players were persistently complaining that the apples the Fresno raisin king was serving were spotted with licorice. They protested to Umpire Nallin and he threw many balls into the discard besides hurling warnings to the Sox dugout.

Whether the balls that Dutch delivered had licorice on them is a matter that somebody else will have to officially determine, but it is a cinch that they had nothing besides the licorice, because the portsider's offerings were soft picking for the visitors, who got 12 hits.

Dutch had good intentions because he likes to win, but beyond that nothing. A little of that old-time effectiveness of his would be as welcome as the flowers that bloom in the Springtime, tra la.

- [Winning pitcher, Coumbe; losing pitcher, Leonard (4–4). Red Sox' standing: 19 wins, 11 losses; in first place.]

Edward F. Martin, *Boston Globe*

[The twenty-six-year-old lefty had been a mainstay of the Red Sox pitching staff for the preceding six seasons. In 1914 Dutch had one of the most brilliant seasons any modern pitcher has ever had, winning 19 while losing only 5, with an incredibly low earned run average of 1.01. This is the best earned run average in major league history for a pitcher with more than 150 innings, a record that may never be broken.

Although he never approached that level of brilliance again, Leonard averaged 16 wins a season from 1913 to 1917, plus two World Series complete game victories.]

Dutch had good intentions because he likes to win, but beyond that nothing.

Leonard is having a bad year. His control has been away off. Twenty-three free tickets in three games is not like Leonard.

Boston Record

Ruth Looks Like Regular Baby in His Hospital Crib

Big Babe Ruth, the Colossus of the Red Sox, worth more than his weight in gold, one of the greatest left-hand pitchers of the decade, also the top slugger and batter in the American League, looked like a real baby yesterday as he lay in bed at the Massachusetts Eye and Ear Infirmary. He was not allowed to talk, and the chances are that had he tried, it would have been like an infant's whisper. His inflamed throat was packed in ice bags, one of the later-day methods of reducing the local inflammation and fever.

But the report from the doctor was encouraging. Babe's great vitality and admirable physical condition have started to throw off the aggravated attack of tonsilitis. The prophecy now is that the big lad will be out of the hospital in four or five days, and that he will be able to go west with the team, ready to play, at the end of the month.

Boston Herald and Journal

Friday, May 24

Sox Get Lone Hit and Lose, 1–0

BOSTON, May 23—Guy Morton of the Cleveland Indians staged a single handed scalping party at the Fens yesterday afternoon. Thanks to a Texas leaguer by Amos Strunk, Guy did not get the no-hitter, but did win the game, 1 to 0. The Indians took two out of the three games in the series, the first time this season the Sox have lost a home series.

It was bat and ball day, with the home club giving 25 percent of its receipts to Clark Griffith's fund providing baseball equipment for soldiers and sailors in the service. The amount that will be given to Griff for his fund will be slightly in excess of $250.

It was a tight game all the way. Sambo [Sam Jones] hurled for the home team for eight frames, and he did very well indeed. It wasn't his fault that his mates, subdued by the shoots and the smoke of Morton, could not make a run.

Morton had Tris Speaker to thank in the fourth. With two out, Whiteman whanged a drive to right centre that had the looks of a double or triple. But the Texan came through with one of his wonderful catches, timing it exactly while going at top speed, one of his old time marvel clutches.

● [Winning pitcher, Morton; losing pitcher, Jones (0–1). Red Sox' standing: 19 wins, 12 losses; in first place.]

Burt Whitman, Boston Herald and Journal

IN THE LAST HALF OF THE 4TH INNING
TRIS SPEAKER MADE ONE OF THOSE CATCHES
THAT MADE HIM FAMOUS OF WHITEMAN'S
SIZZLING WALLOP FOR THE 3RD OUT

Scott, *Boston Post*

I've Quit Game, Says Jackson

WILMINGTON, Del., May 24—Joe Jackson announced today that he is done with professional baseball.

"It makes no difference when the war ends. I shall not attempt to go back to ball playing to make a living. I intend to make my home here and to follow the trade of shipbuilding."

Jackson is peeved over criticism of his quitting the White Sox after being called in the draft. He says he applied here two months ago for a job.

Cleveland Press

Pres. Frazee and Manager Ed Barrow visited Babe Ruth at the infirmary yesterday. Babe is almost completely surrounded by flowers. He says the time to get flowers is when you are alive.

Boston Globe

Would Close Every Place of Recreation in Country

PHILADELPHIA, Pa., May 23—"I don't care if they close all the ball parks." This was the answer of Ban Johnson, president of the American League, when he heard of the order by Provost Marshal Crowder that every man within the draft age must either fight or work.

"I don't believe the government has any intentions of wiping out baseball, but I don't care if they do," he said.

"If I had my way I would close every theatre, baseball park and every other place of recreation in the country. I would make the people realize that we are in the most terrible war in the history of the world. Let us all go to war and buckle in, and fight to the limit."

Boston Herald and Journal

Saturday, May 25

Bush's Bat and Good Arm Win for Red Sox

Pitcher Drives Over Big Run That Beats Chicago, 5–4

BOSTON, May 24—Using the willow as well as his strong right arm effectively, Bullet Joe Bush played a prominent part in that 5 to 4 victory the Red Sox scored over the Chicago World's Champions. His sweet single to center in the ninth drove in the big run that spelled victory.

Joe drove in three of the Sox runs, slammed out two fine hits, fielded his position like an artist, and except for a pair of fielding miscues would have held the White Sox runless until the eighth inning. Seven hits were all that Joe allowed.

- [Winning pitcher, Bush (6–2); losing pitcher, Danforth. Red Sox' standing: 20 wins, 12 losses; in first place.]

Edward F. Martin, *Boston Globe*

Joe Wood's Homer Wins in the 19th

NEW YORK, May 24—A 19 inning game, the longest of the season, was won by Cleveland from New York, 3 to 2, when Joe Wood, the former Red Sox pitcher, hit his second home run of the game.

Boston Globe

[Wood's heroics kept the Indians in second place, two games behind Boston. The Yankees were also hanging tough in fourth place, three games out.]

Babe is almost completely surrounded by flowers. He says the time to get flowers is when you are alive.

Smoky Joe Wood, Cleveland's left fielder

Joe Wood Playing Left

When you pranced upon the hill,
    Smoky Joe,
You could hypnotize the pill,
    Smoky Joe,
So each batsman whiffed the air,
Wrenched his muscles, tore his hair,
Trying to slam it "over there,"
    Smoky Joe.

Now you're shining out at left,
    Smoky Joe.
With a style that's neat and deft,
    Smoky Joe.
If you keep the pace you've set
You will be a Speaker yet,
That's an easy money bet,
    Smoky Joe!

Rex Prouty, *Boston Globe*

[Smoky Joe Wood had been a fabulous pitcher for the Red Sox from 1908 through 1915, winning 116 and losing 57 games. His finest season was in 1912, when he led Boston to the world championship with 34 wins and 5 losses, 10 shutouts, 258 strikeouts, and an earned run average of 1.91. Smoky Joe concluded his dream season with three victories against the New York Giants during the World Series.

Joe came up with a sore arm in 1913, however, and was forced to quit pitching in 1916 at the tender age of twenty-six. But he made an astonishing comeback in 1918 as Cleveland's left fielder, batting .296 with 5 home runs: the former baseball idol was back in the limelight.]

Sunday, May 26

White Sox Beaten in the Tenth, 3–2

Shean Poles Hit That Decides

BOSTON, May 25—The Red Sox won the first extra-inning game of the Fenway season when they shook off the White Sox, 3 to 2, with two out in the tenth.

A long fly over Felsch's head from the bludgeon of Dave Shean accomplished the undoing of southpaw Lefty Williams of the World's Champions.

Shean could have made second easily on his long lift, which landed at the foot of the bank well down into centre field, but he paused at first to watch Schang, who was joyously bouncing in from second with the winning run.

It was a hard fought game, with a lot of credit due to Carl Mays for his unflinching nerve in the pinches.

[Winning pitcher, Mays (7–2); losing pitcher, Williams. Red Sox' standing: 21 wins, 12 losses; in first place.]

Francis Eaton, *Boston Sunday Advertiser and American*

The Year the Red Sox Won the Series

"We'll Get There Yet," Rowland Declares

"We'll get there again!" said Clarence Rowland, manager of the world champion White Sox, yesterday. "In spite of the loss of Jackson and recent injuries sustained by Eddie Collins, Felsch and Cicotte, we are within striking distance of the Red Sox.

"We don't fear the Red Sox at all, and when they begin to play away from home look out for a big slump. The White Sox, in my opinion, will play another World's Series with the Giants in October."

Boston Sunday Advertiser and American

Monday, May 27

IT LOOKS LIKE IT'S UP TO "DUTCH" LEONARD AND EDDIE CICOTTE TO PITCH TODAY.

Scott, *Boston Post*

AMERICAN LEAGUE STANDINGS

	Won	Lost	PCT.	GB
Boston	21	12	.636	—
New York	18	14	.563	2.5
St. Louis	16	14	.533	3.5
Cleveland	18	16	.529	3.5
Chicago	14	14	.500	4.5
Philadelphia	13	17	.433	6.5
Washington	14	19	.424	7
Detroit	9	17	.346	8.5

Colorful Babe Ruth Restored to Health

Babe Ruth, ace of trumps of the pace setting Red Sox, walked out of the Massachusetts Eye and Ear Infirmary yesterday forenoon, a free man. The throat affliction which struck him down disappeared almost as suddenly as it came on, due to his wonderful strength. Soon the cave man will be out there again fighting for the glory of the crimson stockings.

Babe was advised by the hospital physicians to take a complete rest and try to forget baseball for a few days at least. But of course this is impossible. The big boy, who anxiously awaited the news each day of the battles in the Fens while he lay stricken in the hospital, might as well have been asked to stop eating.

He will not be in uniform during the first half of this week if Manager Ed Barrow has his way, but as the hustling manager of the Red Sox put it last night, "It will be a difficult task to keep Babe away from his uniform, from the dugout, and from the long bat he loves so well to swing."

Boston Herald and Journal

RED SOX BATTING

	AB	R	BH	2B	3B	HR	SB	AVG
Ruth, p, lf 54	12	22	9	1	3	1	.407
Hooper, rf 117	21	41	11	2	1	6	.350
Strunk, cf 118	21	39	6	3	0	10	.331
Thomas, 3b 38	6	11	0	1	0	1	.289
McInnis, 3b, 1b 119	14	34	2	1	0	3	.286
Schang, lf, c 63	14	16	5	1	0	0	.254
Shean, 2b 118	14	29	6	0	0	5	.246
Whiteman, lf 66	7	16	5	0	0	6	.242
Scott, ss 118	17	27	3	2	0	5	.229
Hoblitzell, 1b 67	3	9	1	0	0	3	.134
Agnew, c 81	6	10	6	0	0	0	.123

RED SOX PITCHING

	IP	BH	W	L	R	BB	SO
Mays 79.1	67	7	2	29	25	40
Bush 69.1	50	6	2	19	29	20
Ruth 61.2	55	4	3	23	20	11
Leonard 65.1	71	4	4	36	37	25
Jones 17.1	21	0	1	11	3	4

Champions Paste Leonard's Slow One

Hubert's Flirting Results in a Boston Defeat, 6–4

BOSTON, May 27—A Red Sox defeat was the only unpleasant feature of Red Cross Day at Fenway Park yesterday, the World's Champions banging through a 6 to 4 victory because they were able to paste the offerings of Dutch Leonard on the beak.

The Red Cross realized $5,500, this sum representing the gross proceeds and collections by young women members of the organization. Gov. McCall and other dignitaries were present, and but for the poor weather in the forenoon a much larger sum would have been realized.

Leonard did not have anything. He flirted with a slow ball occasionally. Hubert is pitching way off the mark and in only one game this season has shown the real, fancy line of goods that he carries. He should put his slow ball in camphor.

Whiteman had another good day. He drove in two of the Red Sox runs and in the field had a carnival. Once he raced up on the cliff and speared one, à la Lewis. He captured a foul fly on the dead run in the seventh and in the same frame nailed a single on the pickup and threw Risberg out at the plate.

* [Winning pitcher, Shellenback; losing pitcher, Leonard, (4–5). Red Sox' standing: 21 wins, 13 losses; in first place.]

Edward F. Martin, *Boston Globe*

Eddie Cicotte is unable to win for Chicago. Unlike Leonard, however, Cicotte has pitched some fine games only to be on the wrong end. He has lost six straight games and most of them have been close affairs where his mates failed to produce the needed hits or runs behind him.

Eddie Hurley, *Boston Record*

[A 28-game winner in 1917, Cicotte, thirty-four years old, was one of the top trick-ball artists of his era. Eddie's arsenal included a knuckleball, shine ball, emery ball, and spitball.

As the ace of the White Sox staff, Eddie was counted on to lead Chicago to another world championship in 1918. His poor start was a critical blow to the White Sox' chances to repeat.

A vastly underpaid pitcher, Cicotte became one of the ringleaders in the infamous Black Sox scandal of 1919. He hurled two losing games in that World Series and was thrown out of baseball after the 1920 season by the new commissioner, Judge Kenesaw Mountain Landis. Cicotte's brilliant career, with 208 victories against only 149 defeats, was ruined.

Following his exile, Eddie had to change his name to protect his family. He claimed that the only reason he threw the series was because of his low pay. "I did it for the wife and kiddies," he maintained.]

Bush Again Pins Defeat on Chicago, 1–0

BOSTON, May 28—Much to the chagrin of Clarence Rowland & Co., it was Joe Bush day at Fenway Park yesterday. For the second time within four days the skillful pitching and timely swatting of the bullet ball chucker proved the undoing of the World's Champions.

The score was 1 to 0. Bullet Joe drove in the lone tally in the fifth inning, while he held the Cook County delegation to one stingy base hit, a single to short right in the opening stanza, which Happy Felsch registered.

Bush whiffed six of the champions. He whizzed the ball over with everything on it, and his supporting cast stood by him nobly. Joe is pitching great ball these days and his performance yesterday was easily the best job he has turned in this season.

Eddie Cicotte of the Rowland camouflage corps pitched a nice game himself, although he was on the losing end. He pitched good enough to win under ordinary circumstances, but it would have taken a superman and a couple of big brothers to beat Bush.

Three of the Boston hits were registered by Freddy Thomas, who was very much on the job at the hot corner. "Tommy" is looking better every day. He is covering more ground, has great gobs of confidence both at the bat and in the field, and is coming through as one of the gems of the 1918 crop.

* [Winning pitcher, Bush (7–2); losing pitcher, Cicotte. Red Sox' standing: 22 wins, 13 losses; in first place.]

Edward F. Martin, *Boston Globe*

American League Remembers the Boys "Over There"

Recently the Red Cross appealed to President Ban Johnson of the American League for aid in supplying baseball paraphernalia to the wounded soldiers who are convalescing behind the lines "Over There." The American League has answered the call. It was decided to send $5,000 worth of baseball goods to France for the use of American soldiers who are recovering from wounds in battle. The goods consist of 2,000 baseballs, 500 bats, 50 first baseman's mitts, 50 catcher's mitts, 150 infielder's mitts, 100 chest protectors and 50 catcher's masks.

Harry J. Casey, *Boston Record*

Ruppert Offered $150,000 for Ruth

"Col. Ruppert of the New York Yankees asked me if I would sell Babe for $150,000 and I told the colonel I would not," said owner Harry Frazee of the Red Sox." I think the New York man showed good judgment in making such a big offer. Ruth already is mighty popular in New York, and just think what he would mean to the Yankees if he were playing for them every day and hitting those long ones at the leftfield bleachers and the rightfield grandstand!"

Boston Herald and Journal

Sox Capture Double Bill from Senators, 4–2, 3–0

Sam Jones Steals Johnson's Kalsomine Brush and Does a Bit of Painting on His Own

BOSTON, May 29—Clark Griffith played all the trumps he had at the Fens yesterday afternoon, but lost two ball games, with young Sammy Jones getting the decision over the Great Walter Johnson in the second half of the doubleheader.

Wizard Walter had been mowing down everything in sight prior to his appearance in that second game. Already he had beaten the Red Sox three times this season. For 40 innings the Wizard had not allowed anyone to score off his delivery. It looked as if Walter would win as he pleased. But young Mr. Jones, who has been with the Red Sox ever since the spring of 1916, and who never had won a game for them, pitched tip top ball, held the foemen to five hits, shut them out and allowed no man to reach third base.

* [Game one: winning pitcher, Mays (8–2); losing pitcher, Harper. Game two: winning pitcher, Jones (1–1); losing pitcher, Johnson. Red Sox' standing: 24 wins, 13 losses; in first place.]

Burt Whitman, *Boston Herald and Journal*

THE SECOND GAME WAS
A 3 TO 0-SHUTOUT WITH PITCHER
JONES ON THE JOB-

Scott, *Boston Post*

Red Sox Triumph, 9–1, and Then Lose to Senators, 4–0

BOSTON, May 30—It was tit for tat between the Red Sox and the Washington Senators at the Fens yesterday, the home boys gathering in the morning game by the gawky and lopsided score of 9 to 1, with the Toga Toters from the District of Columbia collecting before the big afternoon crowd, 4 to 0.

Dutch Leonard had smooth sailing in the morning game. Doc Ayers, a side-arm, mysterious right-hand pitcher of a freaky, erratic ball, which may be the shine ball or the alcohol ball, had the Red Hose on the hip all the way in the afternoon game. He restricted Barrow's sluggers to six hits. Even the great Babe Ruth, going in as a pinch-hitter in the eighth frame, his first appearance since his sickness and the signal for a grand ovation, could not connect safely.

• [Game one: winning pitcher, Leonard (5–5); losing pitcher, Shaw. Game two: winning pitcher, Ayers; losing pitcher, McCabe (0–1). Red Sox' standing: 25 wins, 14 losses; in first place.]

Burt Whitman, *Boston Herald and Journal*

There was an up-to-date Sir Walter Raleigh in the first base section of the grandstand. He came mighty near breaking his hand stopping a line drive which was aimed directly at his fair lady.

Boston Herald and Journal

Ed Barrow gave Dick McCabe his first big league start in the afternoon and he was hit hard. Dick pitches every day in batting practice and has to stick it over so the boys can tune up their batting eyes. He stuck it over pretty well for the Griffmen yesterday and they indulged in a little batting harmony, too. But no complaint can be made about Dick. Put him into a few more games and he will show something.

Edward F. Martin, *Boston Globe*

[This was the only game McCabe started for the Red Sox in 1918. The twenty-two-year-old righty won just one game in his entire big league career.]

The Red Sox go West at the top of their pile, looking like the best ball club in all big league ball. But there is nothing certain about the game this season. Drafts, enlistments and conscriptions can change the prospects of any business overnight, and baseball is part and parcel of the amusement business.

Bob Dunbar, *Boston Herald and Journal*

Drafts, enlistments and conscriptions can change the prospects of any business overnight, and baseball is part and parcel of the amusement business.

AMERICAN LEAGUE BATTING LEADERS			
	AB	BH	PCT.
BABE RUTH, BOSTON	55	22	.400
Tillie Walker, Athletics	126	46	.365
Frank Baker, New York	149	52	.349
George Burns, Athletics	138	48	.348
George Sisler, St. Louis	136	46	.338

Barrow Is Satisfied with Boston Infield

Barrow thinks he has the best team in the league, "They are leading, not so?" With Ruth again ready to work, his pitching staff is in fine fettle for the western invasion.

Barrow smiled when talking of Ruth. "It is almost impossible to keep him out of a game, as he wants to play somewhere every day. When Babe was sick last week he was about the most disconsolate man to be found anywhere."

The Boston manager is well satisfied with his infield. Although Hoblitzell expects to be called into army service in a short while, the Hubsox are well fortified at first with McInnis. Stuffy has given up trying to play third, as Fred Thomas is making a satisfactory stand at that corner.

Left field is Barrow's biggest problem. He has George Whiteman playing there at present, but the International leaguer's hitting is not exactly up to American League requirements. So he has been shifting Schang and Ruth into the left garden at every opportunity.

Detroit News

It is about time for those wise persons who predicted Ed Barrow's early disappearance as manager of the Red Sox to say, "What'll you smoke?"

Bob Dunbar, *Boston Herald and Journal*

Sunday, June 2

Tigers Defeat Red Hose in Thirteenth Round, 4–3

Riotous Scenes on Navin Field while Players Fight among Themselves and with Umpires; Feud Renewed

DETROIT, June 1—Harry Heilmann caught one of Carl Mays' underhand shoots square on the nose in the thirteenth inning yesterday and smashed the ball to the center field fence. Pep Young, who was on second, walked home and the Tigers were victorious over the Boston Red Sox, 4 to 3.

A year ago the Tigers and Red Sox started a feud that has apparently lost none of its fury. It cropped out afresh yesterday afternoon and several times players were on the verge of committing deeds of violence.

The first break came in the seventh inning. Bush [the Tigers' shortstop], started to swing at a pitched ball, changed his mind and pulled his bat back. Umpire Dinneen called it a ball. The Boston players rushed at Dinneen, gesticulating wildly and yelling. Dick Hoblitzell, Boston first baseman, shoved Dinneen and hit him over the back, but apparently not with the intention of doing him physical injury. The trouble finally subsided, only to appear again in the ninth inning.

The first two Tigers got safely on and Cobb was sent up as a pinch hitter. Schang, catching, walked two feet from the plate and Mays began pitching wide so that Cobb would be purposely passed. Cobb and Mays, who have not been the most intimate of friends since Mays tried to bean Cobb, exchanged some verbal "compliments" as Cobb trotted to first base.

After the inning ended, Mays said something rather provoking to Cobb, who was on his way to the Detroit dugout. Jennings [the Tigers' manager] rushed out and yelled at Cobb to come to the Detroit bench.

"Yes, you'd better go over there," yelled Mays. Cobb replied in subdued tones but Mays did not come over to meet him.

* [Winning pitcher, Cunningham; losing pitcher, Mays (8–3). Red Sox' standing: 25 wins, 15 losses; in first place.]

Tom Powers, Detroit News

[Mays and Cobb had a long-standing feud dating back to the first time they faced each other, in 1915, when Mays was a rookie. He knocked Cobb down twice before hitting him in the wrist. Cobb then threw his bat at the pitcher and vowed revenge, calling Mays a "yellow dog."

Cobb made good on his promise. A few years later, he bunted toward first and spiked Mays in the leg as they crashed together. While Mays lay sprawled on the ground, his pants covered with blood, Cobb threatened to tear apart the other leg.

They were two of the meanest players ever to play ball.]

After Mays went on the rubber both dugouts were in a constant uproar. Umpires Connolly and Dinneen repeatedly had to interfere to stop the verbal abuse. Even the crowd joined in the crusade upon Mays, who enjoys the unenviable reputation here of being a "bean ball" flinger.

Paul Shannon, Boston Post

AS OTHERS SEE THEM

Berndt, New York Journal

The Year the Red Sox Won the Series

[Detroit was supposed to be a contending team but had fallen into last place with a record of 11 wins and 20 losses. Ty Cobb, perhaps the most terrifying hitter in the history of baseball, had led the league in batting in 1917 with a .383 average. But by June 1918, the oft-injured Cobb had slumped to an unthinkable .281. As Cobb went, so went the Tigers.]

Monday, June 3

Ruth Wild, Tigers Trim Sox, 4 to 3

Babe a Little Off Color, Gets His Usual Homer

DETROIT, June 2—Babe Ruth's spirit was willing, but his arm was weak in the opening chapters of the battle in Jungletown this afternoon. Ruth lacked his usual speed, and his control was not what it should have been. He passed two men in the second frame, forcing in a pair of runs.

Manager Barrow pitched Ruth against his better judgment, for the Sox stood a chance of slipping into second place. But Ruth pleaded so hard for a chance to work after his two weeks' layoff that his manager finally yielded.

Rumors of the bitterness shown in yesterday's engagement brought out an attendance of 14,000, but the contest went without any unpleasant incident. This was due to a peace meeting between Mays and Cobb just before the game started and held in plain view from the grandstand. Both men decided to bury the hatchet.

Ruth's poor pitching was partly redeemed by his home run drive into the right field bleachers. It was the hardest hit ball of the year in the local park, although in batting practice yesterday Babe put the ball over the right field wall on to Trumbull Avenue, a feat never accomplished before.

* [Winning pitcher, Erickson; losing pitcher, Ruth (4–4). Home run: Ruth (4). Red Sox' standing: 25 wins, 16 losses; in first place.]

Paul Shannon, *Boston Post*

AMERICAN LEAGUE STANDINGS

	Won	Lost	PCT.	GB
Boston 25		16	.610	—
New York 23		16	.590	1
St. Louis 20		16	.556	2.5
Cleveland 22		20	.524	3.5
Chicago 18		17	.514	4
Washington 17		24	.415	8
Philadelphia 14		23	.378	9
Detroit 12		20	.375	8.5

Dutch Leonard, Red Sox pitcher

Leonard Becomes Baseball Immortal by Holding Tigers Hitless

Sox Win 5 to 0—Ruth Hits Homer

DETROIT, June 3—Dutch Leonard, not an especially brilliant performer in his early games this year, lifted a weight from the mind of his manager today by pitching a no-hit and no-run game. It would have been a perfect exhibition but for a base on balls given to Veach in the first inning.

There were only four balls hit hard. Three were line drives that went almost straight at Ruth or Whiteman. The other was a grounder hit toward second to start the ninth inning on which Scott made a great running pick-up and throw.

It was the second no-hit game for Leonard, who handed one to St. Louis on August 30, 1916. His comeback is especially welcome, as Ruth is needed in the outfield.

[Winning pitcher, Leonard (6–5); losing pitcher, Dauss. Home run: Ruth (5). Red Sox' standing: 26 wins, 16 losses; in first place.]

Boston Herald and Journal

Babe Ruth has toppled from the American League batting lead but he continued to swipe the pill unmercifully. He connected with his fifth home run of the year yesterday by putting the ball into the right field bleachers about the same spot he hit in Sunday's game.

Boston Record

Donie Bush a Sportsman

Donie Bush [the Tigers' shortstop] was the last batter between Dutch Leonard and a no-hit game when he came to bat in the ninth inning yesterday. Leonard, nervous, was showing his first signs of weakness in this inning, getting himself into a hole on each of the first two batters but escaping. The first ball he served Bush was wide and the second was a called strike. Then, to make Leonard sure of his feat, Bush swung wildly at the next two balls. Both were wide and Bush missed them by a foot, proving himself a sportsman and a regular fellow.

Detroit News

[At five-six and 140 pounds, Bush was just a .250 hitter. However, he led the league in walks five times, stole over 30 bases eight times, and scored at least 90 runs eight times for the powerful Tigers.]

Johnny Evers May Go to France as Baseball Leader

NEW YORK—The appointment of Johnny Evers, former major league ball player, as a physical director in the Y.M.C.A. among American troops is being considered.

Boston Record

ROCHESTER—Johnny Evers, lately with the Boston Americans, has accepted the invitation to supervise the athletic work of the Knights of Columbus in France. He will be ready for overseas service as soon as his passports arrive.

Boston Record

Wednesday, June 5

Red Sox Defeat Tigers in Ninth, 7–6

DETROIT, June 4—Timely hitting offset weak pitching for the Red Sox today, and with a great ninth inning rally the Tigers were downed by a 7 to 6 score, giving the Red Sox an even break in the series.

Hooper smashed a wicked drive through Donie Bush at the beginning of the sixth. Harry stole second. Shean poled a pretty hit to right and across came the first run of the game. Taking the chance that Ruth would sacrifice, James served up a high fast one for his first offering. A howl arose from the bleachers as Babe swung hard on the ball and drove it high into the bleachers for the third day in succession.

Rallies in the eighth by both teams found Boston trailing in the last frame. But Hooper's hit tied up the count and Whiteman's third timely drive of the game gave Barrow's men just the margin neccessary to win.

* [Winning pitcher, Mays (9–3); losing pitcher, Boland. Home run: Ruth (6). Red Sox' standing: 27 wins, 16 losses; in first place.]

Paul Shannon, *Boston Post*

Thursday, June 6

Babe Ruth Establishes World's Record of Home Runs in Four Successive Days

Indians Defeat Red Sox, 5 to 4

CLEVELAND, June 5—Boston's errors and Joe Bush's lack of control neutralized the effects of Babe Ruth's seventh home run of the season today.

Cleveland won the game in the tenth inning. With one out, Roth singled, stole second and took third on Schang's bad throw. Roth scored when Schang threw wide again trying to nip him off third.

- [Winning pitcher, Bagby; losing pitcher, Bush (7–3). Home run: Ruth (7). Red Sox' standing: 27 wins, 17 losses; in first place.]

Boston Herald and Journal

> We know of a geezer named Ruth,
> Who slams that old baseball forsooth,
> And after the crash
>   Of aforesaid Ruth's smash
> You hunt for the ball with a sleuth.

Cleveland Press

Ruth Picks Bleachers for Homer

Babe Ruth is already being hailed in the big leagues as the king of home run hitters. He poled out a four-base smash off Johnny Enzmann Wednesday that went clear over the [forty-five-foot-high] right field screen and sailed beyond a house on the other side of the street.

It was his fourth home run in four straight games. It was also Babe's seventh home run of the season as he had an earlier run of three homers in three days.

When Ruth arrived at the Indians' park Wednesday he said he was going to hit a homer during the game. But he picked the wrong spot. He figured on slamming the ball into the left field bleachers on the fly.

Cleveland Press

Babe wants to get back to the infield. He says there isn't enough to do in the outfield. One day after he was shifted from first base to the left garden he came in and complained to Manager Barrow.

"Give a fellow something to do," he pleaded. "I get sleepy out there in the field. It's so slow I just keep yawning."

Cleveland Press

Friday, June 7

Jones Shuts Out Cleveland, 1 to 0

CLEVELAND, June 6—It took 10 innings of a great pitching duel between Sam Jones and Stanley Coveleski before the Red Sox could get the decision this afternoon by a 1 to 0 verdict. Old Cy Young was a witness of the Red Sox victory.

It was the third great game in succession that Jones has pitched and his second shutout. All through today's game he outpitched the Cleveland spitballer. Coveleski was wild at times, but very effective, as he held the Sox to three scattered hits.

Jones held his opponents to five hits and pitched out of a number of bad holes. He passed three men in the ninth, and then retired the side without letting the ball be hit beyond the infield. He received well nigh perfect support.

• [Winning pitcher, Jones (2–1); losing pitcher, Coveleski. Red Sox' standing: 28 wins, 17 losses; in first place.]

Boston Post

At one time Sam Jones was barely noticed. Last winter it was reported that Sam had been drafted. He wasn't even sent a contract by the Hub Hose. The team was at Hot Springs when owner Harry Frazee got a letter from Sam along these lines: "Forgotten me altogether? I'm not worth a contract of any sort? If I am through, let me in on it."

Frazee told Sam to hurry to the Springs. However, his pitching remained a mystery until May 23, when he held Cleveland to one run. Then, on May 29, he startled fandom by beating Walter Johnson and the Senators, 3 to 0. Now he downs the Indians 1 to 0 in 10 innings, allowing but five hits. Verily, one of the chief charms of baseball is its ability to make a prince of a pauper in no time at all.

Bob Dunbar, *Boston Herald and Journal*

[Sad Sam was certainly no pauper. Although this was only his sixth lifetime victory, he went on to record 229 wins during a lengthy career that lasted through 1935.]

Babe Ruth sent his card to the owner of a building across Lexington Avenue in batting practice prior to the game. His card, in this instance, being a drive that broke two windows.

Boston Herald and Journal

Sam Jones, Red Sox pitcher

Captain Dick Hoblitzell has probably played his last game with the Red Sox. Today he was officially notified from Washington that he had been called to the service. Before the team leaves Cleveland he will be on his way to Camp Oglethorpe, Ga.

Boston Post

Ball players might do a lot worse than Joe Jackson did. Suppose they should apply for jobs on the Public Garden swan boats.

Bob Dunbar, *Boston Herald and Journal*

Fohl's Swamp Red Sox, 14 to 7

CLEVELAND, June 7—Dutch Leonard was unable to stand prosperity today. Although his colleagues staked him to a four run lead in the first inning, driving Jim Bagby from the mound, Leonard weakened in the third and followed Bagby off the scene of battle. From then on both sides changed pitchers with reckless abandon, Cleveland finally winning the contest, 14 to 7.

Former Red Sox were important factors in the victory. Tris Speaker made two doubles, stole a base and scored three runs. Joe Wood had a double and two singles, stole a base, scored one run and drove in a few others.

* [Winning pitcher, Coumbe; losing pitcher, Ruth (4–5). Red Sox' standing: 28 wins, 18 losses; in first place.]

Boston Herald and Journal

Sam Jones will be nicknamed Davey if he puts away many more games in his Red Sox locker.

Bob Dunbar, *Boston Herald and Journal*

The fans deserve a certain amount of credit for helping to get Dutch Leonard's goat when he was knocked out of the box Friday in the third round. Leonard has adopted a slow and tantalizing windup in which his arm describes a complete circle four times before he releases the ball.

Fans began to count in a thunderous chorus as Dutch was making his elaborate windups and it seemed to speed him up a bit, also to unsteady him.

Several times he cut his revolutions to three after the fans got to riding him.

Cleveland Press

Shout the glad tidings abroad to the fans —
Tell the sweet news to the rooterish clans —
Speaker is hitting again;
The crack of his bludgeon is sounding immense
And you gotta admit there's a whole lotta sense
In the way that old spheroid is denting the fence
When Speaker gets hitting again.

Cleveland Press

[Originally printed in June 6 edition]

Red Sox Lose Lead by Dropping Game, 3–1

Yankees in Top Berth

CLEVELAND, June 8—Winding up a brilliant pitching performance by striking out Babe Ruth, the leading batsman of the league, Guy Morton registered his second victory of the year over the Red Sox, 3 to 1.

The victory was obtained at the expense of Carl Mays, the submarine hurler, who had beaten the Indians in 13 out of 15 starts. Mays held the Indians to five hits but lost his game when the Indians resorted to bunts.

Despite Morton's brilliant work, the fans worried in the ninth. With two out, Strunk walked, giving Babe Ruth a chance to tie the score with a home run. Few left their seats. They knew Ruth was dangerous and they decided to wait a few minutes.

Morton was nervous. He shot in three that were wide of the plate and the fans looked for him to deliberately walk Ruth. He then whizzed in a couple that were strikes. Ruth fouled off three pitches. The next was over and low. Ruth swung and missed, but the ball had so much on it that Chet Thomas [the Indians' catcher] let it slip from his glove. He picked it up in time, however, to get Ruth at first.

- [Winning pitcher, Morton; losing pitcher, Mays (9–4). Red Sox' standing: 28 wins, 19 losses; in second place, .004 points behind the New York Yankees.]

Boston Globe

IT LOOKS LIKE RATHER ROUGH GOING IN THE PENNANT RACES THIS SEASON.

Scott, *Boston Post*

Leonard Shuts Out Indians 2–0

Sox Lead Again

CLEVELAND, June 9—By dint of great pitching and effective hitting Dutch Leonard downed the Indians by a 2 to 0 score, steering the Red Sox back into the leadership in the American League race.

In the eighth, a bad decision by Umpire Brick Owens caused such a furious demonstration by the Indians that both Ray Chapman and Fritz Coumbe were chased. Chapman claimed that he beat out a grounder but Umpire Owens called him out. On the way to the dressing room Owens was assaulted by a couple of first base bleacherites and the arrest of two men followed.

Just before the game started President Jim Dunn of the Cleveland club was presented with a $300 gold watch by the Indian players. Previously, Dick Hoblitzell was given a handsome gold wrist watch by his teammates as the captain bade baseball good-bye. He left for the training camp in Georgia tonight.

- [Winning pitcher, Leonard (7–5); losing pitcher, Coveleski. Red Sox' standing: 29 wins, 19 losses; in first place.]

Paul Shannon, Boston Post

[Dick Hoblitzell never played another game in the major leagues.]

AMERICAN LEAGUE STANDINGS			
	Won	Lost	PCT.	GB
Boston 29		19	.604	—
New York 27		19	.587	1
Chicago 23		18	.561	2.5
Cleveland 25		24	.510	4.5
St. Louis 21		22	.488	5.5
Washington 23		25	.479	6
Philadelphia 17		26	.395	9.5
Detroit 14		26	.350	11

Babe Ruth is the greatest drawing card in the major leagues.

RED SOX BATTING

	AB	R	BH	2B	3B	HR	SB	AVG
Ruth, p, of	82	19	30	10	2	7	1	.366
Hooper, rf	175	34	58	12	4	1	13	.331
Thomas, 3b	83	12	24	0	1	0	3	.289
McInnis, 1b	167	20	48	3	1	0	4	.287
Strunk, cf	162	24	46	6	4	0	14	.284
Mays, p	37	4	10	1	1	0	1	.270
Shean, 2b	176	22	46	9	0	0	7	.261
Whiteman, lf	106	11	26	7	0	0	8	.245
Schang, lf, c	87	16	21	6	1	0	0	.241
Scott, ss	171	19	38	6	2	0	5	.222
Hoblitzell, 1b	69	4	11	1	0	0	3	.159
Agnew, c	100	6	11	6	0	0	0	.110

RED SOX PITCHING

	IP	BH	W	L	R	BB	SO
Mays	110.2	92	9	4	41	40	48
Jones	36.2	34	2	1	16	14	9
Bush	101.1	74	7	3	28	46	32
Leonard	102.2	103	7	5	48	50	38
Ruth	70	64	4	5	29	25	13
McCabe	8.2	11	0	1	4	2	3

Babe Ruth is the greatest drawing card in the major leagues. The southpaw star of the Red Sox staff, utility outfielder and first sacker, has snatched the crown from Ty Cobb and Tris Speaker.

Here's what one veteran of the American League thinks of Ruth: "I have been going to Detroit for years and never even saw one home run made into those right field seats, where he hit three. Then, to follow up with a clout over the wall at Cleveland is a stunner. He is the most powerful hitter in the game today, perhaps the best of all time."

Harry Casey, *Boston Record*

Tuesday, June 11

Bush Invincible as Red Sox Subdue Chisox, 1–0

CHICAGO, June 10—Bullet Joe Bush opened the Chicago series for the Red Sox today, and the fans, who shivered in the cold, learned why he was given the handle to his name. The warmest thing in Comiskey Park was

Bullet Joe's speed. White Sox fans have never seen this pitcher show more smoke. Neither have the world's champions, who evidently didn't see the sphere. Bush held the White Sox to one hit and no runs.

Dave Shean, a trouble maker for the champions, tripled to right centre in the fourth inning and scored on a passed ball, giving the Red Sox a 1 to 0 verdict.

- [Winning pitcher, Bush (8–3); losing pitcher, Shellenback. Red Sox' standing: 30 wins, 19 losses; in first place.]

Boston Herald and Journal

Wednesday, June 12

Loyal Faber Goes to Slab, Beats Boston, 4–1

CHICAGO, June 11—Red Faber, who already has enlisted at Great Lakes naval station and did not expect to pitch again for the White Sox, asked for his uniform when he learned of Manager Rowland's plight for slabmen. Faber pitched a brilliant game, enabling his pals to lick the Red Sox, 4 to 1.

- [Winning pitcher, Faber; losing pitcher, Jones (2–2). Red Sox' standing: 30 wins, 20 losses; in first place.]

I. E. Sanborn, *Chicago Daily Tribune*

[One of baseball's renowned spitball artists, Faber averaged seventeen wins during each of his first four years with the White Sox, plus three victories as the hero of the 1917 World Series. After the war was over he continued pitching for Chicago through 1933, compiling a career mark of 254 victories and 213 losses with a lot of bad ball clubs. Faber's enlistment in the navy was a big blow to the White Sox pitching corps. He departed with a 4–1 record.

In 1964 Urban (Red) Faber was elected to the Hall of Fame.]

Two White Sox players, Byrd Lynn and Lefty Williams, strolled into Comiskey Park this morning and politely informed President Comiskey their contracts were terminated. They purposed following Joe Jackson into the business of camouflage painting of ships. President Comiskey told the players he was glad they were going, that it was a good riddance. He sent for their uniforms and told these players he was absolutely through with them. When Williams and Lynn said they would loiter around awhile and help him out, Comiskey told them to beat it, the sooner the better. They went.

Boston Herald and Journal

[Lefty Williams had won 17 games in 1917 and was 6–4 in 1918. His departure for the ship-building league decimated Chicago's pennant hopes.]

The White Sox have the best team in the shipyard league.

Bob Dunbar, *Boston Herald and Journal*

Hooper Captain after 10 Years with Boston

After nearly a decade with Boston, Harry Hooper, the favorite right fielder of the team, has been named captain to succeed Dick Hoblitzell, who has left to join the army.

Year after year Hooper has played brilliant ball, always giving his best. There never has been a more popular player among the Red Sox.

Hooper is now playing his 10th season with Boston. There are few players who last as long in the big show. The extraordinary part of it all is that he is going as good, if not better, than when he broke in. Harry is now hitting at a .323 clip.

Boston Record

Thursday, June 13

Mays Shuts Out White Sox, 7 to 0

Submarine Twirler Holds World's Champs to Three Hits

CHICAGO, June 12—Carl Mays and his submarine service were too much for the world's champion White Sox today and the Boston team had little difficulty in winning the 7 to 0 decision.

Backed up by some splendid fielding, especially on Hooper's part, Mays twirled the best game he has pitched on the trip. A little short of control at the start, he settled down as the game progressed, and the White Sox were helpless before him. Not a single one of the locals reached third.

Mays drove in the first run with a lusty three-bagger, but the hitting of Hooper was the big feature of the game. Captain Harry made four fine hits, including a long three-bagger. His catch off Buck Weaver was one of the greatest plays of the year.

● [Winning pitcher, Mays (10–4); losing pitcher, Danforth. Red Sox' standing: 31 wins, 20 losses; in first place.]

Paul Shannon, *Boston Post*

The Rowlands [White Sox] were as helpless as emancipated Russia. Only three of them reached second base and only one of them saw third alive.

Boston Globe

The White Sox had to play in their grey traveling uniforms, as their white ones did not come back from the laundry in time for the game. The league rules prescribe white suits for the home team, but as Boston won the combat there was no chance for a protest by Manager Barrow.

Chicago Tribune

Leonard Pilots Red Sox to 6–0 Win over White Sox

CHICAGO, June 13—Dutch Leonard didn't hurl a no-hit game here today, but he came close to it. He shut out the White Sox, 6 to 0, and only five clear, unsullied safe raps were garnered off him in nine innings. While Dutch was putting the world's champions deeper in dutch with the Chicago fans, his teammates were hammering Eddie Cicotte, shine ball expert, from the hill.

- [Winning pitcher, Leonard (8–5); losing pitcher, Cicotte. Red Sox' standing: 32 wins, 20 losses; in first place.]

Boston Herald and Journal

Everything Goes, Says Griffith

CHICAGO, June 14—Clark Griffith, Washington manager, believes in fighting fire with fire.

"Until the umpires stop the White Sox pitchers from using the shine ball," says Griff, "my pitchers will use it, even Walter Johnson, who really doesn't need it.

"I mean to compel action by Ban Johnson against this illegal delivery, but he'll have to stop every pitcher."

Griff says his players are to smear and shine the ball with all sorts of stuff—paraffin, licorice, oil of tar, talcum, and just plain every day mud.

Boston American

[Although the spitball was the most common trick pitch of this era, it certainly wasn't the only one. A few pitchers used the shine ball, making the ball break sharply by smoothing part of the ball's surface with talcum or paraffin.

Another freak pitch of those days was the emery ball. Pitchers roughened the ball with a small piece of sandpaper, causing it to behave erratically in flight. Ban Johnson was dead set against the pitch and decreed that anyone who tried to turn "our good little American League into a sandpaper league" would be suspended for thirty days and fined a hundred dollars.

In February 1920, the major leagues finally made it illegal to tamper with the ball or apply any foreign substance to it. This, in effect, banned the emery ball, licorice ball, mud ball, and especially the spitball. However, seventeen pitchers were allowed to continue using these illegal pitches until they retired. The last of the old spitballers, Burleigh Grimes, pitched until 1934.

When the trick pitches were finally outlawed, scoring increased markedly and the dead ball era ended.]

Red Sox Lose in Ninth Inning, 5–4

ST. LOUIS, June 14—A pinch hitter, rushed to the rescue of the Browns at the eleventh hour this afternoon, won the verdict for St. Louis by the count of 5 to 4. There were two men on base, two out and two strikes on Pete

THE SNEAK · · · · By Ripley

Ripley, *Boston Globe*

Johns, the relief swatter, when he pounded out the triple that sent the Barrow brigade from Sportsmen's Field [Sportsman's Park] defeated.

* [Winning pitcher, Sothoron; losing pitcher, Bush (8–4). Red Sox' standing: 32 wins, 21 losses; in first place.]

Paul Shannon, *Boston Post*

[Pete Johns played two years in the majors with a lifetime batting average of .196 and five extra-base hits.]

Ruth Finds Batting Orb

Ruth broke his batting slump with two solid raps off Sothoron yesterday. His single in the first counted Shean, while he doubled in the third, scoring Hooper and Shean. Thus, he accounted for three of the visitors' four runs.

St. Louis Post-Dispatch

No Uniform for Barrow

Ed Barrow joins Connie Mack and George Stallings [the Boston Braves' manager] concerning the wearing of a uniform. The Red Sox pilot appeared yesterday decked out in dark trousers, blue shirt and stiff collar. He directs the team from the bench in this attire.

St. Louis Post-Dispatch

Ruth's Smash into Bleachers Winner

Homer with Two on Base Beats Browns, 8 to 4

ST. LOUIS, June 15—Babe Ruth hammered the Browns into submission at Sportsman's Park, the noted slugger driving over five of the eight runs made by the Easterners.

The climax came in the seventh inning, with the score tied at 4, two men on base and two out. On the first pitch to Ruth, the heavy hitter took a mighty swing, but missed the ball and the fans howled with delight. However, their pleasure was short-lived. On the next offering, a little low and down the alley, the ball connected with Babe's bat and sailed like a bullet into the bleachers in right center. Ruth's smash put the game on ice.

[Winning pitcher, Jones (3–2); losing pitcher, Rogers. Home run: Ruth (8). Red Sox' standing: 33 wins, 21 losses; in first place.]

Boston Globe

IT MUST HAVE SURE JARRED THE ST-LOUIS FANS WHEN "BABE" RUTH SENT A HOMER INTO THE RIGHTFIELD BLEACHERS FOR A SCORE OF 3 RUNS IN THE 7TH INNING DOWN ST-LOUIS WAY, SAT-

Scott, *Boston Post*

Johnson's Sprint Beats the Red Sox, 2–1

Races Home When Schang's Low Peg Goes Rolling

ST. LOUIS, June 16—Running wild on the bases in the ninth inning, Ernie Johnson, sub infielder for the Browns, carried off the game from the Red Sox, 2 to 1, after the game had stood one-all for a long time.

Johnson scored the winning run after two were out. He was on first as a pinch runner and made a dash for second. Catcher Schang's throw was low and the ball rolled into right field. Johnson picked himself out of the dust and headed for third, not pausing at that corner, but sailing home. The ball followed him, Shean to Thomas to Schang, just a moment after he slid over the pan.

* [Winning pitcher, Shocker; losing pitcher, Leonard (8–6). Red Sox' standing: 33 wins, 22 losses; in first place.]

Boston Globe

Manager Barrow has worn out three new silk shirts in the dugout since the series began, and he will start on a new batch today.

Boston Record

Austin Sets Fashion for Managers
Gives Johnson Hearty Kiss

Whether they win or lose, give the Browns credit for everlastingly trying and possessing the "will to win." After Ernie Johnson slid across the plate with the winning run in the ninth inning yesterday, Jimmy Austin, coaching at first, and Jimmy Burke, at third, made a rush for the plate.

Burke lifted Johnson out of the dirt and Austin leaped into the air, coming down with both arms around Ernie's neck. Then the manager performed a feat never before seen at a local major league park. He kissed Johnson squarely on the cheek. There wasn't any doubt about it, for the smack resounded in the grandstand.

They're a distinctly different club from the seventh placers of 1917.

St. Louis Post-Dispatch

AMERICAN LEAGUE STANDINGS

	Won	Lost	PCT.	GB
Boston	33	22	.600	—
New York	30	22	.577	1.5
Cleveland	30	25	.545	3
Chicago	26	22	.542	3.5
St. Louis	25	25	.500	5.5
Washington	26	29	.473	7
Philadelphia	19	31	.380	11.5
Detroit	17	30	.362	12

Evers Plays Third in Farewell Game

TROY, N.Y.—More than 5,000 persons turned out to see Johnny Evers, former big league star, play his last game in America before leaving for France. He will direct athletic work among the American soldiers under the direction of the Knights of Columbus. Evers played third base for the Watervliet Arsenal against the Troy team.

When Evers reached the park fans from all parts of New York State were on hand to bid good-by. He autographed a baseball before the game and auctioned it off for $45. Evers gave the proceeds to the Red Cross.

Johnny's double to left field scored two runs in the eighth and brought victory to his team.

Boston Herald and Journal

Ty Cobb must consider this year the day when the regal mantle of baseball will slip from his shoulders.

Cobb ordinarily is a slow starter. He does not extend himself to the limit during the opening weeks of the season, reserving his tremendous resources until warm weather. In addition, this year Cobb has also been handicapped by illness and injuries.

A batting average under .320 for Cobb in the middle of June is a scandal.

Boston Record

[Cobb was hitting .309, tenth best in the league.]

Tuesday, June 18

Mays Shuts Out Browns, 8–0

ST. LOUIS, June 17—Pinch hitters and pinch runners couldn't stop the Red Sox this afternoon, for the Browns couldn't get enough men on the bases to induce any wild pegging. While Mays was making easy work of the St. Louis batters, the Red Sox fattened averages at the expense of four different pitchers, and the Barrow brigade won the closing game of the trip with a verdict of 8 to 0.

Mays was invincible, allowing only four safe hits and permitting only one of the three locals to reach third base. The thermometer in the Boston dugout registered 103 during the game.

[Winning pitcher, Mays (11–4); losing pitcher, Gallia. Red Sox' standing: 34 wins, 22 losses; in first place.]

Paul Shannon, *Boston Post*

The Brownie boys were in the soup,
Because they could not hit;
But with the famous Boston troupe
They got an even split.

They couldn't get to Pitcher Mays,
Who had them in a trance;
And with his underhanded ways
They didn't have a chance.

L. Davis, *St. Louis Post-Dispatch*

The Chicago White Sox recently raised a service flag bearing 13 stars, but Manager Rowland wants it understood that no stars were included for Joe Jackson, Williams and Lynn, who quit the team to engage in shipbuilding.

Harry J. Casey, *Boston Record*

Wednesday, June 19

Everett Scott, shortstop of the Red Sox, is making a notable record in fielding, having gone 24 straight games without an error. Incidentally, his batting has increased with his improved fielding, hitting .270 over the last 24 games. Great work, Scotty.

Bob Dunbar, *Boston Herald and Journal*

Ed Barrow recently had this boost for the Yankees. He said, "The Yankees looked very strong in their games against us, and if Huggins does not lose any boys in the draft he will be the one to fight it out with us at the finish. But I look for Cleveland to be right up there, too. I cannot say that I fear Chicago. They are running short on pitchers and I do not believe they have a chance to repeat. If Huggins can get the pitching he has a great chance, for the Yankees can hit the ball."

Harry J. Casey, *Boston Record*

[New York was in second place, only two games behind the Red Sox.]

Thursday, June 20

Red Sox Bow to Athletics, 5–0

Mackmen Play Like Champions

BOSTON, June 19—Bob Geary, a youngster picked up from the Charleston club of the Carolina league, had the honor of piloting the Macks to their victory over the Red Sox at Fenway Park. The lowly A's

Ty Cobb must consider this year the day when the regal mantle of baseball will slip from his shoulders.

looked like pace-makers of the league, while the crimson hose resembled cellar habitués, the count standing 5 to 0.

Young Geary worked like a master and only one of the hosemen reached third base. Seven hits was the extent of the damage done by the Sox. A remarkable throw by Tilly Walker [Philadelphia's slugging center fielder] to the plate cut off the only threat Boston made.

* [Winning pitcher, Geary; losing pitcher, Bush (8–5). Red Sox' standing: 34 wins, 23 losses; in first place.]

John J. Hallahan, Boston Herald and Journal

[After his terrific debut, Bob Geary posted a career record of three victories and nine defeats.]

Dutch Leonard May Enter Shipyard

Hubert (Dutch) Leonard, sturdy California southpaw and one of the greatest left-handers in baseball, is likely to retire from the Red Sox fold and professional baseball. In fact, he is so close to a decision that he will notify President Frazee, one way or the other, before this afternoon's game.

Leonard is about to follow the example of several other players and become a shipbuilder. He has been assured of a good position at Fore River [Quincy, Mass.] and the chance of pitching weekly on the team in the Steel League.

Boston Post

Friday, June 21

Red Sox Divide with Athletics

BOSTON, June 20—Boston lost the decision in the opening game of yesterday's double-header with the Athletics by the score of 2 to 0. However, the Sox turned the tables in the second battle, and after going scoreless for 23 consecutive rounds, finally managed to bunch enough hits to give them the 3 to 0 decision.

While Sam Jones pitched magnificently for Boston in the first game, he bowed to old Vean Gregg, a Red Sox discard. Sam Jones lost only because Tillie Walker hit a home run in the ninth that broke up a scoreless tie.

In the second game, an injury to Dutch Leonard forced Vincent Molyneaux, the Villa Nova College recruit, to come to the rescue and win his first game for the Sox. Leonard had held Philadelphia to four hits in five innings, when his left thumb was damaged while trying to stop Walker's hit.

Hooper gave the Sox their opportunity to win in the sixth round of the second game by cracking a three-bagger. With nobody gone the Philadelphians closed in to stop a possible squeeze play, but Shean crossed them up by hitting safely to centre, scoring Boston's first run. Ruth was passed intentionally and McInnis landed the second triple of this round, sending two more runs across.

- [Game one: winning pitcher, Gregg; losing pitcher, Jones (3–3). Home run: Walker (Phil.). Game two: winning pitcher, Molyneaux (1–0); losing pitcher, Perry. Red Sox' standing: 35 wins, 24 losses; in first place.]

Paul Shannon, *Boston Post*

[This was the last time Dutch Leonard ever pitched for the Boston Red Sox. He jumped the club after the game to pitch for the Fore River Shipyard team. Leonard had won 90 and lost 63 during his Red Sox career.]

CHICAGO, June 20—Chicago defeated Cleveland, 5 to 4, in 10 innings today. The entire receipts of the game will build a recreation house on the lake front for the benefit of soldiers and sailors.

Before the game three autographed baseballs were auctioned. The first, autographed by Billy Sunday, brought $50; one by Mrs. Woodrow Wilson was sold for $1,450; and one bearing the autograph of the President was sold at $5,650.

Boston Globe

[Billy Sunday was one of America's most prominent evangelists. However, he had been a fleet-footed center fielder with the Chicago White Stockings and the Pittsburgh Alleghenys during the 1880s, stealing 84 bases in his final season.]

Saturday, June 22

Puny Roller Robs Mays of No Hit Honors

Red Sox Humble the Mackmen, 13 to 0

BOSTON, June 21—A little dinky roller down the pitcher's path robbed Carl Mays, the submarine torpedo shooter, from embossing his name in the hall of fame at Fenway Park yesterday afternoon.

The hit was delivered by Jake Munch. It was so soft that ordinarily the fleetest runner in the country would be thrown out at first. Mays, after looking at Schang to make the play, threw late to first.

Dave Shean had a great day with the bat. He was aided by two sun hits, but his other two hits were legitimate. Ruth slammed a three-bagger to right with the bases filled in the fourth and almost killed Burns [the right fielder].

- [Winning pitcher, Mays (12–4); losing pitcher, Adams. Red Sox' standing: 36 wins, 24 losses; in first place.]

John J. Hallahan, *Boston Herald and Journal*

WITH 2 OUT AND THE BASES FILLED ~
"BABE" RUTH TRIPLED (CLEANING THE BASES
THEN SCORED HIMSELF ON A WILD THROW
MAKING 4 RUNS IN THE 4TH INNING ~

Scott, Boston Post

Monday, June 24

AMERICAN LEAGUE STANDINGS

	Won	Lost	PCT.	GB
Boston	36	24	.600	—
New York	32	24	.571	2
Cleveland	35	27	.565	2
Chicago	27	27	.500	6
Washington	31	31	.500	6
St. Louis	27	31	.466	8
Detroit	22	32	.407	11
Philadelphia	21	35	.375	13

[Saturday's game was rained out. Boston didn't play on Sunday.]

Carl Mays, the submarine hurler of the Red Sox, is on his way to a new record. The underhand star has pitched two one-hit games against the Athletics this season and has held his opponents scoreless in the last 32 innings.

Harry J. Casey, Boston Record

RED SOX BATTING

	AB	R	BH	2B	3B	HR	SB	AVG
Hooper, rf 223	44	75	17	7	1	15	.336
Ruth, util 118	25	38	12	3	8	1	.322
Mays, p 47	6	14	2	2	0	1	.298
Shean, 2b 223	38	63	9	3	0	8	.283
Thomas, 3b 133	17	35	2	1	0	5	.263
McInnis, 1b 211	22	55	4	3	0	5	.261
Strunk, cf 210	26	54	7	3	0	16	.257
Whiteman, lf 121	10	30	9	0	0	9	.248
Scott, ss 220	23	54	9	2	0	8	.245
Schang, c 112	22	26	6	1	0	1	.232
Agnew, c 114	6	14	5	0	0	1	.123

RED SOX PITCHING

	IP	BH	Won	Lost	R	BB	SO
Molyneaux 5.1	0	1	0	0	4	0
Mays 137.2	100	12	4	41	46	58
Bush 127.1	119	8	5	38	54	44
Leonard 126	119	8	6	50	60	46
Jones 61.2	58	3	3	26	23	12
Ruth 70	64	4	5	29	25	13
McCabe · 9.2	13	0	1	5	2	3

Tuesday, June 25

Pipp's Mighty Bat Conquers Red Sox, 3–2

NEW YORK, June 24—Wally Pipp, the tall Yankee first baseman, poled a long, high, two-base wallop into the upper tier of the Polo Grounds in the ninth inning yesterday. The hit gave Miller Huggins' clan the honors of their first skirmish with Ed Barrow's Boston Red Sox, by the score of 3 to 2.

Entering the ninth frame the Yankees were lagging in the score by 2 to 1. The crowd was howling for a final inning rally. Roger Peckinpaugh started with a display of patience and drew a pass. Then J. Franklin Baker sent the ball screeching to right field. Peckinpaugh scooted around to third on this blow and scored on Del Pratt's sacrifice fly.

Baker was held to first on the fly, but was confident of Pipp's ability to deliver. Wally responded with his terrific slam close to the top tier of the stands where no one could get it unless ball players add airplanes to their equipment. Ordinarily, Pipp's clout would be recorded as a home run but the scoring rules are different in these situations and the tall first baseman received credit for only a double [as Baker scored the winning run]. Pipp, after rounding the second corner, cut off across the diamond for the dugout amid the thunderous applause of the spectators.

- [Winning pitcher, Mogridge; losing pitcher, Bush (8–6). Red Sox' standing: 36 wins, 25 losses; in first place. New York was in second place, one game behind.]

New York Times

[Wally Pipp became famous as the man Lou Gehrig replaced at first base in 1925. However, Pipp also had an illustrious career, batting .281 with 1,941 hits, including 148 triples. He led the American League in home runs twice, with 12 in 1916 and 9 in 1917.]

Ty Cobb Now Fifth, and Headed for the Top

Here comes Ty Cobb!

The Detroit Demon is at last on his hitting stride and has forged into the American League's Fancy Five. His average is .331 and he ranks only 22 points behind George Sisler.

	AB	Hits	AVG
Sisler, St. Louis 232	232	82	.353
Burns, Athletics 224	224	78	.348
Baker, New York 227	227	77	.339
HOOPER, BOSTON 223	223	75	.336
Cobb, Detroit 172	172	57	.331

Boston American

Wednesday, June 26

Sox Vanquish Yanks, 7 to 3

Ruth Gets Another Homer

NEW YORK, June 25—Tornadic thumps by Babe Ruth, Harry Hooper and Dave Shean in the early innings this afternoon awoke the Yankees from their dream of heading the pennant parade. The Barrow brigade breezed along to an easy 7 to 3 victory.

Babe Ruth was in centre field today, as Amos Strunk injured himself while sliding in the opening game. Ruth got a remarkable ovation from the New York fans when he stepped to the plate in the first inning with George Whiteman resting on first base.

The first ball pitched by Allen Russell was high, fast and on the outside. Babe took a swing and the ball went high, fast and to the upper tier of the right field stands. It was a colossal clout and Babe trotted around the bases to the cheers of the fans.

⁑ [Winning pitcher, Jones (4–3); losing pitcher, Russell. Home run: Ruth (9). Red Sox' standing: 37 wins, 25 losses; in first place.]

Boston Herald and Journal

Ruth's slam was the mightiest ever produced at the Polo Grounds. The ball cracked against the concrete of the upper tier in the furthermost right hand [corner] and caromed deep into centre field.

Boston American

If they were giving automobiles to the best players in the two big leagues this season, it's a certainty that Babe Ruth would get the A.L. buggy. It's equally certain that there would be little left of the machine by the start of the next season. Babe can hit telegraph poles as hard as he hits the horse hide. But we love him just the same.

Bob Dunbar, *Boston Herald and Journal*

LONDON—King George is learning to throw a baseball in preparation for his appearance at a game between American teams on July 4, when he will pitch out the first ball.

Arlie Latham, who will umpire the Fourth of July game, sent him a regulation baseball a few days ago. The next day Latham called at the palace and gave the King a brief lesson as to how the baseball should be handled. Since then he has been practicing in his spare moments on a blank wall in the garden.

The King expressed hope he would be able to throw the ball in a manner to win the approval of the American rooters.

Boston Record

Home Run Baker Has Made 62 Homers in Big League Career

Home Run Baker established a new record in circuit clouts for the American League when his mighty drive in last Saturday's game between the Yanks and the Senators sailed into the right field stands at the Polo Grounds. Ty Cobb ranks second to Baker, with sixty-one four baggers.

Boston Record

[Babe Ruth eventually set the American League record with 708 home runs. (He hit an additional 6 in the National League.)]

Yankees Subdue Red Sox and Draw Near Top

NEW YORK, June 26—Slim Love cast a mystic spell over Babe Ruth up at the Polo Grounds, and the Boston mauler failed to get a home run. With Ruth under subjection, the Yanks went out and won the ball game, 3 to 1. Huggins' crew is now within one game of the Red Sox. If New York should win this afternoon's game, they will hurdle right into the lead.

Ruth made a heroic attempt to inject a stick of dynamite into the fray in the ninth. With one out, Ruth lifted a rocket into right field a mile high. The ball went out of sight and a breathless few minutes followed before the ball came down.

Gilhooley [the Yankees' right fielder] thought he saw a speck which looked like the ball and he ran close to the concrete wall, watching the spot in the sky. When the ball came down it was a few feet short of a home run, and was so close to the wall that Gilhooley could only get one hand on it. The cloudbreaker went for a two-base hit, driving in Boston's only run.

• [Winning pitcher, Love; losing pitcher, Mays (12–5). Red Sox' standing: 37 wins, 26 losses; in first place, one game ahead of the Yankees.]

New York Times

Mays had blanked his opponents for 35 consecutive innings before Love's double drove two runs across in the second inning. He had blanked Cleveland for seven innings and followed up with shut-out victories over Chicago, St. Louis, and Philadelphia.

Boston Herald and Journal

Another good crowd, about 7,000 fans, turned out to see the game. As the Yanks are close enough to take the lead by winning tomorrow, the series shapes up as a big one from an attendance standpoint.

Boston Herald and Journal

Yankees Jolt Red Sox from First Place

NEW YORK, June 27—The Yanks elbowed their way past the Red Sox into first place in the American League race up at the Polo Grounds, winning a topsy-turvy game by the score of 7 to 5.

The game was chockful of spontaneous little thrills, ludicrous errors, and uncertain moments when it seemed as if the Yanks were going to be thumped into subjection. The Red Sox slammed Mogridge for fifteen hits, and were always on the verge of shoving over barrels of runs. There wasn't a chance during the whole game of any of the 8,000 fans falling asleep.

The Yanks were limping in the rear by a score of 4 to 3 in the sixth inning when Ping Bodie inserted a home run against the upper veranda of the grand stand. Wally Pipp was vacationing on first at the time, and the raucous rap pushed the Yanks into the lead, 5 to 4. Although Boston threatened many times after that, Huggins' lads hung onto the lead with a pugnacious grip.

- [Winning pitcher, Mogridge; losing pitcher, Bush (8–7). Home run: Bodie. Red Sox' standing: 37 wins, 27 losses; in second place, .005 behind New York.]

New York Times

The once-upon-a-time joke Senators are now playing as good ball as any team in the American League. They stand but three games behind the Red Sox and local fandom has visions of them moving ahead of the Boston boys.

Boston American

[Washington was running in fourth place, with 35 wins and 31 losses. They had finished fifth in 1917, 25.5 games behind.]

Saturday, June 29

OOCH! HOW SUDDEN!!

9 HITS

7 RUNS

NEW YORK YANKEES

FIRST PLACE

SECOND PLACE

RED SOX

17 HITS

← 5 RUNS

THE NEW YORK YANKEES BUMPED THE BOSTON RED SOX INTO 2ND PLACE, IN THE THURSDAY GAME - BUT MGR BARROW SAYS THEY'LL SOON BE BACK AT THE TOP.

Scott, *Boston Post*

Red Sox Beaten, 3 to 1, by Fast-Going Senators

Ruth's 10th Homer Only Hit

WASHINGTON, D.C., June 28—Babe Ruth's homer, a terrific clout over the right field wall in the seventh inning, was the only dent the Red Sox could make in Harper's pitching here today. Washington continued on its winning way, staging a rally in the eighth that netted two runs and a 3 to 1 victory.

* [Winning pitcher, Harper; losing pitcher, Bader (0–1). Home run: Ruth (10). Red Sox' standing: 37 wins, 28 losses; in second place, one game behind New York.]

Boston Globe

An observing waiter has detected Ruth's weakness. He says that you can get the big fellow if you mix them up. He can't handle tea, coffee and milk at one meal.

Boston Globe

Sunday, June 30

Griffs Falter and Red Sox Win, 3–1

WASHINGTON, June 29—After playing a sensational fielding game for seven innings, showing a defense that made a one run lead look as big as the Washington Monument, the Nationals miscued a game to the Red Sox and lost a chance to get within two games of the American League leaders. The Barrow tribe took the second game of the series, 3 to 1.

After the Griffs got a run in the first inning they had chances to score in the fourth, fifth, sixth and eighth innings, but each time Boston pitching was as deadly to them as a gas attack to unmasked troops. Failing to deliver, they lost an opportunity to take their eighth straight game and get right up in the orchestra seats in the pennant scramble.

* [Winning pitcher, Jones (5–3); losing pitcher, Ayers. Red Sox' standing: 38 wins, 28 losses; in second place, .005 behind New York.]

J. V. Fitzgerald, *Washington Post*

More than $11,000 in war savings stamps were sold before the game. Orator MacFarland got a great hand when he declared in a speech, urging the fans to buy stamps, that there are no better patriots in the country than baseball men and lovers of the game.

Washington Post

Sox Lead League Again, Win 3–1

Babe Ruth Connects with One of Walter Johnson's Fast Ones in 10th for a Homer

WASHINGTON, June 30—The Red Sox went back into first place again this afternoon on the long distance drive of the burly Babe Ruth. The demon slugger's mighty wallop over the right field wall, with a man on base and two out in the tenth inning, broke up the bitter twirling duel between Mays and Walter Johnson and gave Boston the decision by the score of 3 to 1.

The largest crowd that ever attended a Boston game in this city saw Washington outbatted nearly two to one. Not a safe hit was made off Mays until the sixth inning, while Johnson was hit freely throughout the contest.

• [Winning pitcher, Mays (13–5); losing pitcher, Johnson. Home run: Ruth (11). Red Sox' standing: 39 wins, 28 losses; in first place, .001 ahead of New York.]

Paul H. Shannon, Boston Post

Babe Ruth, Boston Red Sox

Babe Ruth's mighty hitting, his homeric smashes, kindles a glow in the hearts of all those who know baseball. In Italy, in Normandy, in Alsace, and in a hundred camps along the firing line, men ask for the latest news of the gifted hitter of home runs. The story of each succeeding circuit clout is received with acclaim. It lightens and breaks the dangerous tension of a soldier's duty.

Bob Dunbar, Boston Herald and Journal

AMERICAN LEAGUE STANDINGS

	Won	Lost	PCT.	GB
Boston	39	28	.582	—
New York	36	26	.581	0.5
Cleveland	39	31	.557	1.5
Washington	36	33	.522	4
Chicago	30	32	.484	6.5
St. Louis	31	35	.470	7.5
Detroit	27	35	.435	9.5
Philadelphia	22	40	.355	14.5

My idea of vee-locity is Babe Ruth knocking a home run off Walter Johnson's fast one.

Bob Dunbar, Boston Herald and Journal

Way Ruth Is Going He'll Own Forty-Four Homers by Fall

Forty-four home runs for Babe Ruth in '18!

That's one sumptuous total, one that has never been made in baseball, and one which probably won't ever be hung up. But—

Were Ruth a regular his collection of four-play slams at the end of the campaign would be forty-four, providing that Battering Babe kept ramming 'em out at his present ratio.

H. W. Lanigan, *Boston American*

Scott, *Boston Post*

Thomas Called in Draft

Fred Thomas, the Red Sox sterling young third sacker, one of the game's best rookies, has been called into the big show. The kid has departed for his home at Weekwonago, Wis., to undergo a physical examination. He's in Class 1 of the draft and has not claimed exemption. So, of course, he goes into the army.

Boston American

[Thomas was batting .257 with one home run. His loss at third base was enormous. Boston never found an adequate replacement that year.]

In 1902 "Socks" Seybold of the Mackmen hammered out 16 home runs, establishing an American League record which many have shot at, but none have even equaled. There is a possibility that the record will be knocked galley west this year by Babe Ruth. The big Oriole boy has pounded out 11 circuit knocks and the season has three months to go.

Boston Globe

LONDON, July 1—American women at the workrooms of the Red Cross put the finishing touches on 300 baseball uniforms and sent them to the American camps in Great Britain, so they can be distributed among the teams which will play baseball on July 4.

The 200 volunteers gave up the whole of Saturday and Sunday to finish the order.

Boston Globe

Wednesday, July 3

Harper Downs Red Sox, 3–0

WASHINGTON, July 2—"Moxie" Harper hung up his second victory of the series against the Red Sox today, 3 to 0, holding the Barrow clan to four scattered hits. Joe Bush succumbed to a vicious assault in the early frames but was effective thereafter.

Babe Ruth vanished after being called out on strikes in the sixth, Stansbury replacing him. Harper's curve ball was too much for the big fellow.

- [Winning pitcher, Harper; losing pitcher, Bush (8–8). Red Sox' standing: 39 wins, 29 losses; in second place, .004 behind New York.]

Boston Herald and Journal

Ruth Is Fined and Benched by Barrow

Ruth can't hit home runs every day, but evidently Manager Ed Barrow thinks he ought to. It hurts the former International League president every time Babe strikes out. Barrow was so pained yesterday that he soaked a $500 fine on his pitching-outfielder for swinging like a gate at some of Harper's offerings. As a result, Babe and his boss had a wordy war.

The slugger left the park in a huff. He threatened to quit the club, and, unless he and Barrow settled their differences on the way to Philadelphia last night, the Sox might be without their prize hitter for a few days. It is certain, however, that Boston club officials are not going to let a fine keep Babe and his big club out of the lineup.

J. V. Fitzgerald, *Washington Post*

Thursday, July 4

Babe Ruth Quits Red Sox

PHILADELPHIA, July 3—The Boston Red Sox outfit was dealt a savage blow today when it learned that big Babe Ruth had jumped the club in a fit of bad temper. Ruth followed the example set by Joe Jackson and others by enlisting under the banner of the Bethlehem Steel Company.

Ruth will enter the shipyard at Chester, Penn. and has agreed to meet this evening with Frank Miller [the shipyard club's manager].

President Harry Frazee of the Boston club is determined to fight this case to a finish.

Paul H. Shannon, Boston Post

"Ruth has signed a contract with the Boston club," said the owner of the Sox, "and must play baseball with us until that contract expires. I shall notify both Ruth and Manager Miller of this, and if they try to use him I shall get out an injunction. After that, I will sue the Chester Shipbuilding Company for heavy damages, and I believe I will win. Ruth can't get away with it. The courts will not stand for a deal like that."

Harry Frazee, quoted in the Boston Herald and Journal

Sore with Barrow

BALTIMORE, July 3—"The whole fuss was started over a play on the field," said Ruth. "I hit at the first ball, and [Barrow] said something about it being a bum play. Then we had some words, and I thought he called me a bum and I threatened to punch him. He told me that would cost me $500, and then I made a few more remarks and left the club."

Boston Post

Not a single player on the team is in sympathy with Babe. The Red Sox are disgusted with the actions of a man they say had his head inflated with too much advertising and his effectiveness impaired by altogether too much babying.

Paul H. Shannon, Boston Post

[The fight between Barrow and Ruth may have been over Babe's refusal to resume pitching. His teammates probably wished he had gone back on the mound, too, because the Red Sox were struggling.]

Macks Blank Red Sox, 6 to 0

PHILADELPHIA, July 3—The Ruthless Red Sox finished a bad second in the ball game with the lowly Mackerels this afternoon, failing to dent the home platter. The Athletics slipped over a total of six perfectly good counters, which was more than enough to win.

The Sox did not look like a ball club when they took the field. Babe Ruth left a gaping hole in the line-up which could not be filled. The infield defence, with Heinie Wagner [the thirty-seven-year-old coach] on second and Wally Schang on third, had the appearance of a leaky sieve. Then, to make the picture complete, they played as badly as they looked, and the home town Quakers and Quakerettes spent a pleasant afternoon.

- [Winning pitcher, Gregg; losing pitcher, Bader (0–2). Red Sox' standing: 39 wins, 30 losses; in second place, .004 behind New York.]

Boston Herald and Journal

Today and Yesterday

July 4. IN OTHER YEARS

July 4. 1918

Boston Record

Friday, July 5

Babe Ruth Rejoins Sox in Quakertown

PHILADELPHIA, July 4—Babe Ruth arrived in Philadelphia at 2 A.M. in tow of Heinie Wagner, who had been sent to Baltimore to bring Babe back to join the Red Sox. Both players went right to bed and were at the ball park for the morning game.

Ruth put on his working togs, but when the batting order was announced his name was not included on the list. Manager Barrow refused to speak to Ruth, who didn't seem highly pleased at not being received with open arms.

At lunch time Babe took off his uniform and declared that he was through for good. Ruth's friends, however, got hold of him and talked him back to reason. Babe showed up for the afternoon contest and played in centre field. He made one hit, drew a pass, popped up a fly and struck out twice, much to the joy of the fans, who took delight in riding him.

Boston Globe

There is a man in Boston town
    His name it is Babe Ruth,
He jumped the Red Sox baseball team
    To build some ships forsooth.
Next day he jumped right back again
    Ere many tears were spilt;
The question now they're asking is—
    How many ships he built.

Cleveland Press

Red Sox Win and Lose in Double Bill with Macks

PHILADELPHIA, July 4—Merlin Kopp's [Philadelphia's left fielder] sacrifice fly, with the bases filled in the 11th, scored the run that decided a brilliant pitchers' battle between Scott Perry and Carl Mays in favor of the local entry, 2 to 1, this afternoon. The Red Sox won the morning free-for-all, 11 to 9.

- [Game one: winning pitcher, Jones (6–3); losing pitcher, Watson. Home run: Walker (A's). Game two: winning pitcher, Perry; losing pitcher, Mays (13–6). Red Sox' standing: 40 wins, 31 losses; in third place, one game behind Cleveland.]

Boston Herald and Journal

Whoopla! Tyrus Cobb Now Leads American League Swat Colony

By the fraction of a percentage Ty Cobb has moved into first place in the American League batting race. Cobb made five hits in six trips to the plate in the second game at Cleveland.

	AB	Hits	AVG
Cobb, Detroit 232	82	.353
Sisler, St. Louis 252	89	.353
Baker, New York 272	95	.349
Burns, Philadephia 263	86	.327

Boston American

NEW YORK YANKEE BUMPS

WASHINGTON SENATORS BUMPS

PHILA ATHLETICS BUMPS

RED SOX

Scott, *Boston Post*

McInnis' Triple Wins in Tenth, 4–3

PHILADELPHIA, July 5—The timely hitting of Stuffy McInnis won an overtime struggle at Shibe Park and gave the Sox an even break in the series with the Athletics. Boston won by the count of 4 to 3.

Babe Ruth made his first appearance on the rubber in many weeks and won the verdict over the clever Geary. Ruth pitched good ball up to the ninth, when Boston was leading by the score of 3 to 1. Here he weakened, grew wild and allowed the locals to tie it up.

In the 10th with two men down, Ruth was purposely passed by Geary. McInnis came through with a long triple to right that sent Babe home and put the Sox in the lead.

• [Winning pitcher, Ruth (5–5); losing pitcher, Geary. Red Sox' standing: 41 wins, 31 losses; in second place, half a game behind Cleveland.]

Paul H. Shannon, *Boston Post*

[Barrow and Ruth had reached a truce. Babe agreed to go back into the pitching rotation and Barrow decided to drop the fine.]

The Red Sox Are Home Again—Babe Ruth and All

The South Sudbury tree chopper is smiling again, for he found his pitching arm in Philadelphia yesterday. His 10th inning win over the Mackmen makes him feel there's fun in being a winning flinger as well as a fence-buster. If Babe's ever had any idea of learning to decorate ships with war paint, it's lost for the time being.

Melville Webb, Jr., *Boston Globe*

The Pennant Race

Wally Schang, the former Mackman, demonstrated his ability as an all-round player. He played a different position in each of the four games here. He was on third in the opener, held down centre field in the A.M. holiday game, went behind the bat after lunch and played in left field yesterday.

Philadelphia Evening Bulletin

"Look out for Fohl [the Indians' manager] and his bunch when Tris Speaker gets to hitting," said Babe Ruth today. "If they can get to the top when Spoke's in a slump, what'll they do when Tris gets going, as he certainly will before long?

"Cleveland doesn't seem to have a weak spot anywhere. It has good pitching, a nice bunch of hitters, about as fast an outfit as there is on the bases, and a fine defensive team."

Cleveland Press

Beaned :-: :-:

T. E. Powers, *Boston American*

The Year the Red Sox Won the Series

Red Sox Regain Lead, 5–4

Ruth's Triple Puts Red Sox in First Place

BOSTON, July 6—When Babe Ruth, Ed Barrow's stubborn child, walked out from the Red Sox dugout in the sixth inning yesterday, swinging two sawed-off bats, an ocean-sounding roar of welcome burst from 5,000 throats. Sergeant Jim Bagby, Cleveland's best pitcher, turned white around the gills.

The score was 4 to 2 in Cleveland's favor, with nobody out, Whiteman on third and Scott on first. The Red Sox needed two to tie and three to go into the lead.

They got them—all three. The shorter of the two sawed-off sticks delivered a curving, drooping liner into right field which [Bobby "Braggo"] Roth missed when he stretched to trap it. The ball rolled to the outfield stand.

Ruth, with the tying runs scoring ahead of him, pulled up at third. But he started home with the winning run when Wambsganss [the Indians' second baseman], handling the throw-in, pegged wide and high to third.

Ruth's hit won the game and restored Boston to the top rung of the pennant ladder, from which the Indians were displaced.

• [Winning pitcher, Bush (9–8); losing pitcher, Coumbe. Red Sox' standing: 42 wins, 31 losses; in first place, half a game ahead of Cleveland.]

Francis Eaton, *Boston American*

"BABE" RUTH CAME THROUGH WITH FLYING COLORS BY A PINCH 3-BAGGER, TYING THE SCORE AND SCORED THE WINNING RUN HIMSELF ON A CLEVELAND ERROR •

Scott, *Boston Post*

WELL-HERE WE ARE AT THE TOP AGAIN

TOP OF THE AMERICAN LEAGUE

1ST PLACE

BOSTON

THE RED SOX SATURDAY 5 TO 4 WIN OVER CLEVELAND, BOOSTED THEM TO 1ST PLACE.

Scott, *Boston Post*

Monday, July 8

AMERICAN LEAGUE STANDINGS

	Won	Lost	PCT.	GB
Boston	42	31	.575	—
Cleveland	43	33	.566	0.5
New York	39	31	.557	1.5
Washington	40	36	.526	3.5
Chicago	35	36	.493	6
St. Louis	36	38	.486	6.5
Detroit	29	41	.414	11.5
Philadelphia	26	44	.371	14.5

Boston fans were handed a surprise package when it was announced that Fred Thomas, the youngster who has been looking after the hot corner for the Red Sox, would be unable to play baseball despite being turned down by Army officials. Thomas is suffering from diabetes and has decided to give up baseball for the time being. Thomas was informed he would have to quit the game if he wished to prolong his life.

Harry J. Casey, *Boston Record*

RED SOX BATTING

	AB	R	BH	2B	3B	HR	SB	AVG
Truesdale, 2b 19	4	9	1	0	0	1	.474
Hooper, rf 275	51	86	20	8	1	15	.313
Ruth, p,1b,lf 156	31	47	14	4	11	1	.301
Shean, 2b 256	39	71	10	3	0	8	.277
McInnis, 1b 260	26	69	5	4	0	7	.265
Thomas, 3b 141	19	37	2	1	1	5	.262
Mays, p 59	6	15	2	2	0	1	.254
Schang, c 150	24	38	7	1	0	2	.253
Strunk, cf 219	26	54	7	3	0	18	.247
Scott, ss 270	28	66	9	2	0	10	.244
Whiteman, lf 165	13	39	11	0	0	9	.236
Bush, p 60	2	14	0	1	0	0	.233
Agnew, c 147	9	20	6	0	0	1	.136
Stansbury, 3b 16	1	2	0	0	0	0	.125

RED SOX PITCHING

	IP	BH	Won	Lost	R	BB	SO
Molyneaux 7.1	2	1	0	0	7	0
Mays 166.1	121	13	6	47	54	73
Jones 83.1	79	6	3	35	33	21
Bush 165	132	9	8	59	66	57
Ruth 80	71	5	5	32	29	16
McCabe 9.2	13	0	1	5	2	3
Bader 15	11	0	2	9	3	8

Cast the dope into the air for the time being, because no manager knows from day to day what team he will have. The dope is changing so fast that it is impossible to figure on anything until Provost Marshal–General Crowder decides whether to stop baseball or to permit the teams to finish the season.

Hugh S. Fullerton, *Boston American*

[Baseball owners and players were nervously waiting for the government to decide the fate of the 1918 season. The decision hinged on whether baseball was an "essential occupation" for the good of the country. If the ruling stated that playing baseball was a non-essential job, most of the twenty-one- to thirty-one-year-old players would soon become eligible for the draft. Such a ruling could quickly end the season.]

Ruth's Drive Gives Sox Split with Indians

Colossal Smash into Right Field Stand in 10th Settles Opener, 1 to 0

BOSTON, July 8—Babe Ruth's home run, high up into the right field bleachers at Fenway Park, which was only a triple, won the first game of yesterday's doubleheader with the Cleveland Indians. Guy Morton held the Sox to three hits in the second game, two of them scratchy. Babe did not "get ahold" of one to his liking, and the invaders grasped the wind-up, 4 to 3.

Zero after zero had been put up on the board [in the first game]. Sam Jones had been pitching powerful ball and Stanley Coveleski's work was not so bad. Shean had been tossed out in the last of the 10th, when Strunk came to bat and singled to right on the first pitch.

The Colossus of Clouters came up swinging his two heavy, new bats. The crowd yelled loudly and long for a home run. Babe took his stance, made his bid on the very first pitch, a curve ball, and, zowee, how it traveled!

Right fielder Bobby Roth made one little turn and then stopped in despair. The ball went up into the realms of eagles, high and higher, far and farther, eventually landing three-quarters of the way up in the right field stand, easily the longest hit to that section ever seen.

But it was only a three-base hit, for when Strunk touched home plate ahead of Ruth, the one run necessary to win the game had been scored and the game was over. Babe has made 11 home runs and it was a shame he could not make it a dozen. It would have been a home run in any ball park in the world.

- [Game one: winning pitcher, Jones (7–3); losing pitcher, Coveleski.
  Game two: winning pitcher, Morton; losing pitcher, Mays (13–7).
  Red Sox' standing: 43 wins, 32 losses; in first place, half a game ahead of Cleveland.]

  Burt Whitman, *Boston Herald and Journal*

[Ruth's circuit clout was scored a mere triple, according to the 1918 rules. If a batter hit a game-winning home run in the last of the ninth or in extra innings, and a runner was on base, only the winning run counted.]

Babe took his stance, made his bid on the very first pitch, a curve ball, and, zowee, how it traveled!

Scott, *Boston Post*

Van Ulm, *Boston Record*

Goose-Egg Samuel Jones

For 10 innings Jones pitched remarkably effectively. He held the visitors to four hits, all singles. In 29 innings this year he has allowed the Indians, his old mates, but one run. Some record for a gent who wasn't considered good enough to take his regular turn in the box until the season was well under way. Give him credit.

Burt Whitman, *Boston Herald and Journal*

STILL GOING

Robert L. Ripley, *Boston Globe*

Fans throughout the league take pride in pointing out some hefty wallops of the young giant from Boston. In Cleveland they point to a shattered window in the top story of a building across the street from the park. A ball from Ruth's bat broke the window after clearing a fence 45 feet high!

They show you the very spot far out in the bleachers in Detroit where the ball landed, and you wonder if you are being told the truth.

In St. Louis, Ruth did not bother about driving the ball into the right field bleachers, but just banged it clear over them into the next block. The big fellow always picks out the upper tier in the Polo Grounds to plant the ball, and he hit it out of the Washington ball park, a remarkable wallop.

In Boston, where the outfield fences are far distant, he hit a sacrifice fly so far that a runner scored from second base after the catch.

Robert L. Ripley, *Boston Globe*

John "Stuffy" McInnis, who is holding down first base for the Red Sox, may be forced out of the lineup for a few days. McInnis is playing under a heavy handicap, as he is suffering from boils on his neck. He played both games yesterday with a bandage around his neck, showing more than ordinary pluck.

Eddie Hurley, *Boston Record*

Mayer's Hit in 10th Beats Cleveland, 1–0

Bush Winner over Bagby in Great Pitching Duel

BOSTON, July 9—Wally Mayer, a mere understudy, provided the big climax, the real thrill, that sent more than 4,000 fans home to dinner happy yesterday afternoon. His slam to left with two down in the 12th inning carried Truesdale over the counting station with the big marker that supplied Bullet Joe Bush with a 1 to 0 decision over Sergt. Jim Bagby.

It was a great game, a thrilling encounter between two clever boxmen, each hurler allowing eight hits, and showing a bunch of stuff in the pinches. Until Mayer planted that fine crack of his, it appeared as if the battle might go on indefinitely.

[Winning pitcher, Bush (10–8); losing pitcher, Bagby. Red Sox' standing: 44 wins, 32 losses; in first place, one and a half games ahead of New York and Cleveland.]

Edward F. Martin, *Boston Globe*

[Mayer was a lifetime .193 hitter. This was the third-string catcher's first hit of the season.]

The picturesque Oriole boy [Babe Ruth] played the first sack yesterday. The boil family is holding a reunion on McInnis' neck and Stuffy did not wish to add to their enjoyment by taking them to the ball game.

Edward F. Martin, *Boston Globe*

Ruth's Smash Wins for Red Sox, 2–0

Drives in Run with Triple; Game Called in 5th

BOSTON, July 10th—Fred Coumbe, puzzling southpaw of the Indian aggregation, tried to slip a fast one past big Babe Ruth in the eventful fourth session of yesterday's abbreviated contest, and he flirted with death when he did so. The burly slugger took one of his famous "cuts" and the pill landed high and dry on the embankment in centre field. Ruth had made his third disastrous triple of the series and the tremendous wallop allowed the Sox to down the Indians for the fourth time in five games.

[Winning pitcher, Bader (1–2); losing pitcher, Coumbe. Red Sox' standing: 45 wins, 32 losses; in first place, two and a half games ahead of New York and Cleveland.]

Paul H. Shannon, *Boston Post*

IN THE 4TH INNING WITH 1-OUT, STRUNK SINGLED TO CENTER,
THEN BABE RUTH SENT A WALLOP TO LEFT CENTER SCORING
STRUNK — REACHING 3RD HIMSELF-WHITEMAN'S HIT SCORED RUTH-

Scott, *Boston Post*

Ruth Brought Despair

The Sox took four out of five from the Cleveland Indians and drove them
back into third place. "Big Babe" Ruth won three of the games single hand-
edly. Twice he delivered triples in the pinch that robbed Cleveland of victory, and his wallop into the bleachers the other day tucked away another
game. Today, Ruth is friendless in Cleveland.

Eddie Hurley, *Boston Record*

Friday, July 12

Mays Applies 4 to 0 Setback to Champions

Ruth Makes Three Doubles

BOSTON, July 11—Babe Ruth swept his range finder around towards the
left field fence at Fenway Park yesterday, practiced all afternoon off the
expert hurling of Eddie Cicotte and got three doubles. The Red Sox beat
the White Sox, 4 to 0.

Someone must have told Cicotte that Babe was a cripple against
pitching that kept the ball on the outside of the plate. The Colossus of
Clouters simply ruined that theory. He spanked the ball with almost non-
chalant ease, twice hitting his two-sacker on the very first pitch. The field in
that direction is the shortest in the park, and if Babe starts raising them,
they'll easily sail over the crest of Lewis Ledge.

[Winning pitcher, Mays (14–6); losing pitcher, Cicotte. Red Sox' standing: 46 wins, 32 losses; in first place, two and a half games ahead of Cleveland.]

Burt Whitman, Boston Herald and Journal

In the ninth inning Ruth capped the most sensational double play of the season at Fenway Park, and he did this stunt entirely unassisted. The White Sox had three men on the sacks, with only one gone, and it looked as though our record of shutting out opposing teams for 26 consecutive innings was to be shattered.

Shano Collins [the Chicago center fielder] drove a scorching grounder toward first base. Babe made a miraculous scoop of the sphere, touched the base runner as he started for second, and then by a sprint and a long slide he beat Collins to first. The play retired the side in the nick of time before Nemo Leibold crossed the plate. So Babe was the big noise again.

Paul H. Shannon, Boston Post

Babe Ruth made four doubles yesterday, three two-base hits and an unassisted double play. They'll be soon calling him the Dublin Kid.

Bob Dunbar, Boston Herald and Journal

Manager Barrow of the Red Sox wears part uniform and part street clothes while on the job. He appears in a baseball shirt, street pants, tennis shoes, and a golf cap.

Chicago Daily Tribune

Saturday, July 13

Babe Ruth's Bat Smashes White Sox to Earth Again, 6–3

BOSTON, July 12—Babe Ruth, the tripling triphammer of the Boston Red Sox, was in another one of his three base moods today and knocked the wearied White Sox flat almost singlehandedly. With a pair of triples and a two-bagger driven out by the stalwart southpaw, the Red Sox won the combat, 6 to 3. Further damage was prevented by a terrific thunder storm which ended the game after seven rounds.

There was nothing fluky about the three baggers. One was a line drive about ten feet from earth that crashed into the terrace in left center. The other was a line drive about eight feet high that went to the corner of right field, close to the foul line. Ruth's two bagger was a short fly to right, which Murphy attempted to catch, but couldn't come in fast enough to reach.

The outfielders seem all crossed up on just what to do when this fellow comes up to bat. Yesterday they played him to pull the ball to right field, and he poled three doubles down the left field line. Today they laid for him in that territory, and he showed them he could hit 'em to all parts of the field. Even his short fly fell safely because the outfielder was playing too deep.

It might have been a close combat if Ruth had been sick in bed or something.

* [Winning pitcher, Jones (8–3); losing pitcher, Benz. Red Sox' standing: 47 wins, 32 losses; in first place, three and a half games ahead of New York.]

James Crusinberry, *Chicago Daily Tribune*

ABOUT TRICK PITCHING

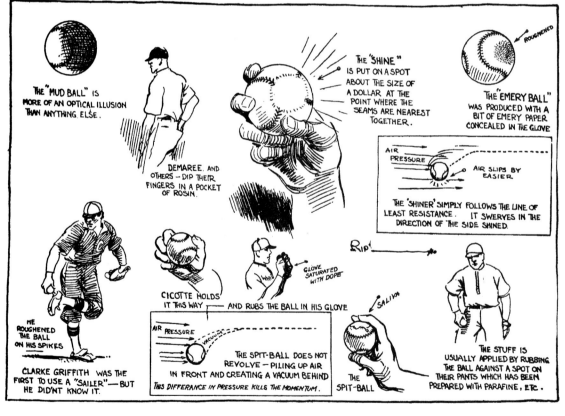

Robert L. Ripley, *Boston Globe*

The Year the Red Sox Won the Series

Walter Johnson Has Swat Duel with Ty

WASHINGTON, D.C., July 12—Ty Cobb and Walter Johnson divided batting honors in a game won by Washington, 5 to 4. Cobb's home run and double sent in three runs, and Johnson accounted for as many with a triple and a single.

Chicago Daily Tribune

[Johnson was playing center field for a depleted Senators ball club. Walter was an excellent-hitting pitcher. His lifetime batting average was .236 with 24 home runs.]

During the past week, Babe Ruth has murdered all sorts of pitching. Ruth's record was:

> July 6 — Triple
> July 7 — Triple and single
> July 9 — Single
> July 10 — Triple
> July 11 — Three doubles
> July 12 — Two triples and a double

During Ruth's batting rampage, he boosted his average from .295 to .316.

Eddie Hurley, *Boston Record*

Sunday, July 14

White Sox Escape at Last from Fenway Bastille

Russell a Mystery as Chicago Wins, 5 to 0

BOSTON, July 13—Rowland's White Sox tunnelled their way out of the Fenway bastille yesterday, 5 to 0. The Red Sox, who have seen very little left-handed pitching, could not do much with [Reb] Russell, who held them to seven hits.

Even the mighty Babe Ruth failed to connect safely. He rolled two grounders to Risberg at first, fanned once (amid incredulous groans from 9,512 fans), and wound up a dismal day by lifting a tremendous fly to right field.

* [Winning pitcher, Russell; losing pitcher, Bush (10–9). Red Sox' standing: 47 wins, 33 losses; in first place, two and a half games ahead of New York.]

Francis Eaton, *Boston American*

The plight of the big leagues is well illustrated in the misfortunes of the world champion White Sox. The Sox are appearing at Fenway now with only seventeen players, the smallest squad in the American League.

Charley Comiskey, master of the White Sox, is apparently so disgusted with the situation that he has abandoned hope of winning the pennant, and is not even trying to strengthen his team with minor league material as other owners are doing.

The [White] Sox are simply staggering through their schedule. Rowland has but six pitchers, two catchers, five infielders, and four outfielders.

Francis Eaton, *Boston American*

"A base on balls is an obstacle in the path of progress. It is a part of the game, all right, but when you are up there crazy to give the old ball a ride and that fellow out there on the mound passes you, it makes you feel as if you could wring his neck. I would rather get a punch in the nose than a base on balls."

Edward F. Martin, quoting Babe Ruth, *Boston Globe*

[Ironically, Babe is the all-time leader in walks, with 2,056. He also had the highest single season total, with 170 bases on balls in 1923.]

Cobb Ready to Quit Baseball for War

WASHINGTON, July 13—Unless the government holds baseball an essential occupation, Ty Cobb will quit the game after this season for the war.

"I am shaping my business affairs so that by the time the season ends I will be able to do my part," said Cobb.

"I don't believe the people care to see a lot of big, healthy young men out on the field playing ball while their sons and brothers are abroad risking their lives to conquer the Huns."

Boston Globe

Monday, July 15

AMERICAN LEAGUE STANDINGS				
	Won	Lost	PCT.	GB
Boston	47	33	.588	—
New York	43	35	.551	3
Cleveland	46	38	.548	3
Washington	41	40	.506	6.5
St. Louis	38	39	.494	7.5
Chicago	38	40	.487	8
Detroit	33	45	.423	13
Philadelphia	30	46	.395	15

"I hear that all the pitchers are trying to find a way to stop Babe from murdering the pill. It's a cinch if they only knew it. If some of those pitchers would throw up half a dozen ham sandwiches, a couple of cigars, a plug of tobacco and a quart of ice cream, Babe would never see that ball. Babe has only one weakness—his appetite."

Eddie Hurley, quoting Dan Howley, Boston Record

[Dan Howley was a former Red Sox coach and had been Babe Ruth's roommate during spring training.]

Tuesday, July 16

White Hose Fall at Boston Again, 3 to 1

BOSTON, July 15—Boston's flying Red Sox made it three out of four from our weary White Sox by taking the final combat, 3 to 1.

The battering Mr. Babe Ruth didn't tear things loose, as is his custom, but the Boston boys won, anyway. Ruth was in something of a batting slump, being limited to two singles in three times at bat. When Battering Babe hits only singles he is way off form.

Carl Mays was on the slab for Boston, coming back to repeat after the first game of the series. He was in his most stylish form, holding the White Sox to four blows and pitching his peculiar underhand curves with deadly effect at all times.

[Winning pitcher, Mays (15–6); losing pitcher, Danforth. Red Sox' standing: 48 wins, 33 losses; in first place, three games ahead of Cleveland.]

James Crusinberry, Chicago Daily Tribune

Danforth, who is an artist at slipping the ball over to first, nailed Babe off the bag twice in the first inning. The Oriole boy was caught cold, but the first time he slipped back to the cushion as Risberg and Eddie Collins were trying to run him down. He was no sooner there when he mooched off again. Over came the ball and he was trapped.

Edward F. Martin, Boston Globe

Wednesday, July 17

Jones Pitches Red Sox to 2–1 Victory over Browns

Shean Scores Winning Run in Ninth
Another Triple for Ruth

BOSTON, July 16—Sam Jones, rising young star of the Ed Barrow Red Sox, piloted his mates to a ninth inning, 2 to 1, win over the Browns at the Fens yesterday.

It was an afternoon of much profit for the Sox, since it increased their lead over the field by a full game. As for Sam Jones, his win makes him the virtual pitching king of the American League, with nine wins and three losses.

• [Winning pitcher, Jones (9–3); losing pitcher, Sothoran. Red Sox' standing: 49 wins, 33 losses; in first place, four games ahead of Cleveland.]

Burt Whitman, *Boston Herald and Journal*

"BABE" RUTH STARTED IN THE 2ND INNING WITH A 3-BAGGER TO LEFT CENTER EMBANKMENT-

Scott, *Boston Post*

AMERICAN LEAGUE BATTING LEADERS

	AB	BH	AVG
Cobb, Detroit 276		105	.380
Sisler, St.Louis 283		98	.346
Burns, Philadelphia ... 308		106	.344
RUTH, Boston 187		61	.326
Baker, New York 326		105	.322

The Year the Red Sox Won the Series

Bush and Ruth Brilliant in Shutting Out Browns

Bullet Slugs in Opener and Wins 7–0, Babe's Two Doubles Register 4–0 Triumph in Aftermath

BOSTON, July 17—Those smashing, slugging Red Sox pitchers are regular devils these days, doing all sorts of things on the mound and at bat in the fight for the A.L. pennant.

Bullet Joe pitched the first game and the visitors did not score. At bat, Joe was a graceful performer, getting two singles and a triple.

In the second game [which was stopped by rain], Babe pitched for the first time since he came back home. He was good enough to hold off the Browns for five innings, in which time they got four hits, all singles.

- [Game one: winning pitcher, Bush (11–9); losing pitcher, Wright. Game two: winning pitcher, Ruth (6–5); losing pitcher, Rogers. Red Sox' standing: 51 wins, 33 losses; five and a half games ahead of Cleveland.]

    Burt Whitman, *Boston Herald and Journal*

The Browns were behind 2 to 0 in the second game when rain clouds were sighted by Jimmy Burke [the Browns' manager] and his boys. Burke put on his latest sketch "Stalling in the Gloaming" so there would not be a legal game played before the rain drops began their pitter patter.

While the stalling act was on in the fourth inning there was a dust storm and it became very dark. A recess of 10 minutes was taken, and when it brightened up play was started again. The Browns did everything to delay the game. They took their time stepping to the plate, threw the ball around carelessly while making no attempt to get Boston baserunners, who never stopped running once they hit the ball. They were trying to get out.

    Edward F. Martin, *Boston Globe*

Babe's fly to Gedeon [the Browns' second baseman] went up so high it came down covered with star dust, but Joe held it.

    Boston Herald and Journal

Some 8,000 fans had plenty of excitement in the finale, which culminated in a fist fight between Wallie Schang and Hank Severeid [the Browns' catcher].

Wallie tapped out an infield hit in the fourth, and never hesitated at first base. The ball was chucked to Austin to stop him at second, and Jimmy nonchalantly dropped it. He didn't try to catch it at all. Wallie kept going, while Jimmy walked after the agate.

He streaked for home, but Jimmy's eventual throw beat him there by a block. As Wallie slid in, Hank put the ball on the back of his neck with much more force than grace. It was a regular K.O. swing.

After Schang picked himself up he took a hop, skip and a jump at Hank. He wrapped one arm around the Brownie's neck and prepared to smite him with his free hand. Hank countered with a couple of left jabs. At this interesting juncture, players, umpires, the announcer and everybody hopped into the scenario.

The bickering athletes were pried apart and exiled, but not until they had shaken hands and declared that everything was lovely again.

Nick Flatley, Boston American

Babe Ruth Must Have His Joke

Yesterday morning Babe hiked along Huntington Ave. bound north, carrying a suitcase. He passed a hotel where Carl Mays and several more of the athletes lived.

"Where are you going, Babe?" shouted Mays.

"Baltimore" said Babe, who hurried on without turning his head or uttering another word.

All Mays could think of was the ship league and he quickly called Ed Barrow on the telephone. Barrow said he did not think Babe intended to leave town and sure enough, he appeared at the ball park when due.

Boston Globe

All of Fred Thomas' friends are elated to hear that "Tommie" has landed successfully in the service. Thomas was strong for the army, but when he could not pass the physical examination he was not down-hearted, but took a try at the navy and managed to get by.

Arthur Duffey, Boston Post

Friday, July 19

Brownies Take 6–3 Leave of Red Sox

BOSTON, July 18—Just when we were beginning to believe the Red Sox were invincible, along came Six-Foot-Six Dave Davenport of the St. Louis Americans. He stopped the Barrowmen dead in their tracks yesterday afternoon at the Fens, the score being 6 to 3.

It was the first defeat of the week and is no cause for alarm. Manager Barrow gambled with one of his second rate pitchers, Lore Bader, a cagey hurler who is not endowed with any great amount of "stuff." Lore was trounced most artistically for six innings.

It was an unusual spectacle to see the Red Sox pitching go blooie. Under ordinary conditions those three runs the Sox made would have won a game in which Mays, Ruth, Bush or Jones pitched, because the opposition has to be extremely fortunate to make three runs off any of that quartet. But Bader is a bird of a different color.

- [Winning pitcher, Davenport; losing pitcher, Bader (1–3). Red Sox' standing: 51 wins, 34 losses; in first place, four and a half games ahead of Cleveland.]

Burt Whitman, *Boston Herald and Journal*

Jimmy Austin [of the Browns] plays in left field when Babe Ruth comes to bat, the only shortstop who does it.

Boston Herald and Journal

Saturday, July 20

Ball Players Must Work or Fight

Only Players Not of Draft Age May Stay in Game

WASHINGTON, July 19—Secretary of War Baker's ruling means that all baseball players within draft age limits [twenty-one to thirty-one] are immediately subject to a call by their draft boards. If they are qualified for service in the army, they must join the fighting forces. Otherwise, they must seek some occupation deemed essential to the prosecution of the war.

Boston Post

Baseball Will Lose Its Brightest Stars

Practically every baseball player of note in both major leagues is affected by Secretary Baker's interpretation of the work or fight order.

Cobb, Speaker, Collins, Ruth, Hooper, Baker, Mays, Scott, Johnson, Sisler—there is no need to continue the list. All must quit baseball.

Boston Post

Will Wreck Red Sox

Under Secretary Baker's work or fight ruling, the Boston Red Sox, prime favorites right now in the American League pennant race, will once again be literally "shot to pieces."

Out of that brilliant array of pitchers and fielders there are but four men in the Red Sox fold who are outside of the draft limit. This quartet includes Frank Truesdale, utility infielder; Dave Shean, the second baseman; George Whiteman, an outfielder; and Heinie Wagner, a coach and utility infielder.

All the rest, from Harry Hooper and Babe Ruth on down, will come within the scope of Provost Marshal Crowder's orders. It looks as though the Red Sox were really hit harder by the latest decision than any of the organizations in either league.

Boston Post

"If the proposition were put up to the fighting men themselves they would vote 1,000 to 1 to have the game kept going here at home."

James C. O'Leary, quoting Harry Frazee, *Boston Globe*

Cleveland Ball Park Will Close

Last Games of Season Tomorrow Is Decision of Club President

CLEVELAND, July 20—Pres. James C. Dunn of the Cleveland American League Club sent the following message:

"We will play a doubleheader with Philadelphia tomorrow and will then close the ball park for the balance of the season. It is our desire to comply promptly with Sec. Baker's ruling on baseball.

"My men told me that they would not care to stand on the field and have leather-lunged fans shout at them to get useful jobs. I heartily agree with them. They are all prepared to step into the new work."

Boston Globe

President Frazee of Red Sox Will Stick to the Finish

When informed that Dunn threatened to wreck the American League by suspending the Indians for the season, Frazee showed great surprise.

"When was Jim Dunn appointed to run the American League?" he asked. "He hasn't got a chance to quit. He will be forced to stick to the finish.

"It takes the unanimous consent of the eight club owners to suspend the playing season, and it's impossible to secure unanimous consent because I will not quit. I'm in this thing until the finish, and I will be the last club owner in the country to throw up the sponge."

Eddie Hurley, *Boston Record*

Carl Mays Takes Pelts of Ty-Less Tigers, 5 to 0

BOSTON, July 19—Those Ty-less Tigers of Detroit were skinned and their hides hung up to dry in the hot summer sun at the Fens yesterday when, with Carl Mays pitching one of his best underhanded games, the Red Sox won, 5 to 0.

Cobb missed the midnight train, something he had not done for many years. There were about 6,000 out there yesterday, and most of them wanted that peek at Ty and a chance to compare his wonderful batting with those of our own Colossus of Clouters, Babe Ruth. The fans wanted to pay homage to Ty, maybe yell a few pleasantries at him and see him march around with that near-Indian pussy-foot gait of his.

* [Winning pitcher, Mays (16–6); losing pitcher, Bailey. Red Sox' standing: 52 wins, 34 losses; in first place, five and a half games ahead of Cleveland.]

Burt Whitman, Boston Herald and Journal

Sunday, July 21

Shut Parks, Ban Johnson Orders

American League to Suspend Till War Ends, Says President

CHICAGO, July 20—American League baseball parks will close their gates for the duration of the war [after Sunday's games], unless unexpected developments occur. This announcement was made by Pres. Johnson.

No attempt will be made to finish the season with teams recruited from veterans above the draft age or amateurs below the draft age.

In speaking of the chaotic situation, Pres. Johnson said:

"I hope the great majority of our players will put on uniforms and shoulder a rifle. They are trained athletes and capable of bearing any physical hardships."

Boston Globe

Ban Johnson, American League president

Red Sox Won't Abide by Ruling to Wind Up Season Today

President Frazee does not think the Baker decision will be final. He thinks baseball should be permitted to run a little longer instead of being crushed out so abruptly. "We should be given a little time," he said. "I don't see why they could not let us finish the season or play until Labor Day, anyway."

Boston Globe

American League Ends Season Today

The gates of all the American League baseball parks will be closed with a bang and locked for the duration of the war, unless unexpected developments occur.

And nothing is expected to occur.

Before the end of the week it is probable that the parks of the National League teams will also be closed, and, with the minor leagues passing out of existence, the United States of America will be absolutely bereft of its national pastime except as it is played by amateur teams.

Boston Post

Biggest Crowd of the Year Sees Sox Win, 5–1

BOSTON, July 20—Before 13,525 fans, the largest crowd that has seen a game in Fenway Park this season, the Red Sox beat Tyrus Cobb and the other Junglemen, 5 to 1.

The fans were glad to see Tyrus in the game and the Georgian gamely went through the nine innings. He gave the fans one of the thrills they were looking for when, with Walker, he pulled a double steal in the sixth inning. Tyrus made one hit and did not have a chance in the field.

George Dauss turned Babe Ruth back without a base blow, but passed the Oriole boy in the eighth. It was in the field that Babe was conspicuous. He accepted five chances and some of them were not easy, particularly one off Cobb in the opening stanza, when he had to jump to snare the agate.

Sam Jones pitched for the Red Sox and he held the Junglemen to seven hits. Behind the Woodsville grocer the Sox played faultlessly.

[Winning pitcher, Jones (10–3); losing pitcher, Dauss. Red Sox' standing: 53 wins, 34 losses; in first place, five and a half games ahead of Cleveland.]

Edward F. Martin, *Boston Globe*

Capt. Harry Hooper called the boys together in the dressing room before the game, the players finally deciding to be guided by whatever action Pres. Frazee and Manager Barrow took.

Some of the boys felt the jig was up. It will not be a surprise if some of them get out from under, and the fans may hear any day of a new trail to the shipyard.

Boston Globe

Steel Plants Try to Land Stars

DULUTH, Minn.—As a result of the federal work or fight order, Ty Cobb, Walter Johnson, "Home Run" Baker, George Sisler, and Ray Schalk [the White Sox' star catcher] have been sent telegrams to come and join the Duluth-Masseba baseball league and work at local steelplants and shipyards on government contracts.

Detroit News

WHY SHOULDN'T HE BE CONTENTED?

Berndt, *Detroit Sunday News*

[The Cubs were having an outstanding season, with 56 wins and 28 losses, four and a half games in front of the New York Giants.]

Monday, July 22

AMERICAN LEAGUE STANDINGS

	Won	Lost	PCT.	GB
Boston 53	34	.609	—
Cleveland 50	42	.543	5.5
New York 45	40	.529	7
Washington 46	41	.529	7
St. Louis 40	45	.471	12
Chicago 39	46	.459	13
Detroit 36	48	.429	15.5
Philadelphia 36	49	.424	16

Keep Playing, Says Big Man

WASHINGTON, July 21—Manager Clarence Rowland of the Chicago American League club received a telegram from President Johnson directing him to play all games scheduled until further notice.

Manager Ed Barrow of the Red Sox said last night that he had not received word from Johnson to continue with the schedule, but added that the Red Sox would go on until compelled to stop.

Boston Herald and Journal

[Ban Johnson backed off on his edict to shut down the American League because he was alienating some of the owners.]

Both major leagues are in a badly demoralized state. Many of the players on different clubs have assumed that a suspension is inevitable and are ready for a stampede. They have jobs picked out in steel and shipbuilding plants. Some of them, it is said, have already jumped.

The next couple of days will decide the fate of major league baseball.

James C. O'Leary, *Boston Globe*

Talk that Babe Ruth will jump away from the Sox and that Carl Mays will do the same, is scoffed at by Manager Barrow. He told me last night that both of these boys are game to the core and do not know the meaning of the word "fear."

Big Ed had several clubhouse meetings Saturday over the "work or fight" ruling as it applied to his men. He made it plain to them that they were not involved as yet and there was no reason for them getting hysterical.

Boston Herald and Journal

Baseball Licked

The game is licked.

We hate to sing the swan song of the old game. It has been a wonderful thing for the general run of folks. But it doesn't compare with the war, and other big things. Everybody in the world, except the magnates and the players, knows that.

In times to come, the pastime will come back. There will be big crowds and heroes. But from now until the end of the war, baseball is over. Proposals of abbreviated world's series and such things merely make the end more certain. There aren't enough old timers left to finish the season.

Nick Flatley, *Boston American*

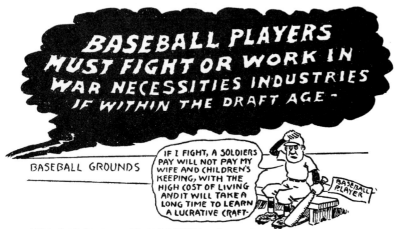

BASEBALL PLAYERS MUST FIGHT OR WORK IN WAR NECESSITIES INDUSTRIES IF WITHIN THE DRAFT AGE —

BASEBALL GROUNDS

IF I FIGHT, A SOLDIERS PAY WILL NOT PAY MY WIFE AND CHILDREN'S KEEPING, WITH THE HIGH COST OF LIVING AND IT WILL TAKE A LONG TIME TO LEARN A LUCRATIVE CRAFT·

BASEBALL PLAYER

IT'S A GLOOMY OUTLOOK FOR BASEBALL, THE NATIONAL GAME ·

Scott, *Boston Post*

RED SOX BATTING

	AB	R	BH	2B	3B	HR	SB	AVG
Ruth, p, 1b, lf	202	42	66	20	10	11	2	.327
Hooper, rf	326	54	97	20	9	1	18	.298
McInnis, 1b	283	28	78	6	4	0	7	.276
Bush, p	71	4	19	0	2	0	0	.268
Shean, 2b	305	45	80	13	3	0	10	.262
Whiteman, lf	185	16	48	11	0	0	9	.259
Mays, p	73	7	18	3	2	0	1	.247
Strunk, cf	269	33	66	8	5	0	18	.245
Schang, c, lf	169	26	41	8	1	0	3	.243
Scott, ss	312	31	74	9	3	0	11	.237
Agnew, c	163	9	23	7	0	0	0	.141
Stansbury, 3b	37	3	5	1	0	0	0	.135
Jones, p	34	3	4	0	0	0	0	.118

RED SOX PITCHING

	IP	BH	Won	Lost	R	BB	SO
Jones	128.1	100	10	3	40	40	26
Mays	202.1	140	16	6	52	62	82
Bush	195	159	11	9	64	72	70
Ruth	85	65	6	5	32	30	18
Bader	26	26	1	3	14	7	10
Molyneaux	10.1	3	0	0	1	8	0

Double Shutout Is Handed to Tigers

Red Sox Win First Game by 1 to 0, Second 3 to 0

BOSTON, July 22—It was sentiment alone that brought out many of the 10,592 fans who saw the Red Sox vanquish the Junglemen of Jennings in a twin bill yesterday. Sitting under that glaring sun, which beat down mercilessly upon the Fenway, were many who came feeling that they might never have another opportunity to see Cobb, Hooper, Ruth, Mays, Scott, Jennings and the others, and they showed their approval of the athletes in no small measure.

There were two rattling, fine ball games. If the double pastime yesterday turns out to be a swan song it will be one well worth remembering.

* [Game one: winning pitcher, Bush (12–9); losing pitcher, James. Game two: winning pitcher, Mays (17–6); losing pitcher, Kallio. Red Sox' standing: 55 wins, 34 losses, six and a half games ahead of Cleveland.]

Edward F. Martin, *Boston Globe*

As the concluding innings of the second game were played, a hush came over the multitude. They seemed to realize that here they were getting the last peeks at their baseball favorites.

As Babe Ruth, Harry Hooper, Carl Mays, Everett Scott, Ty Cobb and the other topliners of the national game went to bat for what the fans realized was the last time of the day, mayhap for all times, fresh cheers went up; cheers that were so lavishly given they swelled into an ovation.

It tore the heartstrings—the change from the tired hush of the sultry summer afternoon to the rising chorus of hail and farewell.

H. W. Lanigan, *Boston American*

Carl Mays won his 17th game of the season yesterday and he is going like a combined Mathewson-Johnson-Alexander. If the season goes through to the finish and Carl is not drafted, I expect him to win 30 games.

Bob Dunbar, *Boston Herald and Journal*

Big Babe Ruth did not get a hit in either game, much to the disappointment of the crowd of 10,000 fans on hand to see what they thought might be the last big league game until after the war. However, Babe had a big day afield, and his classy running catches of line drives brought forth rounds of applause from his many followers.

Boston Post

Frazee's Views

Harry H. Frazee, president of the Red Sox, in a talk over the long distance phone from Cleveland, states he is confident there will be a world series, even if it has to be played right away.

"I believe we have a fair chance to play out our schedule. But if we must close up shop, tell Sox rooters to get ready for a championship series," said Frazee. "Yes, we'll be in it, for sure. Our current lead is plenty big enough to keep us in front, even if we go through until October.

"However, if the curtain is rung down, we'll be ready for the Cubs or the Giants."

Boston Record

Harry Hooper Is First Hub Player to Reach 100 Mark

Field Captain of Red Sox Says This Is His Last Year on the Diamond

Harry Hooper, field captain of the Red Sox, in his 10th season with the Boston club, seems to be reaping more laurels than ever. Hooper is at his best this year and there is not a more valuable player on the team than the popular, unassuming captain and sun fielder.

Hooper has been above the .300 mark all year with the war club and he has the distinction of being the first Boston player to reach the century mark in base hits.

He has always been the idol of the fans in the bleachers, and Harry regards the boys who sit through the nine innings in the blazing sun as his own pals. They are always ready to accord him a reception any time he turns in the necessary bingle. They've had plenty of opportunities to give him a hand this year for he has done most of his hitting in the pinches.

Boston fans may never see the popular right fielder again after the present season. Hooper claims he will retire from the game at the end of the 1918 season. He has notified Harry H. Frazee of his intentions and says he will take life easy at his home in Capitola, California.

Eddie Hurley, *Boston Record*

[The thirty-one-year-old star outfielder went on to play seven more years, retiring from the Chicago White Sox after the 1925 season with 2,466 hits and a .281 lifetime batting average.]

Wednesday, July 24

Caught Between the Bases

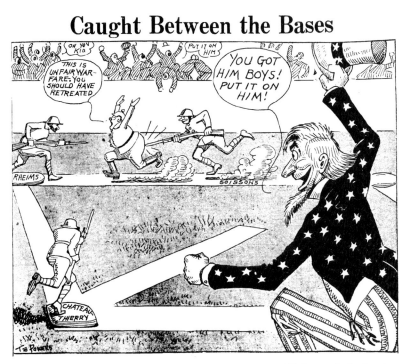

T.S. Powers, *Boston American*

In Washington the case of baseball, as regards the "work or fight" ruling, gets its final hearing from Gen. Enoch Crowder and War Secretary Newton D. Baker. Unless a respite of a month or 60 days is given, big league ball will vanish from the face of the earth, and will not reappear until Mars' high heeled boots no longer bruise Europe's soil.

Bob Dunbar, *Boston Herald and Journal*

Out of 17 games played during the home stand, the Red Sox won 14 of them. Sam Jones was the big pitcher, winning four straight games without a defeat, while Carl Mays and Joe Bush won four out of five games.

The Sox pitchers handed their opponents eight shutouts, while they were blanked only once. They allowed 26 runs while the Red Sox scored 54.

This is pennant winning pitching, and if the Red Sox hurling artists keep up their work along the western front, there is little doubt that they will return home in first place.

Eddie Hurley, *Boston Record*

Thursday, July 25

Robert L. Ripley, *Boston Globe*

DULUTH, Minn., July 24—Walter Johnson, Washington baseball pitcher, was wired terms by the management of the Duluth baseball team of the Head of the Lakes circuit today. The telegram offered Johnson at least $300 a game to pitch here if organized baseball disbands.

Boston Globe

If the government ruling says all players of draft age must go to work immediately, players will be scattering to all parts of the country by tonight or tomorrow. There's a big demand for workers in the harvest fields of the middle west, and all the ship yards and munition plants of the country need men.

James C. Crusinberry, *Chicago Daily Tribune*

Friday, July 26

Chicago Defeats Red Sox, 4–2

CHICAGO, July 25—With the final verdict from Washington still pending, the Red Sox started the first series on the Western trip with a defeat at the hands of Rowland's White Sox this afternoon. Lefty Russell did not have enough speed to break a pane of glass, but with superb support he downed the leaders by the score of 4 to 2.

The White Sox hit Carl Mays far harder than the submarine hurler has been hit for many a day. Big Chick Gandil [the White Sox' first baseman] was mainly responsible for Mays' defeat. He scored Chicago's first run and drove in the other three.

- [Winning pitcher, Russell; losing pitcher, Mays (17–7). Red Sox' standing: 55 wins, 35 losses; in first place, six games ahead of Cleveland.]

Paul Shannon, *Boston Post*

[Gandil became the leader of the Chicago Black Sox scandal during the 1919 World Series. He was banned from organized baseball in 1921.]

It was the speediest game of the season, all over in 1:23.

Boston Herald and Journal

Hibbing, Minn., Team Is After Babe Ruth

DULUTH, Minn.—George H. Ruth of the Boston Americans has been offered a contract to pitch for the Hibbing, Minn., team of the Head of the Lakes league. It is said he will accept if Sec. Baker closes down big league baseball.

Boston Globe

Saturday, July 27

Baker Gives Baseball Till Sept. 1 to Wind Up Season

WASHINGTON, D.C., July 26—Organized baseball was given a respite until Sept. 1 by Secretary of War Baker today. Mr. Baker suspended enforcement of the work or fight order in the cases of players of draft age, but declined to extend the period of exemption until the close of the season on October 15.

The Year the Red Sox Won the Series

The baseball magnates have stated that they will close the parks when the order goes into effect. This means that the schedule of games will be concluded on Sept. 2 [Labor Day], thus shortening the season six weeks.

Arthur Sears Henning, *Chicago Daily Tribune*

CINCINNATI, Ohio, July 27—Ban Johnson, president of the American League, said that he was pleased with the outcome of the conference at Washington.

"The major leagues," said Johnson, "will play their last game September 2, and the world series will follow immediately."

Boston American

Eddie Cicotte Has His Laugh at Last

Twirls White Sox to 7–2 Victory over Boston

CHICAGO, July 26—Another display of their world championship punch gave the White Sox a victory over the league leading Red Sox, 7–2.

Superlative pitching by the veteran shine ball expert, Eddie Cicotte, along with concentrated batting by his mates made it an easy matter to trim the headliners for the second straight time.

Cicotte faced the mighty Babe Ruth four times and did not allow him to get even a single. However, on Babe's last attempt he hit a ball so far that for a time it seemed the scoreboard beyond center field was in danger. Fortunately, the wind had shifted and brought the ball down before it did any damage.

- [Winning pitcher, Cicotte; losing pitcher, Jones (10–4). Red Sox' standing: 55 wins, 36 losses; in first place, five games ahead of Cleveland.]

Boston Globe

Will Not Let Players Dodge Army Draft

CHICAGO, July 26—President Comiskey, owner of the Chicago American League club, received a letter today which said the government would not permit ball players to dodge the Army draft by entering the employ of shipyards and munitions plants to play baseball.

Boston Post

Walter Johnson will not desert the Senators. Johnson declared today he had declined seven offers from munitions plants and ship leagues. "So long as the American League gates are open I'll remain," he said.

Chicago Daily Tribune

Boston's Three Runs in Seventh Beat White Sox, 6 to 4

CHICAGO, July 27—Realizing that a pennant and world series were close at hand, Boston's hustling Red Sox gingered up a bit in the third combat against the well-worn White Sox and won with a seventh inning rally by a count of 6 to 4.

The White Sox made quite a gallant fight against the first placers and might have won a third straight victory if it hadn't been for the prowess of Mr. Joe Bush, who not only hurled a steady game after a bad first inning, but produced the staggering blow with his bat in the seventh inning.

When the seventh inning arrived the White Sox were leading by a scant one run and Wally Schang was shoved into the combat as a pinch hitter with orders to start something. He delivered a safe poke for one base, whereupon Mr. Bush stepped up and drove a two bagger out to left center. This put Schang on third and Joe on second, and the White Sox lead of one run wasn't worth shucks. Immediately, Hooper slammed a single to right, sending his two mates home, after which the White Sox crumbled.

- [Winning pitcher, Bush (13–9); losing pitcher, Danforth. Red Sox' standing: 56 wins, 36 losses; in first place, five games ahead of Cleveland.]

James Crusinberry, *Chicago Daily Tribune*

THE RED SOX LANDED A 6 TO 4 WIN ON THE "WINDY" CITY WHITE SOX, IN SATURDAY'S GAME, AFTER TWO DEFEATS—

Scott, *Boston Post*

Reb Russell Trips Red Sox Once More

Blanks Leaders, 8 to 0, and Wields Mighty Bat

CHICAGO, July 28—Reb Russell, White Sox hurler, once more blocked the road of progress for the Boston Red Sox, the result being a defeat, 8 to 0. Reb was at his best, to the dismay of the Bostonians. Not only did he keep them from reaching third, but he struck out six, turning the trick against the mighty Babe Ruth twice.

Carl Mays opposed Russell and came back for revenge for the trimming he took in the first game of the series. Russell failed to show the proper respect and poled out a couple of two baggers, one with the bases loaded in the sixth. All three men came home, and it was more than enough to spill the Boston beans.

[Winning pitcher, Russell; losing pitcher, Mays (17–8). Red Sox' standing: 56 wins, 37 losses; in first place, four and a half games ahead of Cleveland.]

Boston Globe

Ruth walked off the field after he struck out in the eighth inning. His reputation for long distance clouts had been severely jolted and apparently he had no heart to walk out in front of that taunting gang in the left field bleachers again.

James Crusinberry, *Chicago Daily Tribune*

Cobb Will Be 1918 Champion

With the shortening of the baseball season by government decree, there is little likelihood that Cobb can be beaten in the batting race now. The 1918 championship will give him a new record for seasons' leadership, [ten] in his own league and [eight] in which he has outstripped the batters of all major circuits.

AMERICAN LEAGUE STANDINGS			
	Won	Lost	PCT.	GB
Boston 56	37	.602	—
Cleveland 52	42	.553	4.5
Washington 50	42	.543	5.5
New York 46	42	.523	7.5
Chicago 42	48	.467	12.5
St. Louis 41	49	.456	13.5
Detroit 40	51	.440	15
Philadelphia 37	53	.411	17.5

His lowest rating since he became a regular was .324 in 1908. Cobb's highest averages were in 1911 and 1912, when he finished at .420 and .410 respectively. This season's mark of .376 is not likely to be greatly reduced.

Boston Post

Hooper and Ruth Star in 3–2 Defeat of Browns

Ruth Lines Out Triple, Gives Browns Four Hits

ST. LOUIS, July 29—Babe Ruth, the demon slugger of the Boston Red Sox, took a turn on the pitching mound this afternoon at Sportsman's Park and hurled and batted his team to a 3 to 2 victory over St. Louis.

The husky southpaw held Burke's men to four hits, three of them being bunched in the sixth for the St. Louis scores.

At bat Ruth traveled below his speed, getting only one hit in four times up. But this bingle was a triple to left center that drove over the visitors' first run, which proved to be the margin by which they won.

Harry Hooper was as responsible for the Browns' defeat as any other individual, scoring one run, driving over another and fattening his batting average by hitting safely on each of his four trips to the plate.

* [Winning pitcher, Ruth (7–5); losing pitcher, Sothoron. Red Sox' standing: 57 wins, 37 losses; in first place, five games ahead of Cleveland.]

Boston Globe

One wonders just how great an interest will develop in a World Series when only 6,000 spectators attend a Sunday game in Chicago between the champions of 1917 and the leading team for the 1918 honors. The weather was pleasant, too.

Boston Globe

Red Sox Treat Brownie Pitchers Shamefully

Sam Jones Breezes as Sox Win, 11–4

ST. LOUIS, July 30—A good old-fashioned slugging bee, where singles, doubles and triples meet the fast ball and curve, featured the Red Sox performance against the Browns today. It was a walkaway, with the final count 11 to 4. The Red Sox faced all sorts of pitching and they treated 'em all alike.

Strunk contributed a single, double and triple; Ruth was held to three singles; while Hooper gathered a single and a double. While all of this was going on, Samuel Jones was breezing along the avenue with a hook that fooled the Browns. Now and then Sam teased the home side with a walk or a base hit, but as the Red Sox had six scores at the end of the fifth, Barrow did not even send anyone to the bullpen.

[Winning pitcher, Jones (11–4); losing pitcher, Bennett. Red Sox' standing: 58 wins, 37 losses; in first place, four and a half games ahead of Cleveland.]

Boston Herald and Journal

Sadder Budweiser

Going-going, almost gone—the attendance today was around 750.

Boston Herald and Journal

The closing of the baseball season on Sept. 1 won't worry the St. Louis fans. The season is always over in our town long before that date.

L. C. Davis, *St. Louis Post-Dispatch*

The gambling squad supplied the real sensation of the day. Approximately 20 bettors were arrested, trotted to the rear in real prisoner fashion and loaded into a waiting patrol.

Boston Globe

[Bookies frequented ballparks in 1918 and occasionally were arrrested if their transactions were too flagrant.]

Scott, *Boston Post*

Robs Babe of Chance

The curtailment of the season will cheat Babe Ruth out of his big chance to hang up a new record for home run hitting. The big Oriole boy has not hit one for nearly a month now, his last circuit smash having been registered in Washington on June 30th. If it were a normal season and the show were running on until October 5, G. Babe might have turned the trick, but it is too big a task for him to go through with now.

Boston Globe

[Babe had eleven home runs at this point; the American League record was sixteen in a season.]

Bullet Joe Is a Whole Show

Bush's Bat Beats Browns, 8 to 4; Hits 'Em Far and Often

ST. LOUIS, July 31—The pesky Browns had an idea that they were going to sprinkle the Red Sox path with a defeat today, when in the eighth round, Sisler tied the score with his first home run of the season. But the first-placers put on a little speed in the ninth, gathered four runs and made it three straight, 8 to 4.

Besides pitching a nifty game, Joey Bush was the prime swatter for the first-placers. All Joe did was compile two singles and two doubles. He drove in two with a single in the third while his double in the ninth was responsible for three more scores.

* [Winning pitcher, Bush (14–9); losing pitcher, Gallia. Home run: Sisler. Red Sox' standing: 59 wins, 37 losses; in first place, four and a half games ahead of Cleveland.]

Boston Herald and Journal

Sisler Emerges from Slump, Hits Triple and Homer

George Harold Sisler apparently has emerged from the batting slump which has contributed to the sinking of Jimmy Burke's Browns to seventh place.

Of the four runs scored for the locals, Sisler drove in three and scored two. In the eighth, after Tobin had beaten out an infield hit, Bush shot a fast ball squarely across the plate on the first pitch to Sisler.

George connected and the ball cleared the right field fence, hit about halfway up the bleachers and bounded back onto the track. It was a home run, the first of the season for Sis, and tied the score.

St. Louis Post-Dispatch

[An outstanding fielding first baseman, "Gorgeous George" Sisler was one of baseball's top hitters with a lifetime batting average of .340. The twenty-five-year-old rising star was on his way to a .341 average in 1918, with a league-leading 45 stolen bases.]

Sisler's greatest years were still ahead of him. From 1920 through 1922 he hit .407, .371, and .420. He still holds the major league record for base hits in a single season with 257. Ty Cobb, who rarely handed out compliments to his opponents, called Sisler the nearest thing to a perfect ballplayer.

George Sisler was elected to the Hall of Fame in 1939.]

Friday, August 2

Sox Clean Up Browns, 2-1

ST. LOUIS, Aug. 1—Another step toward the hall of fame for George Ruth. The big boy gained fame as an iron man of the hill today when he choked the Browns, 2 to 1, in a fancy exhibition, earning his second victory in four days. He scattered five hits, walked two and fanned three.

* [Winning pitcher, Ruth (8–5); losing pitcher, Leifield. Red Sox' standing: 60 wins, 37 losses; in first place, five and a half games ahead of Cleveland.]

Boston Herald and Journal

Babe Ruth is in a peculiar predicament in St. Louis. When he drives the ball to the fences the crowd goes into ecstasies, while when he swings lustily and vainly at a pitch, the outburst is as whole-souled as before. Anything he does is perfectly acceptable to everyone. Cobb and Speaker do not receive the ovations that Babe does.

Boston Globe

Ping Bodie and Wally Pipp Quit New York Yankees

Take it from James Miller Huggins [the Yankees' manager], running a ball club isn't the softest job in the world in these times. Just when it appeared that Huggins might have a chance to cop the American League bunting, a hurricane of offers from shipyards and steel leagues blew up and devastated his club.

Francisco Bodie, otherwise known as "Ping," is the latest member of Huggins' Yankees to take the hurdles. Fear of the "work-or-fight" order is the reason for Bodie's flop to a shipbuilding concern near Hoboken, N.J. Bodie [a veteran outfielder] believed if he did not obey Uncle Sam's work ruling he might be forced to fight for his country, which is considered quite an honor in some quarters.

St. Louis Post-Dispatch

[Wally Pipp, the Yankees' star first baseman, was batting .304 when he enlisted in the Naval Aviation Corps. Two key Yankee pitchers, Allan Russell and Herbert Thormahlen, had already jumped to the shipyards earlier in the year.

Since June 27 the Yankees had won only 13 of 33 games. They fell from the lead on July 4 and had dropped to fourth place, ten games behind Boston.]

The curtailment of the season will cheat Babe Ruth out of his big chance to hang up a new record for home run hitting.

Indians' Big Drive On

The biggest series of the American League season is here in Cleveland. The arrival of the Boston Red Sox Friday opens hostilities in the four games that'll determine whether the Indians are really in the pennant race.

Each side has saved its ace for this opening game which finds Stanley Coveleski, spitballist, pitted against Carl Mays, chief purveyor of the submarine ball and a main factor in keeping Boston up there on top.

Boston starts this series five and a half games ahead but the Tribe refuses to be despondent. It'll take four straight victories to put the Tribe anywhere close to the Red Sox, but three out of four will still give Cleveland a fighting chance.

Cleveland Press

Just as Johnny Evers was about to sail for France the Germans beat a hasty retreat—evidently fearing a deadly gas attack when Johnny reached the far side of the Marne.

Bob Dunbar, *Boston Herald and Journal*

A Popular Song

A player of the major leagues was packing up his grip,
    And making preparations for a weary ocean trip;
An edict had been issued that he'd have to fight or toil,
    To help his Uncle Sam-u-el defend his native soil.

He wasn't used to working, so, he said he'd rather scrap;
    In fact he would enjoy it, being quite a husky chap.
So he was not downhearted as he packed his clothes away,
    And as he bid his friends farewell
    He chirped this roundelay:

CHORUS

"Oh, for years I've been in clover,
    But I'll soon be going over;
I have heard the call of duty and
    I'll soon be on my way.

But believe me when I say it,
    I will learn the game and play it,
And for all my tribulations
    Kaiser Bill will have to pay.

He has knocked my bankroll silly,
    And I have it in for Willy,
So I've laid aside the spangles
    For a khaki suit of dun;

Kaiser Bill I'm not afraid of
    And I'll show the stuff I'm made of,
For I've put away the willow
    For a bayonet and gun."

L. C. Davis, St. Louis Post-Dispatch

Saturday, August 3

Indians Whip Red Sox, 6–3

CLEVELAND, Aug. 2—Cleveland fans will endorse the declaration of Sec. of the Navy Daniels that the submarine menace has been curbed. There was a time when all Carl Mays had to do to down the Indians was to throw his glove into the diamond, but today the Tribe registered its third victory of the season off him, 6 to 3.

It was first blood for the Redskins in the battle for first place and tonight Boston is only four and a half games ahead of the Clevelanders, who have not given up hope of being in the World Series.

The Redskins went after Mays' scalp or it might be more proper to say his periscope, from the start.

  [Winning pitcher, Coveleski; losing pitcher, Mays (17–9). Red Sox' standing: 60 wins, 38 losses; in first place, four and a half games ahead of Cleveland.]

Boston Globe

Defeated by 'Dusting'

That merry little art, known endearingly to ballplayers as "dusting 'em off," proved the undoing of Carl Mays, premier of the Red Sox hurling staff and the greatest submarine hurling artist in captivity.

Joe Wood and Bobby Roth [the Indians' second baseman and right fielder] were inconsiderate enough to duck out of the way of a pair of beanballs that came in their direction.

Exactly three runs scored on the wild pitches, and that's precisely the margin by which the Indians won the opener of the biggest series of the year.

Cleveland Press

They're cutting down the baseball sched
With Boston still some laps ahead,
So Indians sure will have to scurry
If they're to cause the Red Sox worry.

Cleveland Press

Ty Cobb Almost at .400 Batting Mark

Ty Cobb has clubbed his way to within seven points of the .400 mark. Getting seven hits in his last four games, he boosted his average to .393. Harry Hooper has tied Cobb for honors in scoring, each having registered 61.

Boston Globe

Sunday, August 4

Indians Swamp Sox in One Big Inning, 5 to 1

Savage Attack Routs Sam Jones

CLEVELAND, Aug. 3—Overzealousness on the part of the Indians today cost them at least three runs, but they still had enough markers left to trounce Boston, 5 to 1, and reduce Boston's lead to three and a half games. The Redskins indicated right from the kick-off that they were after the scalps of the Red Sox. They led Sam Jones into an ambuscade in the fifth and figuratively tied him to the stake while they scored four runs, cinching the contest.

In the attack on Jones, Chapman made two singles and a double, and Speaker a single and two doubles.

● [Winning pitcher, Bagby; losing pitcher, Jones (11–5). Red Sox' standing: 60 wins, 39 losses; in first place, three and a half games ahead of Cleveland.]

Boston Globe

Will Play Ball Until Sept. 2

CLEVELAND, O., Aug. 3—The American League baseball schedule will be played out until Sept. 2 without any readjustment and the World Series staged, starting Sept. 3 or 4, it was decided at today's special meeting of American League club owners.

Boston Post

Monday, August 5

Ruth's Pitching Saves Sox from Double Defeat

Babe Hero of 12-Inning 2 to 1 Victory

CLEVELAND, Aug. 4—Cleveland made it three out of four from the pace-makers of the league. Boston took the first game, 2 to 1, in 12 innings, while Cleveland gathered in the second, 2 to 0, in six innings, a rainstorm obligingly making its appearance and stopping the contest just after the Indians scored the only runs of the game.

Both were royal battles, as might be expected from the two teams that are way out in front and battling each other for the pennant in the shortest campaign the American League ever has held.

Babe Ruth was the Red Sox hurler in the opening fray. He battled the Indians to a standstill and was the most obstinate puzzle the Indians have tackled this year. He allowed two hits in the third and no more until the eighth, when a reserve squad of pinch hitters unsteadied him for a moment or so. Two of them delivered, tying the score.

In the top of the 12th Cochran [the Red Sox' third baseman] reached first on a force play with two down. He stole second. Then Mayer, the Boston catcher who soon goes to war, singled to left; and one of the greatest battles of the year at League Park was ended, as the Tribe could do nothing with Ruth in its half of the final round.

- [Game one: winning pitcher, Ruth (9–5); losing pitcher, Enzmann. Game two: winning pitcher, Coveleski; losing pitcher, Bush (14–10). Red Sox standing: 61 wins, 40 losses; in first place, three and a half games ahead of Cleveland.]

Boston Herald and Journal

It was Bullet Joe Bush against Stanley Coveleski in the second game. Aided by lowering clouds that threatened to open at any moment, Bush with his great speed was able to keep the Indians away from the plate for five innings. But to the accompaniment of the cannonading of the skies, the Redskins chased two runners across the plate in the sixth, giving Covey his second victory of the series.

Boston Herald and Journal

[Coveleski was in the midst of a brilliant 22–13 season. The spitballer went on to win 215 games while losing 142. He was inducted into the Hall of Fame in 1969.]

Everett Scott May Be Called "Deacon," But—

CLEVELAND, Aug. 4—Jack Graney [the Indians' left fielder] and Everett Scott almost came to blows in the 12th inning of the first game today. Jack went into second with his spikes unnecessarily high in the air and Scott retaliated by giving Graney a kick. As Graney arose they "mixed" and were about to stage a one-round affair, but were separated by teammates. Umpire Connolly informed them the boxing laws of this state forbade fistic encounters on Sunday.

Boston Herald and Journal

AMERICAN LEAGUE STANDINGS

	Won	Lost	PCT.	GB
Boston	61	40	.604	—
Cleveland	58	44	.569	3.5
Washington	55	45	.550	5.5
New York	48	49	.495	11
Chicago	47	51	.480	12.5
St. Louis	45	53	.459	14.5
Detroit	44	56	.440	16.5
Philadelphia	39	59	.398	20.5

More than 18,000 fans paid their way into the park to witness the two games, 2,000 being forced to find seats on the field.

Boston Herald and Journal

Sox Lose Their Batting Power

The Red Sox are finishing their Western tour in a batting slump, with a bit of unsteady fielding and weak pitching added to it for good measure. While they won a majority of their games last week, the falling off of their all-round play bodes ill for their chances of finishing the season in the lead.

Boston Post

RED SOX BATTING

	AB	R	BH	2B	3B	HR	SB	AVG
Bush, p	81	8	25	3	2	0	0	.309
Hooper, rf	370	62	113	21	10	1	21	.305
Ruth, p, lf, 1b	248	43	74	20	11	11	3	.298
McInnis, 1b	330	33	89	7	5	0	7	.270
Shean, 2b	335	47	86	13	3	0	11	.257
Whiteman, lf	193	17	49	10	0	0	9	.254
Mays, p	83	7	21	3	2	0	1	.253
Mayer, c	24	6	6	1	0	0	0	.250
Strunk, cf	318	38	79	11	6	0	17	.248
Schang, c, lf	183	29	43	8	1	0	3	.235
Scott, ss	351	34	81	10	3	0	11	.231
Stansbury, 3b	52	4	8	1	0	0	0	.154
Agnew, c	175	9	24	7	0	0	0	.137
Jones, p	41	4	5	0	0	0	0	.122

RED SOX PITCHING							
	IP	BH	Won	Lost	R	BB	SO
Mays	230	167	17	9	69	70	92
Bush	229	191	14	10	74	81	89
Jones	149	125	11	5	56	50	27
Ruth	115	78	9	5	36	34	27

Baseball Is Often Like This as September 1st Approaches

Scott, *Boston Post*

Big Salaries Thing of Past, States Mack

Pilot of Athletics Says $5,000 Is Enough for Major League Star

"The day of big salaries is doomed, and it is likely there will be an ironclad agreement among the magnates not to pay even the biggest star in the game more than $5,000 a year.

"No ball player who ever lived is worth more than that amount for a season's work. Inflated salaries have done more to hurt the game than anything else. There is no other work in the world where a man receives greater compensation for less effort than he does in baseball, but the end has come.

"Of course, there will be a yell from some of the present day stars, but they will get in line and sign up when they see that the club owners mean business."

Connie Mack, quoted in the *Boston Record*

Babe Ruth's sterling pitching has aided the club tremendously on the road. The Oriole boy won two games against St. Louis and then set back the Fohlmen [Cleveland]. Babe has now pitched five consecutive winning games.

Edward F. Martin, *Boston Globe*

Red Sox Upset Tigers, 7 to 5

DETROIT, Aug. 6—With the thermometer registering 115 in the coolest spot in the park, the Red Sox and Tigers went into 10 innings before a decision was returned in favor of Carl Mays.

Boston staged a great rally in the eighth inning, scoring three runs and pulling into a tie. The Tigers were held in the eighth and ninth; then in the 10th Barrow's crew got started.

Gonzalez started it off by walking. Schang was safe when Kallio [the Tigers' pitcher] threw late to first. Mays walked, filling the bases. Then Kallio heaved Hooper's bunt into the stands in an attempt to get Gonzalez at the plate and two runs went over.

[Winning pitcher, Mays (18–9); losing pitcher, Kallio. Red Sox' standing: 62 wins, 40 losses; in first place, three and a half games ahead of Cleveland. The Indians defeated Washington, 1 to 0, in 10 innings.]

Boston Post

[Eusebio "Papo" Gonzalez, the Cuban third baseman who scored the winning run for the Red Sox, was playing in his first major league game. He batted five times in his brief career with Boston, with two base hits and two runs scored.]

Babe Ruth pulled the ball a little too much to the right or he would have had another home run to his credit. In the eighth inning he belted the ball towards the bleachers and for a moment it appeared as if it would go into the seats. But instead, it struck the concrete side wall and bounded back, the fence breaker reaching second.

Tom Powers, *Detroit News*

If they win, Babe Ruth ought to be given 50 per cent of the team's share, as he has won this pennant almost alone by his hitting and pitching.

My count shows nineteen games in which Ruth has turned the tide by his own efforts. Without him, even with a first class substitute, the team would be down in fourth or fifth place.

Ruth undoubtedly has been the great individual star of the season.

Hugh S. Fullerton, *Boston American*

Red Sox Lose to Tigers, 11 to 8

DETROIT, Aug. 7— The Tigers handed Joe Bush a terrible thumping in the first inning and continued their rampage on through the succeeding rounds. Jennings' men won out, although the Sox gave them quite a battle before conceding the victory, 11 to 8.

In spite of the defeat the Red Sox didn't lose any ground in the race for the pennant. Washington turned back the Indians, so the pace-setters are still ahead by a margin of three and a half games.

- [Winning pitcher, C. Jones; losing pitcher, Bush (14–11). Red Sox' standing: 62 wins, 41 losses; in first place, three and a half games ahead of Cleveland.]

Boston Post

Cobb had a big day. Up four times, the King poled three hits, one a double, and tallied four runs.

Boston American

As the war progresses several of the Red Sox players are following the movements of the allies by means of maps clipped from various newspapers. Every evening Hooper, Mayer, Strunk and a few more, gather after dinner to see what improvement the day's doings have produced over there.

The other evening, as the team was boarding the boat at Cleveland, Walter Mayer [the Sox' catcher] came rushing on board with an extra in his hands. "Good news!" he yelled. "Fismizz has fallen!" The news was greeted with acclaim. It only needed Whiteman's statement that "Sweesons" had also been taken to make the joy of the strategy board complete.

Arthur Duffey, *Boston Post*

Papo Gonzalez, the new recruit corralled by the Red Sox, is pining to figure in a World Series even if only to run for someone else. He states that if he gets this opportunity he will be a bigger man than the governor of Havana when he returns home in October.

Arthur Duffey, *Boston Post*

My count shows nineteen games in which Ruth has turned the tide by his own efforts.

Ruth's Pitching Trims Tigers, 4 to 1

DETROIT, Aug. 8—The hustling Red Sox won today's encounter, 4 to 1, through Ruth's excellent work in the box. Babe was touched up for seven hits, but they were scattered.

The Tigers' habit of hitting in the direction of Everett Scott gave that chap plenty of work. With seven assists and two putouts he had the honor and glory of putting the Detroit pastimers back with dazzling regularity.

[Winning pitcher, Ruth (10–5); losing pitcher, Boland. Red Sox standing: 63 wins, 41 losses; in first place, three and a half games ahead of Cleveland. The Indians defeated Washington, 8 to 4.]

Boston Post

Out on the trails the Barrow brigade collected eight wins while losing seven times. Five of the victories were won by Babe Ruth's pitching, the illustrious Batterer proving once more that he is really the complete ball club.

Nick Flatley, *Boston American*

THE BASEBALL FIREWORKS WILL COME OFF AT FENWAY PARK TILL THE SEPT. 1ST SEASON CLOSING –

Scott, *Boston Post*

Umpire Billy Evans will be in the double bill at the Fens this afternoon. If it is hot and Billy works behind the plate he wants Babe Ruth to bat as often as possible. Said Evans last night, "In Detroit that awfully hot day, Babe came to bat and struck out a couple of times. I was behind the plate and he surely did keep me cool. That swing of his is like our cooling wind off the Atlantic."

Bob Dunbar, Boston Herald and Journal

[Evans was elected to the Hall of Fame as an umpire in 1973.]

ONLY AN INCIDENT WHEN
THE RED SOX PLAY BASEBALL-

Scott, Boston Post

Sunday, August 11

Yankees Take Both Games from Red Sox

Spread a Bunch of Gloom in Fenway Double-Header

BOSTON, Aug. 10—Col. Jake Ruppert's Broadway crepe hangers, who knocked the Red Sox pennant prospects flat last September, spread another bunch of gloom around the Fenway when they grabbed both sections of the twin bill from the Barrowmen. A batting fusillade by the Yankees decided the first contest in their favor in the 10th stanza, 5 to 1, and they took the second game, 4 to 1.

George Nemesis Mogridge pitched the first game for the Yankees. Mogridge has been beating the Sox consistently since 1915, and his win yesterday was the fifth he has hung up against them this season.

Joe Bush gave Mogridge quite a battle in the first game until the final inning, when the visitors banged the ball hard. Joe fanned 10 of the Yankees but the remnants of "Murderers' Row," Baker, Pratt and Gilhooley, swatted the ball. The Trapper Farmer [Home Run Baker] slammed out four hits in the contest.

More than 7,800 fans saw the twin bill, and in spite of the Arctic weather they were enthusiastic, even though the Sox were on the losing end. The presence of such a crowd on a punk day seemed to prove that there is some interest left in baseball.

[Game one: winning pitcher, Mogridge; losing pitcher, Bush (14–12). Game two: winning pitcher, Caldwell; losing pitcher, Mays (18–10). Home run: Hyatt (N.Y.). Red Sox' standing: 63 wins, 43 losses; in first place, three games ahead of Cleveland. The Indians lost to Chicago, 6 to 2.]

Edward F. Martin, Boston Globe

Mogridge and Caldwell effectively tamed Babe Ruth, Boston's big slugger. In the fourth inning of the first game. Ruth came up with three on base and none out and proceeded to fan. Mogridge also struck out Ruth in the second inning and Caldwell fanned him twice in the second game.

New York Times

A poisoned arrow was shot into the ranks of the Red Sox yesterday when it was learned that in all probability Carl Mays, submarine hurler extraordinary, will be unable to continue twirling the team to victory. His loss would be a stunning blow to the Sox.

Before he went into the box he said, "Well, boys, it looks as though this will be my last game for some time."

The big underhand pitcher has been called for examination by his home draft board and he expects to leave for Mansfield, Mo., today or tomorrow. Manager Barrow will find it impossible to fill the gap made by his departure.

Eddie Hurley, Boston Record

Eddie Collins to Join the Marines

Gives Up $15,000 Salary

Eddie Collins, second baseman for the Chicago Americans, will play his last game this season at Boston next Thursday, leaving that night to join the Marines. He is 31 years old, married and has two children.

Collins is the third member of the World Champion White Sox to announce his determination to enlist within the week. Pres. Comiskey, on learning that Collins had decided to enlist, wired his congratulations.

Boston Globe

[Photos of Collins depict an odd-looking, thin man with huge ears and a generous nose. But he was a beauty at second base! Eddie played for twenty-five years, from 1906 to 1930 with six pennant-winning clubs in Philadelphia (the A's) and Chicago, smacking out 3,315 hits for a .333 career batting average. His worst season, however, was 1918, with an average of .276 and only 12 extra-base hits. He was one of the top base stealers in the history of baseball, with a total of 743 thefts, including six in one game. Eddie also led the league in fielding nine times, a record for second basemen.

Eddie Collins was elected to the Hall of Fame in 1939.]

Monday, August 12

AMERICAN LEAGUE STANDINGS

	Won	Lost	PCT.	GB
Boston 63	43	.594	—
Cleveland 61	47	.565	3
Washington 58	48	.547	5
Chicago 52	53	.495	10.5
New York 50	52	.490	11
St. Louis 48	58	.453	15
Detroit 47	59	.443	16
Philadelphia 42	63	.400	20.5

[Boston didn't play on Sunday, while Cleveland split a doubleheader with Chicago, leaving the Red Sox with a three-game lead.]

Even the most optimistic of the owners has no thought that baseball will be played in its organized form next season. They are preparing to junk their immense plants, or turn them to other uses for the period of the war.

The Brooklyn owners have decided to make a huge government war storage plant of Ebbets field. It will cease to be a ball orchard.

Hugh S. Fullerton, *Boston American*

On or before September 3 we must bid farewell to the present generation of baseball stars. Unless the war ends suddenly this generation of athletes never will be seen again.

Cobb, Speaker, Johnson, Cicotte, Hooper, Bush—scores of the older players would be passé after even a year out of the game. Some of the younger generation probably would return to baseball if the game is resumed in 1920, but it is doubtful if they would be great again.

Hugh S. Fullerton, *Boston American*

[World War I raged on in Europe. Although it seemed as if the fighting would continue indefinitely, the armistice would be signed on November 11, 1918, and peace was finally restored. An estimated ten million people were killed in the most bloody war in history.

Baseball resumed the next season, the stars returned to play ball, and major league attendance increased from 3 million fans in 1918 to 6.5 million fans in 1919.]

Tuesday, August 13

Yankees Clean Up Sox as Babe Gets Careless

Two Runs off Colossus Give New Yorkers 2 to 1 Victory and Three Straight over Skidding Leaders

BOSTON, Aug. 12—Even Babe Ruth nods occasionally. The New Yorkers made two tallies before the Colossus woke up to what was going on, and, try as dernedly as possible, the Red Sox could not overcome that two-run obstacle. The Yanks won 2 to 1.

It was a disastrous loss, since the second-place Cleveland Indians gained a full game by walloping the White Sox. Two games separate the Hub Hose and the Indians.

Those Yankees are soft pickings for some teams, but not for the Red Sox. It is the sad duty of the historian to recount that the Yanks have won 10 out of 15 this season from the Ed Barrow team.

[Winning pitcher, Robinson; losing pitcher, Ruth (10–6). Red Sox' standing: 63 wins, 44 losses; in first place, two games ahead of Cleveland. The Indians defeated Chicago, 11 to 2.]

Burt Whitman, *Boston Herald and Journal*

Ed Barrow undoubtedly will throw away that soft felt hat he has been wearing since the Sox came home. It covers a multitude of woes.

Boston Herald and Journal

The end of the battle found Ruth hitless and disgusted as well. The slugger toed the plate in the ninth with two out and the fans imploring him to start a rally with one of his famous clouts. Babe took a vicious swing, broke his bat, and popped a weak fly which Fournier [the Yankees' first baseman] grabbed after going back a few feet.

New York Times

When Ruth flied to Fournier for the last out of the game, the Colossus hurled his bat beyond second base and then grinned, just like a kid.

Boston Herald and Journal

While all eyes are watching Cleveland, Washington is not out of the race by a long shot. Griffith has his team working under full steam, and the Senators are but a few games [four and a half] behind the leaders.

The Senators are playing plucky ball with wonderful pitching. If the season were not so short, Washington might break a long existing record and win the pennant.

Eddie Hurley, *Boston Record*

[Washington had had only four winning seasons since their birth in 1901. The Senators' best finish was second place in 1913, six and a half games out. Thus the saying "Washington, first in war, first in peace, and last in the American League."]

Wednesday, August 14

Washington Pushes Up Nearer the Top

Johnson Wins Own Game

PHILADELPHIA, Aug. 13—Washington twice defeated the Athletics today, 6 to 3 and 6 to 1. Walter Johnson was responsible for the first victory. He cracked out a home run with Lavan on second in the fourth inning and singled with the bases full in the ninth, scoring two runs.

Boston Globe

[Johnson was having a brilliant season. He finished with a league-leading 23–13 record, 8 shutouts, 162 strikeouts, and a 1.27 earned run average.

This sweep pulled the third-place Senators to within three and a half games of Boston.]

3-ASPIRANTS FOR THE 1918 AM LEAGUE PENNANT—

Scott, *Boston Post*

I have never felt that the Cleveland team was dangerous.

Hub Hose Fear Only Senators

"Washington is the team I am watching every day," admitted manager Ed Barrow last night.

"I have never felt that the Cleveland team was dangerous. The Senators have some great pitchers and finish up at home. The schedule is so arranged that we will not have a chance to play them again this season. I am sorry about that, as I believe we could knock them out in a three or four game series. As it is, we will have to rely on the other teams to take care of Griffith's team."

Boston Herald and Journal

Red Sox Ordered to Useful Jobs

BOSTON, Aug. 13—Babe Ruth, batting Colossus of the Red Sox, catcher Sam Agnew, and outfielder Amos Strunk today received notices from their draft boards that they must get into useful occupations by Sept. 1.

The players are becoming more and more disturbed over the "essential occupation" regulation. Even if the Red Sox win the pennant, it appears doubtful whether several of the stars would be in a world series lineup.

Chicago Tribune

Thursday, August 15

Hub Hose, Behind Jones, Win 5 to 3

BOSTON, Aug. 14—The Rebel Russell bubble was punctured yesterday by the Red Sox, with Sam Jones and Everett Scott doing most of the pricking. The White Sox were beaten by the Hub Hose, 5 to 3. As a result the league lead seems a mite safer in the custody of the Barrowmen.

The score was two-all in the last of the sixth, Miller [the Red Sox' rookie left fielder] was on first base and there was one out. Scotty came to bat. He stepped back and whanged Russell's offering to right field, Hack Miller easily scoring and the Deacon hot-footing it most scandalously to third and taking a good overrun.

Chick Gandil [the White Sox' first baseman] ran out to get the relay, muffed the ball and it rolled into the infield. Scotty put on another burst of speed and scored.

Those two runs were enough to salt away the game, because the White Sox made only one more run.

[Winning pitcher, Jones (12–5); losing pitcher, Russell. Red Sox' standing: 64 wins, 44 losses; in first place, two games ahead of Cleveland, four and a half games ahead of Washington. The Indians defeated the Yankees, 7 to 2, while the Tigers defeated the Senators, 5 to 3.]

Burt Whitman, *Boston Herald and Journal*

Sam Jones pitched for the Sox and did well considering that he has been considered non-essential for nearly a fortnight. Sam evidently did not have his range finder with him, as he franked five of the Cook County boys and hit another. There were times when it looked rather dubious for Sam but he succeeded in weathering the storm.

Edward F. Martin, *Boston Globe*

Friday, August 16

Eddie Collins in Farewell Game Helps Beat Boston, 6–2

BOSTON, Mass., Aug. 15—The White Sox displayed their appreciation of the courage and patriotism of Eddie Collins by making his last day in the American League a pleasant one.

With Jack Quinn on the slab, the world's champions mauled Carl Mays for ten hits and halted the league leaders by the count of 6 to 2.

Collins, playing as if there were no tomorrow, flashed one of his brilliant games. In the field he accepted every chance cleanly. At bat, Eddie smote a single his first time up and repeated upon his second trip. On the bases he displayed speed, pilfering second and daringly rushed to third when Schang's bad throw rolled to center.

[Winning pitcher, Quinn; losing pitcher, Mays (18–12). Red Sox' standing: 64 wins, 45 losses; in first place, two games ahead of Cleveland, three and a half games ahead of Washington. The Yankees defeated the Indians, 3 to 2, while the Senators defeated the Tigers, 6 to 2.]

Chicago Daily Tribune

Eddie Collins threw out Everett Scott in the ninth yesterday, the last play of the game. Eddie ran over to Chick Gandil, got the ball and shoved it into his hip pocket, a souvenir of his last game. A million kids, more or less, tried to beg that ball from Eddie, but there wasn't a scintilla of a chance. Eddie will keep that ball, and I would not be surprised if the marines use it in a game of ball at the front, over near the Rhine, in a few months.

Bob Dunbar, *Boston Herald and Journal*

There were many good plays in the game. Harry Hooper made one of his half-diving, half-sliding catches on a line drive, followed by a rubber-ball recovery and a throw to Stuffy McInnis at first base, which retired another man, an unusually brilliant double play.

Burt Whitman, *Boston Herald and Journal*

[Hooper perfected a sliding catch by folding his left leg under him with his right leg trailing behind. He was able to bounce back onto his feet immediately, ready to throw the runner out.]

Here come the Clevelands for the series that may settle this year's American League race once and for all. It should be as near a World's Series as we shall see at Fenway Park.

Boston Globe

Red Sox Shut Out Chicago in Final, 2–0

Tackle Indians Today with Lead of Two Games

BOSTON, Aug. 16—It took the Red Sox just one hour and 45 minutes to hang up a 2 to 0 win in the final combat with the world's champions yesterday, which pleased the Chicago bunch because it permitted them to grab the 5:15 rattler for New York and escape a night in the sleepers.

Joe Bush held the Rowlands to five scattered whacks, while only three of the Cook County boys got as far as the keystone hassock.

There was considerable first-ball hitting, the athletes being eager to get it over with.

• [Winning pitcher, Bush (15–12); losing pitcher, Cicotte. Red Sox' standing: 65 wins, 45 losses; in first place, two games ahead of Cleveland, four and a half games ahead of Washington. The Indians defeated the Yankees 12 to 4, while the Tigers dealt a severe blow to the Senators by scoring six runs in the ninth and beating Washington 8 to 7 in sixteen innings.]

Edward F. Martin, *Boston Globe*

Scott, *Boston Post*

Frazee Denies the Report that Sox Must Quit Game

NEW YORK, Aug. 16—Harry Frazee, president of the Red Sox, denied the report that three of his players, Babe Ruth, Sam Agnew and Amos Strunk, had been notified by their local draft boards to get essential work by Sept. 1, preventing them from taking part in a World's Series if the Boston club wins the pennant.

"None of my players has received such a notification," said Frazee, "and if the Red Sox win the pennant we will most certainly proceed with the World's Series."

Boston Record

Red Sox Repel Indians, 4–2

Biggest Crowd of Year

BOSTON, Aug. 17—With Big Babe Ruth at his best and the entire Red Sox team playing as though the result of this one battle settled the title to the 1918 championship, Barrow's leaders stopped the Indians yesterday and won the opening game of this crucial series of the year, 4 to 2.

Ruth opposed the brilliant Morton, who was in equally good form, and the duel that resulted had every one of the 15,000 odd watching every play with tense eagerness from start to finish.

Thanks to Ruth's splendid pitching, his gilt-edged support and the timely hits of McInnis, Miller and Strunk, the Western title chasers were halted.

* [Winning pitcher, Ruth (11–6); losing pitcher, Morton. Red Sox' standing: 66 wins, 45 losses; in first place, three games ahead of Cleveland and six games ahead of Washington. The Senators' flickering pennant hopes collapsed with a disastrous doubleheader loss to the Browns, 3 to 0 and 3 to 1.]

Paul H. Shannon, *Boston Post*

The big break in the game [with Boston leading 2 to 1] occurred when Smoky Joe Wood, after opening the seventh with a two-bagger, assumed that Bescher's liner to right would not be caught.

Wood put his head down and dug for home. Lee Fohl [the third base coach] yelled at him as he rounded third, but it was not until he was informed by Umpire Evans at the plate that Joe realized his fate. Hooper had taken the hard liner and pegged to Scott for a double play that was a life saver.

Francis Eaton, *Boston American*

The strategy employed by the visitors helped to lick them. [Boston was leading the tense game 2 to 1], with men on third and second in the eighth, one out and Ruth up. "Fadeaway Jim" Bagby was instructed to purposely frank the Oriole boy, and then along came modest Stuffy McInnis, who ripped a single to left, driving in two runs.

Edward F. Martin, *Boston Globe*

It was a noisy crowd, ready for fun. The bleacherites on the first base side loudly invited Sergeant Campbell of Boston's finest to pursue foul balls which landed in their midst, after he had rescued one similarly hit pellet from the left field stand.

Francis Eaton, *Boston American*

All of Cleveland's remaining seventeen games must be played on the road, whereas the Red Sox practically finish their season at home, playing thirteen of their remaining fifteen games at the Fenway.

Francis Eaton, *Boston American*

Monday, August 19

AMERICAN LEAGUE STANDINGS				
	Won	Lost	PCT.	GB
Boston 66		45	.595	—
Cleveland 64		49	.566	3
Washington 62		52	.544	5.5
New York 53		55	.491	11.5
Chicago 54		57	.486	12
St. Louis 53		57	.482	12.5
Detroit 49		62	.441	17
Philadelphia 44		68	.393	22.5

Ruth Saturday's Hero

Babe Ruth was the hero of his own game Saturday and the victory he turned in just about clinches the gonfalon for the Sox. No, the Colossus didn't bust out one of his circuit drives. But by beating out a slow tap to Terry Turner [the Indians' second baseman] in the fourth canto he set the stage for what proved the winning rally.

Ruth went up after Strunk expired. Babe tapped an ordinary grasser to Turner and ol' Terry, electing to play it safe, backed up so as not to get the ball between hops. He made a clean stop all right, but Ruth dug down to first at top speed and reached the bag a half step ahead of Turner's throw.

The game, and the pennant as well, in all likelihood, was won then and there. Next, Evans [the third baseman] overran McInnis' bunt. Then Hack Miller, the Sox' husky new outfielder, poled a line single to left, and McInnis followed Ruth across the plate. [This hit put the Red Sox ahead 2 to 0 and they never lost the lead.]

The whole game would have been played differently if Ruth had not stolen his hit in the fourth.

H. W. Lanigan, *Boston American*

RED SOX BATTING

	AB	R	BH	2B	3B	HR	SB	AVG
Ruth, p, lf 285	285	46	86	23	11	11	4	.302
Hooper, rf 420	420	69	123	22	11	1	21	.293
Bush, p 91	91	8	26	3	2	0	0	.286
McInnis, 1b 374	374	36	102	8	5	0	8	.273
Mays, p 90	90	7	24	3	3	0	1	.267
Shean, 2b 382	382	51	98	16	3	0	11	.257
Strunk, cf 366	366	45	91	14	7	0	17	.249
Whiteman, lf 199	199	17	49	10	0	0	9	.246
Schang, c 193	193	31	47	9	1	0	3	.244
Scott, ss 395	395	37	89	10	4	0	11	.225
Mayer, c 44	44	6	9	3	0	0	0	.205
Coffey, 3b 76	76	9	15	0	2	0	2	.197
Agnew, c 183	183	9	27	7	0	0	0	.148
Jones, p 43	43	5	6	0	0	0	0	.140
Cochran, 3b 39	39	7	5	0	0	0	2	.128

RED SOX PITCHING

	IP	BH	Won	Lost	R	BB	SO
Mays 258	258	201	18	12	84	80	102
Bush 250	250	217	15	12	86	85	104
Jones 158	158	129	12	5	59	55	31
Ruth 142	142	104	11	6	41	45	35

Tuesday, August 20

Two-Hit Jones Humbles Indians and Cinches Flag, 6–0

BOSTON, Aug. 19—Sam Jones effaced the Cleveland Indians, 6 to 0, at the Fens yesterday afternoon. He pushed his old chums off the face of the earth, held them to two hits, put them four games behind the Sox and made

Maybe He's Crowing Too Soon

Cleveland Press

it all but a mathematical certainty, almost in the class with death and taxes, that Ed Barrow's Hub Hose will win the American League championship of 1918, and take part in the World Series.

The Sox played thrilling, flawless baseball behind Sam, giving him all the inspiration in the world to pitch his young head off. The Hubmen were full of ambition, pepper, hustle and aggressiveness. Gone was all the uncertainty of a week or more ago, when it seemed as if the Sox had lost faith in their ability to "come through." Their four game lead, with 14 to play, looks like the Rock of Gibraltar.

* [Winning pitcher, Jones (13–5); losing pitcher, Coveleski. Red Sox' standing: 67 wins, 45 losses; in first place, four games ahead of Cleveland.]

Burt Whitman, *Boston Herald and Journal*

If you ask the 7,500 fans what the outstanding feature of the game was, they'll answer you:

"Oh, boy, you should have seen that smash which Babe Ruth hit to right field in the last of the eighth. Joe Wood, the right fielder, was stationed over in East Boston. He dropped back still farther and caught the ball at the very edge of the bleacher fence, after the ball had been up in the air so long that it came down coated with frost. Sure, it was a fly out, but a gosh-awful whack just the same!

"Then in the ninth Babe evened it up with Smoky Joe. Woodie smashed a drive to left field, up toward that corner which is usually good for two, sometimes three bases. Babe ran over, stuck out his mitt hand, and there the ball stuck, even though he crashed into the left field bleacher barrier the next jiffy."

Burt Whitman, Boston Herald and Journal

Babe Ruth has not been able to get a hold of that old apple in the pinch. He was passed twice on Saturday and twice yesterday. It's the right dope even though the fans groaned and shrieked at Cleveland's methods.

Passing Ruth was the undoing of the Indians yesterday as Stuffy McInnis laid on the "cripple" and sent two big runs across that made the game safe. It was the second time in the series that Stuffy has hit after Ruth has been passed.

Eddie Hurley, Boston Record

Indians came to Boston town
Nursing pennant hopes,
Red Sox knocked 'em galley west,
Sent 'em to the ropes;
Now those selfsame Indians
Lucky will be reckoned
If they finish out the season
Landing high as second.

Wampus, Cleveland Press

Walter Johnson fanned 12 batsmen [in a 3–2, fourteen-inning win over the St. Louis Browns] yesterday. It was the fifteenth extra-inning game he has pitched this season.

Boston Globe

Wednesday, August 21

Cleveland Hammers Ruth, 8–4

BOSTON, Aug. 20—Babe Ruth tried to come back after his admirable victory of Saturday, but his playmates refused to give him the right sort of support. The Indians hammered the ball, and the grand total was Cleveland 8, Boston 4, which brings down the Sox lead over the field to three full games, with 13 to play.

Babe was so provoked last night that he could bite two-penny nails, three at a time. He not only was marked down as the losing pitcher, but he failed to get a hit in four trips to the plate. Once he was passed by Jim

Bagby, but the three other times Babe took his healthy [cuts] and did not come through.

Stuffy McInnis was another busy boy. If his team had held down the Indians, he would have been the hero of his third straight game. He personally drove over three of the four runs the domestics made.

• [Winning pitcher, Bagby; losing pitcher, Ruth (11–7). Red Sox' standing: 67 wins, 46 losses; in first place, three games ahead of Cleveland.]

Burt Whitman, *Boston Herald and Journal*

Babe can do almost anything in athletics, but beating the next best team on Saturday and then being expected to repeat on Tuesday was evidently too much even for him.

Nick Flatley, *Boston American*

MONARCHS OF SWATDOM			
	AB	H	AVG
Cobb, Detroit	372	139	.374
Burns, Philadelphia . . .	448	153	.342
Sisler, St. Louis	399	134	.336
Speaker, Cleveland . . .	431	138	.320
Baker, New York	448	136	.304

Boston American

"Sam Jones is the best pitcher Boston has," is the eloquent praise which Tris Speaker handed out yesterday to the modest right hander of the Barrow forces. "Those two years Sam sat on the bench made him. He simply absorbed everything that went on in the games. He's smart and learns rapidly. That slow ball of his simply floats up there and you swing your head off, and then he has a fast one that is on top of you before you realize it. In addition, he has as good a curve ball as anyone in the league. Yes, I believe he's the best pitcher on the team."

Bob Dunbar, *Boston Herald and Journal*

It is almost assured that the series will start Sept. 4. Chairman Herrmann [of the National Baseball Commission] has received word from both Chicago and Boston that the local draft boards will not interfere with the members of these two teams during the series.

Boston Post

The Year the Red Sox Won the Series

Mays Pitches His 19th Win for Sox

Beats Browns, 4–1

BOSTON, Aug. 21—While Red Sox base hits were just about as plentiful as promotions among the Police Headquarters, the Barrowmen succeeded in winning their opening combat with the Browns, 4 to 1, Carl Mays hanging up his 19th win of the season.

Dixie Sothoron, the spitballer, held the Sox to two hits in seven innings. One of these was a scratch, but the other was a home run to deep center by Jack Coffey in the fifth. [It was the Red Sox third baseman's only major league home run.]

Sothoron had a very tough afternoon. The boys in the Red Sox dugout were riding him, and when some pert remark was passed he blamed Wally Mayer, who was coaching on the first base line. Later he discovered that he had Wally wrong, but not until after he started over to mix it up with him.

Sam Jones got chased off the bench for chucking persiflage around with reckless abandon.

• [Winning pitcher, Mays (19–12); losing pitcher, Sothoron. Home run: Coffey (1). Red Sox' standing: 68 wins, 46 losses; in first place, three games ahead of Cleveland. The Indians defeated the Senators, 5 to 3.]

Edward F. Martin, *Boston Globe*

Scott, *Boston Post*

It was Shriners' Day at Fenway Park. A big representation from Aleppo Temple donated smokes to the players who made base hits, as well as to the soldiers and sailors in the grandstand.

Paul H. Shannon, *Boston Post*

Heinie Wagner did not make a base hit for the Sox yesterday, but he looked at the free cigars so approvingly that Ed Barrow presented him with his own box.

Boston Globe

The 1918 world's series purse promises to be leaner than an Ozark shoat.

St. Louis Post-Dispatch

THE GREATEST SPORT OF ALL
By RIPLEY

Robert L. Ripley, *Boston Globe*

The Year the Red Sox Won the Series

Red Sox Shut Out, Failing in the Pinch

Browns Get to Bush in the Fifth, Scoring 1–0 Victory

BOSTON, Aug. 22—After the decorations had been passed around yesterday, every St. Louis player having been supplied with membership in the widely known Order of the Tin [the Shriners], the Browns turned around and licked the Red Sox, 1 to 0, big Dave Davenport shading "Bullet" Joe Bush in an interesting tilt.

Carelessness and failure to produce in the pinch hurt the Sox. The defeat knocked them out of an opportunity to gain a little ground as the Fohlmen were being plastered in Washington.

* [Winning pitcher, Davenport; losing pitcher, Bush (15–13). Red Sox' standing: 68 wins, 47 losses; in first place, three games ahead of Cleveland.]

Edward F. Martin, Boston Globe

Players of St. Louis Ball Team Fired

Ten days' notice of unconditional release was handed to each member of the St. Louis Browns before the game yesterday. After Sept. 2 every one of the players, including the great Sisler, will be free agents. From the way things shape up now, it looks as if the boys would be all dressed up with no place to go.

Boston Globe

World Series Certain

WASHINGTON, Aug. 22—When asked whether the work or fight order would interfere with the world's series this year, Secretary of War Baker indicated his strong opinion that the series would be and should be played.

Since only two teams would take part, the Secretary thought the number of men affected would be very small, and moreover, the soldiers in France were intensely interested in the results.

Boston Post

Pershing's Boys Can't See Why Athletes Get Big Salaries, While They Fight for America

There is no place left for the Cobbs, the Ruths, and the Johnsons in the ease and safety of home when the Ryans, the Smiths, the Larsens, the Bernsteins and others are charging machine-guns and plugging along through shrapnel or grinding out 12-hour details 200 miles in the rear.

Back home the sight of a high fly drifting into the late sun may still have its thrill for a few. But over here the all-absorbing factors are shrapnel, high explosives, machine gun bullets, trench digging, stable cleaning, nursing, training back of the lines and other endless details throughout France from the base ports to beyond the Marne.

Milton Bronner, *Stars and Stripes*
(reprinted in the *Boston Record*)

Ty Cobb vs. Germany

Ty Cobb has joined the gas and flame;
When Ty gets in the fighting game
    He'll make the Germans swear.
He'll steal up on the Huns in France
And steal the Kaiser's coat and pants
    When he gets "over there."

He'll bat the Crown Prince from the box
And steal his hat and shoes and sox
    And everything in sight.
He'll steal a march upon the Huns
And steal their mustard gas and guns
    When he gets in the fight.

He'll steal a mile or two of trench,
And put the Kaiser on the bench,
    When he gets in the scrap.
He'll steal the watch upon the Rhine,
He'll steal Von Hindy's famous line
    And wipe it off the map.

He'll lead the league in batting Huns,
He'll show those German sons-of-guns
    They have no chance to win.
He'll go through villages and towns
Like going through the famous Browns
    Until he hits Berlin.

In point of fact the Georgia Peach
A lesson to those Huns will teach
    That they will not forget;
For cover they will quickly hike
When Tyrus Raymond starts to spike
    Their guns already yet.

When Tyrus Raymond hits his stride
Unter den Linden he will slide
    And score the winning run.
That famous battery Me und Gott
He'll hammer all around the lot
    Until the game is won.

L. C. Davis, *St. Louis Post-Dispatch*

[Unter den Linden is a main boulevard in Berlin.]

Saturday, August 24

Double Steal Paves Way to Sox Victory

Boston Beats St. Louis in the Ninth, 6–5

BOSTON, Aug. 23—Ace Sam Jones had a deuce of a day yesterday, yet he managed to squeeze through a 6 to 5 win over the Browns. There were two out in the ninth when Severeid [the Browns' catcher] chucked high to Maisel [their third baseman], trying to break up Ruth and Strunk's double steal, the latter skipping in with the winning run.

Sam was not up to his usual form, letting a three-run lead slip away from him in the fifth. He made some sweet fielding plays and soaked the apple [two hits], but he was often in trouble. But that Sam is a regular ace there can be no question.

• [Winning pitcher, Jones (14–5); losing pitcher, Houck. Red Sox' standing: 69 wins, 47 losses; in first place, three games ahead of Cleveland. The Indians defeated the Senators, 6 to 2.]

Edward F. Martin, *Boston Globe*

IN THE 9TH INNING.
STRUNK ON 2ND BASE AND RUTH ON 1ST
MADE A DOUBLE STEAL AND A WILD THROW
TO 3RD SCORED STRUNK FOR THE WINNING RUN.

Scott, *Boston Post*

In Babe Ruth, Boston has one of the greatest left-handers in the history of the game. Like the late Rube Waddell, Ruth has terrific speed and a beautiful curve. A southpaw needs no more.

Billy Evans, American League Umpire, Boston Post

Ruth Hurt but Recovers, Red Sox Trim Brownies, 3–1

BOSTON, Aug. 24—The Red Sox took the game they needed, 3 to 1, at the Fens yesterday in the farewell series with the St. Louis Browns.

Ruth twisted his right knee in a play at the plate, when he avoided Nunamaker's tag in the second inning [while stealing home].

"There goes Boston's chances in the World's Series," groaned a grandstand gloom as the Babe, falling flat, began to roll over and over in evident pain.

Ruth was assisted to the dugout, and Carl Mays arose in the bull pen and began to warm up. But at the beginning of the next inning the Babe limped out to the mound and received the cheer.

Although partly crippled, Ruth was able to field his position cleverly while pitching effectively, and by striking out Sisler in the eighth inning he reduced the only dangerous salient that bulged out into the Barrow trenches.

The Browns, as if in search of a cooler spot than Boston, hurried through the game, hitting at the first ball if anywhere near the plate.

And if the Brownies failed to hit the first ball, they were just as ready to hit at the second ball and then the third ball. Result—a game played well within an hour and a half, and an early start for the beaches.

• [Winning pitcher, Ruth (12–7); losing pitcher, Leifield. Red Sox' standing: 70 wins, 47 losses; in first place, four games ahead of Cleveland. The Indians lost to the Senators, 4 to 0.]

Francis Eaton, Boston American

It's All Over! Flag for Cubs!

CHICAGO, Aug. 24—The Cubs drove the ultimate spike into the 1918 National League pennant yesterday when they trounced Brooklyn in both ends of their double header by scores of 8 to 3 and 3 to 1. The two edged victory gave the Mitchell tribe a lead of eleven and a half games over the Giants.

I. E. Sanborn, Chicago Tribune

[The red-hot Cubs had a record of 78 victories and only 40 losses, a .664 winning percentage.]

Chicago Fares Well in World's Series

CHICAGO, Aug. 24—The first three games of the World's Series will be played in Chicago, starting Wednesday, Sept. 4, it was announced here tonight by Pres. Johnson of the American League. The remaining contests will be played on the home grounds of the American League pennant winning team. War charities will share in the receipts.

Because of the demands made upon the public for the investment in Liberty Bonds and thrift stamps, the commission decided to reduce prices of admission to enable patrons to attend the games at reasonable prices.

The price of box seats, which a year ago sold for $5, was reduced to $3. Grandstand reserved seats will sell for $1.50, pavilion seats for $1 and bleacher seats at 50 cents.

Pres. Johnson announced that the National Commission would cable reports and features of each game to the American and Canadian troops overseas.

Boston Globe

Limit Share for Each Player

Even had times been normal the players would not get as much bonus money from the series as in the past, for a new rule was established last winter limiting the amount to $2,000 for each winning player and $1,400 for each losing player. The balance of the players' pool will be apportioned to teams in the first division of each league. Because of the cut in prices and the general decline in interest this season, it is possible the players' purses will be more like those of ten and twelve years ago.

James Crusinberry, *Chicago Tribune*

Ty to Quit Baseball, Off to War Oct. 1

NEW YORK, Aug. 24—Tyrus Raymond Cobb, who for more than a dozen years has been baseball's most sensational figure, played for probably the last time at the Polo Grounds this afternoon. After the war is over Cobb doesn't expect to return to the game. He is retiring at a time when he is still the greatest player in the national pastime.

After the first Yanks-Tigers game, when the crowd was all worked up to a high pitch of enthusiasm over the war savings stamp drive, it called on Cobb for a speech. Tyrus climbed onto the roof of the Detroit bench and made an impressive plea for the stamp drive, and then he said that he would soon be on his way to France. Cobb said that he had bought $250 worth of war stamps.

Chicago Tribune

[Ty played ten more seasons, retiring after the 1928 season at the age of forty-one.]

THESE TWO SATURDAY EVENTS SURE GIVE THE
RED SOX A BOOST FOR THE 1918 PENNANT-

Scott, *Boston Post*

AMERICAN LEAGUE STANDINGS

	Won	Lost	PCT.	GB
Boston	70	47	.598	—
Cleveland	67	52	.563	4
Washington	67	54	.554	5
New York	56	57	.496	12
Chicago	57	62	.479	14
St. Louis	54	61	.470	15
Detroit	50	66	.431	19.5
Philadelphia	48	70	.407	22.5

The Red Sox have the pennant cinched—
They told me so
A week ago.
And yesterday and day before
They told me just the same twice more.

And now today
I find that they
Still tell me Boston cannot lose
As if that were some startling news—

I hope the next gazabo's lynched
Who tells me that the flag is cinched.

Says Wampus, *Cleveland Press*

[A gazabo is an eccentric man.]

The Year the Red Sox Won the Series

IN THE WORLD SERIES
THE FIRST THREE GAMES
WILL BE PLAYED IN THE
WINDY CITY—

Scott, *Boston Post*

Frazee Refuses to Play First Three in Chicago

Owner Harry Frazee of the Red Sox does not propose to knuckle down to any Ban Johnson plan for the world series which provides for the first three games being played in Chicago.

"If the Boston club wins the American League pennant," he declared, "I will refuse to abide by the schedule arrangements for the world series as given out by President Johnson on Saturday. Such a schedule is not only very unfair to the Boston club, but it is an insult to Boston fans and to the best baseball town in the American League.

"I do not mind playing the first two games in Chicago and then coming to Boston for two games. But I am absolutely opposed to playing three games in Chicago, and then, as President Johnson says, 'playing the remaining games, if any, in Boston.'"

Burt Whitman, *Boston Herald and Journal*

[The standard procedure was to play the first two games in one city, with games 3 and 4 in the other city. Games 5, 6, and 7 switched back and forth. This created the possibility of four trips.

To limit wartime transportation costs the proposed arrangement involved only one trip.]

Early in the season Everett Scott, the Sox shortstop, played over a long stretch of games without making an error. Now he has completed another big string of perfect play, going 22 games without a miscue. All year, in his 117 games, Scotty has been charged with only 15 errors. By all odds he has been the most efficient fielding shortstop in the league. "Consistency" is his middle name.

Boston Globe   Everett Scott, Red Sox shortstop

Father of Babe Ruth Is Killed

BALTIMORE, Aug. 25—George H. Ruth, 45 years old, father of Babe Ruth, pitcher for the Red Sox, died at the University Hospital early today as the result of a fractured skull, which he received in a fight with his wife's brother, Benjamin H. Sipes.

Sipes was arrested later and is being held pending the action of the coroner.

According to the police, Sipes called at the home of Ruth, shortly before midnight Saturday and told the latter that he was not treating his sister right. Words soon followed and Sipes left the house.

Sipes went over and stood in front of Ruth's café. Ruth came out and swung his fist, catching Sipes in the face. The blow staggered the man for a moment and as he recovered he was hit a second time by Ruth.

Then, according to witnesses, Sipes struck his assailant in the face. Ruth collapsed and fell to the sidewalk, his head striking the curbing. He was carried into his house and first aid treatment was administered. When he didn't respond he was rushed to the hospital, where he died.

Boston Post

Tuesday, August 27

Tigers Depth Bomb Our Carl, 6–3

BOSTON, Aug. 26—Carl Mays went out to win his 20th ball game, but on his way to Victory Knoll he bumped into a flock of Tigers, led by Georgian Ty Cobb, and they mauled Blonde Carl, 6 to 3, getting 11 hits.

The Red Sox missed the mighty bat of Babe Ruth, Colossus of Clouters. The big fellow left last night for Baltimore to settle many matters connected with the tragic death of his father.

[Winning pitcher, Cunningham; losing pitcher, Mays (19–13). Home run: Cobb (3). Red Sox' standing: 70 wins, 48 losses; in first place, three and a half games ahead of Cleveland. The Indians split a doubleheader with the A's.]

Burt Whitman, *Boston Herald and Journal*

Ty Cobb, who reported late for the start of the game, made up for any time he had lost. Donie Bush was on in the third, when Ty faced his "little pal" Mays. He showed his affection for the blond beaver by putting the ball deep into the outfield for a home run. Cobb has made two home runs on consecutive days, bringing his total up to three.

Detroit News

Giving out a statement at Chicago last night, Pres. Ban Johnson said:

"There will be no change in the schedule for the World's Series unless Pres. Harry Frazee of the Boston club, who protested against its alleged unfairness, obtains the consent of the War Department to arrange special trains. It was our idea to conserve transportation in every way possible."

Boston Record

"Some day Frazee will learn that the United States is engaged in a desperate war, the winning of which is the only thing that matters to the American public."

Ban Johnson, quoted in the *Chicago Tribune*

BOSTON, Mass., Aug. 26—Harry H. Frazee, president of the Boston American League club, said tonight he was satisfied with the explanation of the World Series arrangements made by President Ban B. Johnson. He added that he was now willing to go on with the series as arranged.

Chicago Tribune

Cubs to Donate to War Fund

CHICAGO, Aug. 27—Members of the Cubs have unanimously voted to donate 10 per cent of their share of the world's series receipts to war charities, as suggested by the National Commission.

President Ban Johnson of the American League states that he will hand over the $250 allotted him for his personal expenses to the good cause.

Boston American

Wednesday, August 28

Bush Fans 13, but Loses 2–1

BOSTON, Aug. 27—Minus Ty Cobb and despite the remarkable pitching feat of Joe Bush in fanning 13, those yowling, howling Michigan Tigers behaved abominably at the Fens yesterday afternoon, clutching a 2 to 1 win from the weak hitting Red Sox, prolonging the wrestling match between old Doc Mathematics and Kid Certainty. As Cleveland won, the margin twixt the Hubmen and the field is now two and a half games, with seven to go.

- [Winning pitcher, Kallio; losing pitcher, Bush (15–14). Red Sox' standing: 70 wins, 49 losses; in first place, two and a half games ahead of Cleveland.]

Burt Whitman, *Boston Herald and Journal*

[Cobb had gone back to Detroit to settle his business and personal affairs before entering the army as a captain in the Chemical Warfare Service.]

It was a tough game for Bullet Joe to lose. His 13 strikeouts is the season's record. He was mowing the Tigers down with ease and pitching airtight ball.

In the first three innings Joe fanned eight batters, getting the side in the first and third. It looked as if he might hang up a big record until Col. Jim Slattery, the sage of the Press Gallery, asked what the American League record was. That jinxed Joe for fair.

Edward F. Martin, *Boston Globe*

[The American League record for strikeouts in a game was sixteen, set by Rube Waddell in 1908.]

Cleveland 8, Philadelphia 6

PHILADELPHIA, Aug. 27—Cleveland won today's game, 8–6, making a four run rally in the sixth. Speaker was called out on a close decision at the plate in the fifth and was finally ordered out of the game.

Boston Globe

[Their comeback victory kept Cleveland's flickering pennant hopes alive, pulling them to within two and a half games of Boston. However, one of their best pitchers, Guy Morton, received his draft notice and left the team. He had a record of 14 wins and 8 losses. Morton's departure left the Indians with only five pitchers on their staff.]

Tris Speaker Hangs One on Ump's Jaw

PHILADELPHIA, Aug. 27—Imagine Tris Speaker hanging one on Umpire Tommy Connolly's jaw! Tris came in with what he thought was the tying run in the game against the Athletics, but the sage of Natick counted him out. Tris did not wait to argue the point but started a haymaker and the ump nearly took the count.

Boston Record

Any further gains by the Tribe are likely to cause the Red Sox to put in an S.O.S. for the return of Babe Ruth, who was called away by the death of his father, killed in fisticuffs with his brother-in-law. Ruth has been absent from the Red Sox lineup for two days and Boston dropped both games.

Cleveland Press

World Series Players to Wear Old Uniforms

Owner Charley Weeghman of the Chicago Cubs will economize in the coming world series by request of his players.

He was so tickled at winning the pennant that he wanted to make presents of new uniforms to every one of his men. But they refused his offer and told him that, in these wartimes, they'd rather keep on wearing the old suits in which they copped the National League flag.

Cleveland Press

Frazee said he wouldn't play
If they didn't let him have his way;
Thoughts of all that cash, you'll find,
Quickly made him change his mind.

Cleveland Press

Tris Speaker Gets "Can" Indefinitely

PHILADELPHIA, Aug. 28—Tristram Speaker was notified today that he has been indefinitely suspended as a result of his clash with Umpire Connolly yesterday.

Boston Post

There never was a club that ever entered a world series as weak at third base as the Red Sox. Manager Barrow is unable to say who will hold down the job. Fred Thomas was going big while he was here, but he was forced to quit. Since he left the club has been up against it. Jack Coffey and George Cochran are the third sackers on the club now.

Coffey is a good fielder and he seems to hit harder than Cochran. Coffey is a hard luck hitter, however, as most of his drives are made right at some waiting fielder.

Eddie Hurley, *Boston Record*

[Jack Coffey was playing in the majors for the first time since 1909 and was batting .186. George Cochran was hitting a puny .106 in his rookie season. Fred Thomas was training at the Great Lakes Naval Base near Chicago and hadn't played for two months.]

IN THE 3ʳᵈ INNING, HOOPER
MADE A CLASSY RUNNING CATCH
OF DAUSS' LONG FOUL -

Scott, *Boston Post*

Hooper-Jones Combine Flays Man-Eaters, 3–0

Handsome Harry Factor in All the Runs, Lithe Sam Gives But Three Hits

BOSTON, August 28—Harry Hooper is the captain of the Red Sox and he proved it was a well-deserved title yesterday when he smashed out two doubles and a triple, providing all the dynamite for the explosion which gave the Hubmen a 3 to 0 victory over the Tigers.

As the A's set down the Speaker-less Clevelanders, the Barrowmen advanced one full game nearer the certainty of being A.L. pennant winners. The margin this morning is three and one-half games, with but six to play.

Sam Jones, whom slugger Tris Speaker stamps as the best pitcher Ed Barrow has, held the Tigers to three hits.

A good curve ball, change-of-pace pitcher is Sam Jones, my dears, and do not be surprised if he opens the series against the Cubs. He has the courage, the heart, the stuff and the general equipment to stop Mann, Paskert, Killefer and Merkle, and need have no fear of the slugging of the left-hand batting Hollocher, Flack and Tyler.

[Winning pitcher, Jones (15–5); losing pitcher, Dauss. Red Sox' standing: 71 wins, 49 losses; in first place, three and a half games ahead of Cleveland. The Indians lost to the Athletics, 1 to 0.]

Burt Whitman, *Boston Herald and Journal*

"HE'S OUT!"

L. Satterfield, *Boston Record*

NEW YORK, Aug. 28—Percy Guard, a betting commissioner, was offering $10,000 to $9,000 that Chicago wins the World's Baseball Series. Some small bets were made. Guard states there is plenty of Chicago money, but very little Boston.

Boston Globe

CHICAGO, Aug. 28—The World Series will be played at Comiskey Park, the home of the Chicago American League club.

Comiskey Park was the scene of the 1917 World's Series between the Chicago White Sox and the New York Giants, and has a seating capacity of 30,000. The capacity of the Chicago Nationals' park does not exceed 16,000.

Boston Post

Friday, August 30

THERE WAS NOTHING DOING AT FENWAY PARK YESTERDAY, BUT A DOUBLE-HEADER IS BILLED FOR TODAY.

Scott, Boston Post

Winning six straight games is an almost impossible task for Cleveland in their crippled condition. The loss of Speaker will be a blow to the club.

Eddie Hurley, Boston Record

The Big Four of the Red Sox pitching staff must come through in the doubleheaders today and tomorrow to make the pennant a certainty. The Sox are still three and a half games ahead of Cleveland and they need three more victories to clinch the American League title. Manager Barrow is anxious to nail down the pennant in the series with the Mackmen. He does not want to take any chances with the Yankees in the two games on Labor Day.

Eddie Hurley, Boston Record

Jim Vaughn to Face Red Sox the First Game of Big Tilt

CHICAGO—Red Sox players and Boston fans can rest assured that Manager Fred Mitchell of the Cubs will start Big Jim Vaughn, his massive left-hander, against the American League champions in next Wednesday's opening World's Series battle here.

Boston Record

[Vaughn was the top pitcher in the National League, with 22 wins against only 10 losses. He also led the league with 148 strikeouts and a 1.74 earned run average.]

Here's a Hunch on the World's Series Games

John McGraw [the New York Giants' manager] is a strong booster of the Cubs. A few days ago he came out with the statement that the Cubs would have little trouble in defeating the Red Sox in the fall series.

McGraw is the inventor of a baseball game played with the ordinary pack of cards, and on the recent jump from the West to New York he persuaded Heinie Zimmerman [the Giants' third baseman] to try his hand at the game. Zimmerman upheld the Red Sox and won four of the five games. Babe Ruth was selected to pitch the first game for the Sox, and the big fellow won his own game with a home run.

If you like to play a hunch, go to it.

Harry J. Casey, *Boston Record*

Saturday, August 31

Mays Puts Pennant Almost in Sox' Hands

Iron Man Stunt, Pitching and Winning Two Games

BOSTON, Aug. 31—It was Oregon Day at Fenway Park yesterday and almost 5,000 fans saw Mr. C. Mays, the blond propeller of the submarine ball, do an iron-man stunt against the Conniemacks. The first game was a romp, the Sox registering a 12 to 0 victory, while they copped the second 4 to 1.

Mays had a fine day, pitching and hitting well [five base hits] and fielding his position with his usual class. The Oregonian has now earned 21 victories, and he will probably not work in any more games between now and the close of the season.

Babe Ruth returned to the combat and his double in the first inning of the first game pushed two runs over. He made some good catches, and the entire Boston club played smartly in the field all day.

[Game one: winning pitcher, Mays (20–13); losing pitcher, Johnson. Game two: winning pitcher, Mays (21–13); losing pitcher, Perry. Red Sox' standing: 73 wins, 49 losses; in first place, three and a half

Carl Mays, Red Sox pitcher

games ahead of Cleveland. The Indians swept a doubleheader from the Tigers, 2 to 1 and 4 to 2, to remain barely alive in the pennant race.]

Edward F. Martin, Boston Globe

If the Sox win one of their four remaining games, the pennant is cinched mathematically. If the Indians lose one game their slim chance of getting into the classic goes to the land of sunk U-boats.

Burt Whitman, Boston Herald and Journal

Mays had an exceptionally easy time of that first game. The A's, demoralized and playing a miserable fielding game [eight errors], were hitting the first ball and Carl breezed through triumphantly, merely lobbing the ball over at times.

Manager Barrow's plan was to use Babe Ruth in the second game. But Ruth was a trifle soft after his lay-off and Mays said that he was in rare trim, did not mind pitching the second game, and away he went.

Burt Whitman, Boston Herald and Journal

Scott, Boston Post

Babe Ruth Will Go against Mackmen

Victory Means Flag for Sox

George Babe Ruth, husky son of swat, will be handed the honor of clinching the pennant at Fenway Park today, in the first game of the doubleheader with the Mackmen.

"Babe's bat has been prominent all season while his pitching has also helped out, and he is deserving of the chance to clinch the pennant," said Ed Barrow this morning. "We need just one more victory to make the pennant beyond Cleveland's reach, and it's up to the big fellow to come through this afternoon," continued the manager.

Eddie Hurley, *Boston Record*

There is no more need to worry over that third base job. Fred Thomas, who quit the team in mid-season, will be on the job in the title games. Barrow was trying to keep it a secret, but it leaked out. Thomas has secured a furlough from the Navy and will report to the club on Labor Day.

Eddie Hurley, *Boston Record*

Cobb Quits Game as Batting Champion

CHICAGO, Aug. 31—Capt. Tyrus Raymond Cobb, who this week stepped from baseball into the chemical division of the Army, took with him the 1918 batting honors of the American League. He has taken these honors every year since 1912 with the exception of 1916, when Tris Speaker beat him out.

Boston Globe

Sunday, September 1

Babe Ruth's Victory Gives Pennant to Sox

Colossus Wins Deciding Game

BOSTON, Aug. 31—Babe Ruth closed the door in the face of pudgy old Doctor Mathematics with a bang yesterday by personally piloting the Red Sox to a 6 to 1 win over the Athletics in the first game of the doubleheader. [The Athletics won the second game, 1 to 0.]

The first game was a dandy. Babe Ruth, who had done so well all season, was the hero. At bat his terrific driving, high, far flies, caused the crowd to rock back and forth with delight. In the fifth Babe smashed a drive to far right centre field. It would have gone into the bleachers for a home run but for the wind from the east which held it back.

Rarely will one see such a whack. Acosta [the center fielder] backed into the bleacher fence and then dropped the ball. He thought it was going into the seats and was all flustered when the wind brought it out a mite.

[First game: winning pitcher, Ruth (13–7); losing pitcher, Watson.
Second game: winning pitcher, Watson; losing pitcher, Bush (15–15).
Red Sox' standing: 74 wins, 50 losses; clinched first place, three games
ahead of Cleveland.]

Burt Whitman, *Boston Herald and Journal*

[Boston scored three times during the fifth-inning rally of the opener, breaking open a tight
game. Ruth put the finishing touch on his brilliant season by pitching a three-hitter to clinch
the American League pennant.]

Hanging the Ribbon Aloft!

BOSTON	AB	R	BH	PO	A	PHILADELPHIA	AB	R	BH	PO	A
Hooper, rf	3	1	1	1	1	Jamieson, rf	4	0	1	2	1
Shean, 2b	3	0	1	3	3	Kopp, lf	4	1	0	1	1
Strunk, cf	2	0	2	3	0	Acosta, cf	2	0	0	2	1
Ruth, p	4	1	2	0	4	Burns, 1b	4	0	2	11	1
McInnis, 1b	4	2	3	14	0	Gardner, 3b	3	0	0	0	1
Scott, ss	3	0	1	2	6	Perkins, c	3	0	0	3	4
Cochran, 3b	3	0	1	0	3	Dykes, 2b	3	0	0	3	5
Schang, c	4	0	0	4	1	Dugan, ss	2	0	0	2	1
Whiteman, lf	1	2	1	0	0	Watson, p	3	0	0	0	3
Totals	27	6	12	27	18	Totals	28	1	3	24	18

Innings	1	2	3	4	5	6	7	8	9	R
Boston	0	1	1	1	3	0	0	0	x	- 6
Philadelphia	1	0	0	0	0	0	0	0	0	- 1

Errors—Shean, Dykes. Two-base hits—McInnis, Whiteman, Ruth. Stolen bases—Kopp,
Acosta. Sacrifice hits—Hooper, Scott, Shean. Double plays—Hooper to Scott to Shean;
Dykes to Burns; Shean to Scott to McInnis; Burns to Dugan to Burns. Left on base—Boston
5, Philadelphia 4. First base on balls—off Watson 5, off Ruth 4. Struck out, by Ruth 3, by
Watson 1. Time 1 h. 30 m. Umpire-in-chief, Connolly. Umpire on bases, Nallin.

Boston Herald and Journal

Boston Fans Take Harry Hooper's Work for Granted

Harry Hooper, captain and right fielder of the Red Sox, is about to lead his
teammates in the world's baseball classic.

In the three world series the Red Sox have won in the last six years,
Hooper's work has been outstanding. He has scored more runs, totaled
more bases, made more spectacular plays than any other outfielder.

Harry Hooper, Red Sox right fielder

A batsman who is cool and heady, a good base runner and a remarkable judge of a fly ball, with an arm of steel, Hooper is a combination of Frank and Dick Merriwell.

Fred Hoey, *Boston Herald and Journal*

[The Merriwells were fictional, all-American athletes in teenage novels of the day.]

The end of the baseball season marks the end of many careers. We probably have watched for the last time such great players as Cobb, Speaker, Johnson, Collins and Cicotte. When baseball is revived again after the war, most of the present stars will be missing.

A year or two of idleness will render all of the old stars unfit for further greatness on the diamond. Military life or essential occupations will develop new muscles at the expense of the old ball-playing ones.

Robert L. Ripley, *Boston Globe*

We probably have watched for the last time

such great players as

Cobb, Speaker, Johnson, Collins and Cicotte.

End-of-the-Season Marks Final Passing
of Some of the Stars

ON THEIR WAY

Robert L. Ripley, *Boston Globe*

BOSTON, Mass., Aug. 31—[Special]—The Boston Red Sox of 1918 look
to be the weakest outfit that has represented the Hub in the American
League in the past ten years. The team never would have finished in
the first division but for the tremendous clouting ability of the versatile
Babe Ruth.

Paul Shannon, *Chicago Tribune*

Monday, September 2

IT'S A CASE OF "OVER THE TOP" FOR THE RED SOX NOW—

Scott, *Boston Post*

Johnny Evers to Teach Poilu Baseball

PARIS, Sept. 1—Johnny Evers has just returned from a French camp, where he gave the first lessons in baseball to French soldiers. Evers spent nine days giving the rudiments to a class just called to the colors. This included pitching, batting, and passing the ball around.

The young Frenchmen were barely escaping severe casualties because they could not learn to use their hands. Evers' assistant threw a grenade six meters farther than the best throw of the Alpine Chasseurs, which is why General Vidal favors baseball training.

Evers is having baseball rules translated into French, has laid out a diamond, and left enough equipment for three teams.

M. F. Murphy, *Chicago Tribune*

[A Poilu was a French soldier in World War I.]

Tuesday, September 3

Red Sox Finish by Dividing with Yanks

NEW YORK, Sept. 2—In the final games of the American League season, the Red Sox broke even with the Yankees, winning the first game 3 to 2, with Sam Jones pitching. The Red Sox have only won two games here this season.

To tune up the Sox for Tyler and Vaughn [the Cubs' star lefties], Manager Huggins used southpaw Slim Love and "Nemesis" George Mogridge. It was the sixth time Mogridge has beaten the Sox this season. [The Yankees won the second game, 4 to 3.]

Ruth and McInnis were slightly injured. The former was hit on the arm by Love in the first game, and Stuffy turned his ankle chasing a foul fly in the last inning of the second game.

Hooper and Scott did not miss playing in a league game all season.

• [First game: winning pitcher, Jones (16–5); losing pitcher, Love.
Second game: winning pitcher, Mogridge; losing pitcher, Dubuc (0–1).
Home runs: Whiteman (1), Baker (6).]

Edward F. Martin, *Boston Globe*

Babe Ruth dearly wished to finish over the .300 mark. His first time up he was hit by a pitched ball. Then he walked. But his third trip to the plate saw him get a scratch infield hit.

Burt Whitman, *Boston Herald and Journal*

[Ruth finished the 1918 season with a .300 batting average.]

Ty Cobb batted .600 his last day in baseball with six hits in 10 times at bat [in a doubleheader against Chicago].

Boston Globe

[Cobb concluded the 1918 season with a league-leading .382, thirty points higher than his nearest rival.]

FINAL AMERICAN LEAGUE STANDINGS

	Won	Lost	PCT.	GB
BOSTON	75	51	.595	—
Cleveland	73	54	.575	2.5
Washington	72	56	.563	4
New York	60	63	.488	13.5
St. Louis	58	64	.475	15
Chicago	57	67	.460	17
Detroit	55	71	.437	20
Philadelphia	52	76	.406	24

FINAL BATTING LEADERS

	AB	Hits	AVG
Cobb, Detroit	421	161	.382
Burns, Philadelphia	505	178	.352
Sisler, St. Louis	452	154	.341
Speaker, Cleveland	471	150	.318
Baker, N.Y.	504	154	.306
Pipp, N.Y.	349	106	.304
Weaver, Chicago	420	126	.300
RUTH, BOSTON	317	95	.300

HOME RUNS
RUTH, BOSTON 11
Walker, Philadelphia 11
Burns, Philadelphia 6
Baker, N.Y. 6

RUNS BATTED IN
Veach, Detroit 78
Burns, Philadelphia 70
RUTH, BOSTON 66
Wood, Cleveland 66

RUNS
Chapman, Cleveland 84
Cobb, Detroit 83
HOOPER, BOSTON 81
Bush, Detroit 74

STOLEN BASES
Sisler, St. Louis 45
Roth, Cleveland 35
Cobb, Detroit 34
Chapman, Cleveland 30

FINAL PITCHING LEADERS

	Won	Lost	Pct.
JONES, BOSTON 16		5	.762
RUTH, BOSTON 13		7	.650
Johnson, Washington . . 23		13	.639
Coveleski, Cleveland . . 22		13	.629
MAYS, BOSTON 21		13	.618

STRIKEOUTS
Johnson, Wash. 162
Shaw, Wash. 129
BUSH, BOSTON 125
Morton, Clev. 123
MAYS, BOSTON 114

EARNED RUN AVERAGE
Johnson, Wash. 1.27
Coveleski, Clev. 1.82
Sothoron, St. L. 1.94
Perry, Phil. 1.98
BUSH, BOSTON 2.11

SHUTOUTS
MAYS, BOSTON 8
Johnson, Wash. 8
BUSH, BOSTON 7
JONES, BOSTON 5

BOSTON RED SOX—FINAL HITTING STATISTICS

	AB	R	BH	2B	3B	HR	RBI	SB	AVG
Babe Ruth 317	50	95	26	11	11	66	6	.300
Harry Hooper 474	81	137	26	13	1	44	24	.289
Carl Mays 104	10	30	3	3	0	5	1	.288
Joe Bush 98	8	27	3	2	0	14	0	.276
Stuffy McInnis 423	40	115	11	5	0	56	10	.272
George Whiteman 214	24	57	14	0	1	28	9	.266
Dave Shean 425	58	112	16	3	0	34	11	.264
Amos Strunk 413	50	106	18	9	0	35	20	.257
Fred Thomas 144	19	37	2	1	1	11	4	.257
Wally Schang 225	36	55	7	1	0	20	4	.244
Everett Scott 443	40	98	11	5	0	43	11	.221
Sam Jones 57	6	10	1	0	0	1	0	.175
Sam Agnew 199	11	33	8	0	0	6	0	.166
Eusebio Gonzalez 5	2	2	0	1	0	0	0	.400
Frank Truesdale 36	6	10	1	0	0	2	1	.278
Hack Miller 29	2	8	2	0	0	4	0	.276
Wally Mayer 49	7	1	4	0	0	5	0	.224
Walter Barbare 29	2	5	3	0	0	2	1	.172
Jean Dubuc 6	0	1	0	0	0	0	0	.167
Dick Hoblitzell 69	4	11	1	0	0	4	3	.159
Jack Coffey 44	5	7	1	0	1	2	2	.159
Jack Stansbury 47	3	6	1	0	0	2	0	.128
George Cochran 63	8	8	0	0	0	3	3	.127
Heinie Wagner 8	0	1	0	0	0	0	0	.125
Lore Bader 9	2	1	0	0	0	0	0	.111

The Year the Red Sox Won the Series

FINAL PITCHING STATISTICS

	IP	BH	Won	Lost	BB	SO	ShO	ERA
Carl Mays	293	230	21	13	81	114	8	2.21
Sam Jones	184	151	16	5	70	44	5	2.25
Joe Bush	273	241	15	15	91	125	7	2.11
Babe Ruth	166	125	13	7	49	40	1	2.22
Dutch Leonard	126	119	8	6	53	47	3	2.71
Vince Molyneaux	11	3	1	0	8	1	0	3.27
Lore Bader	27	26	1	3	12	10	1	3.33
Dick McCabe	10	13	0	1	2	3	0	2.70
Jean Dubuc	11	11	0	1	5	1	0	4.09
Walt Kinney	15	5	0	0	8	4	0	1.80
Bill Pertica	3	3	0	0	0	1	0	3.00
Weldon Wyckoff	2	4	0	0	1	2	0	0.00

Part 4 The World Series

WHICH TEAM WILL WIN IT? IS THE BIG QUESTION—

Scott, *Boston Post*

World Series Starts Today

Cubs Fear Ruth

CHICAGO, Sept. 3—The mighty shadow of Babe Ruth falls athwart Chicago tonight like a menace. Take him out of the way and the Cubs would have enough confidence to do harsh things to the men from Massachusetts. But there he is, a huge, horrifying prospect for Mitchell [the Cubs' manager] and his men. He is the difference between defeat and victory.

Burt Whitman, *Boston Herald and Journal*

WHOOPLA! THE WORLD BASEBALL CHAMPIONSHIP FIREWORKS START TODAY.

Scott, *Boston Post*

Babe Pines for Action

Ruth absolutely lacks the nervousness which has hampered so many great pitchers on the eve of the title series. He says, "I'd pitch the whole series, every game, if they'd let me. Of course I can do it. Why, I used to pitch three games in one day when I was at school. I pitched a 13 inning game one Saturday with Baltimore [in the minors] and then pitched a double-header the next day, with the second game another 13 inning one."

Burt Whitman, *Boston Herald and Journal*

The Red Sox have been torpedoed amidships on the eve of the first battle with the Chicago Cubs in the 1918 baseball classic. The crash came in the short practice session of the Red Sox yesterday at Comiskey Park. Dave Shean split the middle finger of his throwing hand and this morning was wearing the digit in a splint.

An injury to Shean at this time would prove fatal beyond the shadow of a doubt. He is the pivot of the Sox infield and has been the brains of the defence.

Boston Record

Bullet Joe Bush, Carl Mays and Sam Agnew, who constituted the Sherlock Holmes committee that looked over the Cubs at Philadelphia on the holiday [Labor Day], arrived in advance, not too greatly impressed by what they saw.

The only possible [Cubs] pitcher they are a bit wary of is George Tyler. They admit they can hit him, but not easily. As for the rest, they don't seem to care the well-known tinker's, whatever that is.

Boston American

Babe Ruth Is a Better Southpaw Than Vaughn or Tyler

Manager Barrow: "We have the steadier team, the one which is more experienced in a world series. Man for man we excel the Cubs in the majority of positions. Our pitching staff is better balanced and Ruth is a better southpaw than either Vaughn or Tyler. We are absolutely confident of the outcome."

Manager Mitchell: "We will outhit the Sox and outfight them. We will be able to hit their pitchers, and I believe that Vaughn and Tyler, who will do most of our pitching, will be able to stop Ruth's batting. The Sox are a one-man team, and his name is Ruth. But we have studied his ways and his mental processes so much this season that we will spike his guns."

Babe Ruth: "I hope I don't have to sit on the bench a single inning of the series."

Boston Herald and Journal

The Sox are a one-man team, and his name is Ruth.

The Year the Red Sox Won the Series

Seaman Fred Thomas joined the Red Sox at the Hotel Metropolis late this afternoon. He was in the regalia of our fighting seamen, and today starts a 10 day furlough. He will play third base tomorrow, bolstering up one of the weak spots in Manager Barrow's fighting front.

Burt Whitman, *Boston Herald and Journal*

This will be the fifth world's series for Fred Merkle [the Cubs' first baseman], who played with the Giants in title games in 1911, 1912, 1913 and in 1916 with Brooklyn.

Arthur Duffey, *Boston Post*

[Although he was a fine fielder and batted .297 in 1918, Merkle will always be remembered for pulling the bonehead play that cost the New York Giants the pennant in 1908.

In a key game against the Cubs during the 1908 pennant race, Merkle ran from first base to the center field clubhouse, without touching second, while the winning run crossed home plate. As the fans mobbed the field, Johnny Evers, the Cubs' second baseman, retrieved a ball and touched second for the force out. The umpires were brought back from their clubhouse to make the out call on Merkle, nullifying the run and ending the game in a tie. The Cubs eventually beat the Giants in a makeup contest on the last day of the season to win the 1908 pennant by one game.

Fred went on to amass 1,580 hits and a lifetime batting average of .273 during his sixteen-year career. Nevertheless, he was haunted by that awful mistake the rest of his life.]

PLAYERS	CUBS		RED SOX	
Catchers	Killefer	.233	Schang	.244
			Agnew	.166
Pitchers	Vaughn	22–10	Mays	21–13
	Hendrix	20–7	Jones	16–5
	Tyler	19–8	Bush	15–15
	Douglas	10–9	Ruth	13–7
1st Base	Merkle	.297	McInnis	.272
2nd Base	Pick	.326	Shean	.264
	Zeider	.223		
3rd Base	Deal	.239	Thomas	.257
Shortstop	Hollocher	.316	Scott	.221
Outfielders	Mann	.288	Ruth	.300
	Paskert	.286	Hooper	.289
	Flack	.257	Whiteman	.266
	Barber	.236	Strunk	.257
Club Batting		.265	. . . .	.249
Stolen Bases		159	. . . .	110
Home Runs		21	. . . .	15
Club Fielding		.967	. . . .	.966

Boston Herald and Journal

World Series Information

A is for Agnew; his mates call him Sam.
   He catches for Boston, if you care a d--n.

B is for Bush; he is called Bullet Joe.
   The reason for which is a thing I don't know.

C is for Coffey, of Boston's fine team.
   I like lots of sugar, but not so much cream.

D is for Dode, as George Paskert is known.
   I play better golf when I play all alone.

E is for Everett Scott of the Sox.
   And after two rounds I can eat like an ox.

F is for Flack and his first name is Max.
   I always get called when I bet on two jacks.

G is for George; he's a Pullman car porter.
   Some athletes say: "George, have you change for
   a quarter?"

H is for Hollocher, Hendrix, and Hooper.
   You'll see them all play if you're not in a stupor.

I is for Irving E. Sanborn and I.
   I hail him as fly, but I never knew why.

J is for James Crusinberry; some name.
   He drives with a clunk, but gets there just the same.

K is for Killefer, native of Mich.
   When it isn't baseballs he is catching, it's fish.

L is for Leslie, whose last name is Mann.
   When the bases are full don't you hope he won't fan?

M is for Manager Mitchell, or Mitch.
    He looks at his pitchers and tells which'll pitch.

N is for nothing, which we have to pay
    To see the first game of the series today.

O is for Otto Knabe, whose job
    Is to make all Cub baserunners think they are Cobb.

P is for Pick, who is awfully quick,
    And slick with the stick when he doesn't feel sick.

Q is for quarter, which I want to bet.
    But do not know how I will bet it just yet.

R is for Red Sox and also for Ruth.
    I play better golf when I don't tell the truth.

S is for Schang and for Shean and Strunk.
    A Swiss S, however, is just for a drunk.

T is for Tyler, left handed but sane.
    Those birds who shoot ninety give me a pain.

U is for umpires; in other words, Umps.
    They're almost as funny sometimes as the Gumps.

V is for Vaughn, known as Hippo and Jim.
    I believe I shall risk my whole quarter on him.

W's for Wertman and Whiteman, both subs,
    and most of the birds who own stock in the Cubs.

X is for Xperts; their number is legion.
    Jack Lait is undoubtedly best in this region.

Y is for you, and I don't know your name,
    But I'll wear a carnation and you do the same.

Z is for Zeider from down Indiana.
    Stand up when the band plays the S. S. B.

Chicago Tribune

Good Weather Promised

A cloudless sky, with a bracing wind sweeping out of the northeast, is the weather forecast for the opening game.

Paul H. Shannon, *Boston Post*

[Out-of-town fans followed the World Series in theaters and arenas by watching simulations appearing on large boards. The running account of each game was provided via Western Union telegraph messsages.]

Thursday, September 5

OLD JUPE PLUVIUS WAS ON THE JOB AT CHICAGO YESTERDAY.

Scott, *Boston Post*

The weather bureau was crossed by the storm which blew into Chicago yesterday morning. It spilled so much water on the south side ball park that the impending battle was called off before 11 o'clock.

I. E. Sanborn, *Chicago Tribune*

Pastiming on Rainy Days

While it was a long day, it was by no means a dreary one for the Red Sox. This is especially so in the case of Samuel Jones, who collected $44 and expressed the hope it will rain some more tomorrow. For a fellow who only broke into the poker league in 1916, Sam is showing everything.

Edward F. Martin, *Boston Globe*

"It only postpones the killing for another day," chirped Babe Ruth yesterday, when he learned that the first game had been put over.

Boston Record

War Is Biggest World's Series Just Now

Scott, *Boston Post*

Boston Wins First World Series Game

Babe Ruth Pilots Red Sox to 1–0 Victory over Chicago Cubs

CHICAGO, Sept. 5—Not the blasting big black bat of Babe Ruth, but his potent left arm quelled the Chicago Cubs, 1 to 0, in the opening game of the war-time World Series at Comiskey Park. Twice the colossus fell down on strikes at the bat, but his fiery southpaw service, fast ball and curve alike, proved more than enough to smash the haughty champions of the National League.

Search through the big book of history of world series games and you will never find the yarn of such a contest. It was a battle of mighty flingers, both left-handers, both proven demi-gods of the hill, huge and powerful beyond the average of the diamond.

The Cubs outwacked the American League champions, six hits to five. But this means little, since Ruth was potent in the pinches when the Cub threatened to become a bear.

The only run of the contest came in the fourth inning. Shean walked, Strunk popped up in a futile attempt to sacrifice, and Arlington Dave scored on successive base hits by George Whiteman and John Stuffy McInnis.

[Winning pitcher, Ruth (1–0); losing pitcher, Vaughn (0–1). Boston leads the series 1–0.]

Burt Whitman, *Boston Herald and Journal*

1ST INNING. 2 OUT, BASES FILLED WITH CUBS-WHITEMAN CAUGHT PICK'S FLY FOR THE 3RD OUT-

"BEANED"

Scott, *Boston Post*

Caging the Cubs!

First Game

BOSTON	AB	R	BH	PO	A	CHICAGO	AB	R	BH	PO	A
Hooper, rf	4	0	1	4	0	Flack, rf	3	0	1	2	0
Shean, 2b	2	1	1	0	3	Hollocher, ss	3	0	0	2	1
Strunk, cf	3	0	0	2	0	Mann, lf	4	0	1	0	0
Whiteman, lf	4	0	2	5	0	Paskert, cf	4	0	2	2	0
McInnis, 1b	2	0	1	10	0	Merkle, 1b	3	0	1	9	2
Scott, ss	4	0	0	0	3	Pick, 2b	3	0	0	1	1
Thomas, 3b	3	0	0	1	1	Deal, 3b	4	0	1	1	3
Agnew, c	3	0	0	5	0	Killefer, c	4	0	0	7	2
Ruth, p	3	0	0	0	1	Vaughn, p	3	0	0	3	5
						*O'Farrell	1	0	0	0	0
	—	—	—	—	—		—	—	—	—	—
Totals	28	1	5	27	8	Totals	32	0	6	27	14

Boston	0	0	0	1	0	0	0	0	0	-	1
Chicago	0	0	0	0	0	0	0	0	0	-	0

Errors—none. Sacrifice Hits—McInnis, Hollocher, Strunk. Left on bases—Boston 5, Chicago 8. First base on balls—Off Ruth 1, off Vaughn 3. Hit by pitcher—By Ruth (Flack). Struck out—By Ruth 4, by Vaughn 6. Time—1:50.

[Run batted in—McInnis.]

*Batted for Pick in the 9th.

Boston Herald and Journal

Big Jim Vaughn's best is his fast one. His curve ball is more or less dinky. You can see it coming and handle it fairly well. But his buzzer, the speedball, is a mighty breeze and is difficult to hit.

Burt Whitman, *Boston Herald and Journal*

Cannot Fool Dave

Shean drew two passes during the afternoon. The important one was in the fourth. Vaughn tried hard to get Dave by pitching on the inside, but the Arlington lad just looked them over with that calm, gentlemanly, reproving way of his.

Amos Strunk, left-handed batter and very fast in getting down to first base, was told to bunt. He dropped his bat a little too far and the ball popped innocently to Jim Vaughn. It was only alert, heads-up base running by Shean that prevented a double play.

Georgie Whiteman, grizzled veteran of many big and little league campaigns, who was playing ball for money before Freddie Thomas got pennies for running errands for ma and the woman upstairs, already had hit one clean single to centre field. With the count 2 and 1, Whitey hit a curve ball, one of those dinky things, to centre field. Dode Paskert played the ball rapidly and held Shean to second.

Then McInnis called the turn. A high fast one whizzed by and ump-in-chief Hank O'Day called it a ball. Stuffy was not looking for a pass, but for the old base blow.

Sure enough, he got that same dinky curve ball and was ready for it. He slammed it to left field and Shean, who did not wait to see if the ball might be caught, started a mad dash for the plate and made it ahead of Les Mann's frenzied throw.

Burt Whitman, *Boston Herald and Journal*

[Dave Shean's injured hand didn't prevent him from scoring the winning run.]

Babe Ruth, Red Sox pitcher

On his first trip to the plate Babe soaked the apple to center, Paskert getting under it after flopping around the pasture for a while. The next two times that the Oriole boy faced Hippo he fanned and looked stupid, as he was missing bad balls. The fans applauded him every time he stepped to the plate. He was a picture even when he was striking out, but the kind of picture that no Boston artist would seek to paint.

Edward F. Martin, *Boston Globe*

Ruth had bewildering speed, a great curve and was as cool as a radiator in an apartment house. He worked the batters perfectly, and, on the three occasions when a hit meant a run, turned back the hostiles with consummate ease.

Nick Flatley, *Boston American*

Mrs. Ruth Hears Returns

Mrs. Ruth, wife of the Red Sox star, was in a good-sized crowd who followed the progress of the game in Chicago yesterday on the special board at the Boston Arena. She was one of the most enthusiastic fans as Babe covered himself with glory.

Boston Globe

Five hits for the Browns, three for the Macks and six for the Cubs has been the allowance of Babe Ruth against his last three opponents. His winning scores were 3–1, 6–1 and 1–0. Two runs and 14 hits in 29 innings pitched is pretty fine work.

Boston Globe

"It was anybody's ball game all the way. They got their hits at the right time and we didn't. The base on balls to Shean at the start of the fourth beat us. Pick almost sent us off in front in the first when he hit that one with the bases filled. It was a corking drive but right straight into Whiteman's hands. It was tough on Vaughn to pitch a game like that and lose because his mates couldn't get a run."

Fred Mitchell, the Cubs' manager, quoted in the *Chicago Tribune*

Great Drop in World Series Attendance

CHICAGO, Sept. 5—War made its hand felt in the first game of the World's Series.

The attendance today of 19,274 was nearly 13,000 less than the crowd which jammed Comiskey Park for the initial contest between the Giants and White Sox a year ago.

The receipts—$30,348—were less than half the amount taken in for the first game a year ago, as the prices this year were reduced, the choice box seats selling for $3 as compared with $5 in 1917.

Boston Post

Vacant Seats and Lack of Cheers Show War's Effects

CHICAGO, Sept. 5—One of the smallest crowds which ever turned out for a World's Series opening saw today's game.

The effect of the war was everywhere, especially in the temper of the crowd. There was no cheering during the contest, nor was there anything like the usual umpire baiting.

War taxes, the high cost of living, the curtailed season and the shadow of the war accounts for the indifference of the public. The dyed-in-the-wool fans were there, but not the general public.

Boston Globe

Before the contest started a big floral horseshoe, as well as a bundle of roses, was presented to Manager Mitchell at the home plate.

James Crusinberry, *Chicago Tribune*

The left field bleacher space, usually given over to the virtues of a certain chewing gum [Wrigley's], admonished the crowd to "Keep the Glow in Old Glory," and the right field space commanded "Buy War Savings Stamps, and Do It Now."

Boston Globe

At one time there were six [army] planes over the field. Occasionally one of them would do a nose dive or a tail spin just to let us know they were ready for a flight to Berlin.

James Crusinberry, Chicago Tribune

Ticket Lost by Young Fan, but He Sees Game

All summer long three youngsters saved nickels and pennies and denied themselves many a luxury, until they accumulated enough coins to pay for one ticket [apiece] to the World's Series games. One of them, Harry Fox, was delegated to purchase the prize.

Harry went to the Cub park on Monday to obtain the tickets. On the "L" train going home, the tickets disappeared and there were three desolate homes in Chicago that night. But Harry reported the loss [to the Cubs].

A couple of detectives volunteered on behalf of the three kids yesterday. They watched the seat until an adult man was ushered to it, then tapped him on the shoulder and asked him to explain how he obtained the ticket. He convinced the detectives that he purchased it innocently off an "L" guard, and was released under promise to produce the guard today.

Meantime, Harry Fox saw yesterday's game from the coveted seat and his two pals will see the other two games of the series.

Chicago Tribune

The great moment of the first World's Series game came during the seventh inning stretch. As the crowd of 19,274 stood up to take the afternoon yawn the band broke forth to the strains of the Star Spangled Banner.

The yawn was checked and heads were bared as the ball players turned quickly about and faced the music. First the song was taken up by a few, then others joined, and when the final notes came, a great volume of melody rolled across the field. It was at the very end that the onlookers exploded into thunderous applause and rent the air with a cheer.

New York Times

[This performance was repeated during every game of the 1918 World Series. "The Star-Spangled Banner" became an integral part of baseball, although it didn't officially become the national anthem until 1931.]

Saturday, September 7

Chicago Wins Second Game of Series, 3–1
George Tyler Outpitches Joe Bush
Tyler's Bat Knocks in Brace of Runs

CHICAGO, Sept. 6—It took the wide, sweeping, swishing, left-handed curve ball of George [Lefty] Tyler; it took more than a few adverse breaks, and it took a big inning to give the Cubs a 3 to 1 victory over the Red Sox at the South Side Park this afternoon.

Tonight all Chicago rocks with World Series fervor, for the series is now a 50–50 proposition, each team mightily serene and confident in its ultimate success.

- [Winning pitcher, Tyler (1–0); losing pitcher, Bush (0–1). Boston and Chicago were tied at one game apiece.]

Burt Whitman, Boston Herald and Journal

[Lefty Tyler had his greatest season in 1918, with 19 wins and 8 losses, 8 shutouts, and a 2.01 earned run average. But this was Lefty's last big year. The twenty-eight-year-old Tyler retired three years later, with a lifetime record of 127 victories against 118 losses.]

The Boston men bubbled with good nature as they went through their practice stunts, jigging when the band played rag time, jostling their opponents and showing their confidence to repeat yesterday's victory.

Boston Post

Cubs Win Game in Second Inning

The perverse little devils of the diamond mocked the Bostonians in the second. Bush made the fatal mistake of working carefully to Fred Merkle, a very dangerous batter. Joe got Merkle to three and two and walked him.

Then followed the crash of luck. Pick sent a hopper down in the general direction of third base. The ball would have been a putout if it had not taken a funny little skip just as Fred Thomas of the Navy, rushing in fast, stooped down to field it. The ball rolled beyond third base and went as a base hit, Merkle stopping at second.

Lefty Tyler, Chicago Cubs pitcher

AND THE CHICAGO CUBS ROMPED THROUGH THE 2ND GAME WITH A 3 TO 1 WIN-

Scott, Boston Post

Chuck Deal, next batter, is a fair bunter, but Bush pitched high and fast and not too close. Chuck twice fouled and with two strikes could not chance a sacrificial push. So he swung and Shean caught his easy pop.

Bill Killefer swung at the very first pitch and sent it careering to the far right field territory, just inside the foul line, for two bases, Merkle scoring and Charley Pick holding up at third base.

One run over and men on second and third, with the pitcher up. Tyler took one strike and then, just as if Bush underrated the Cub flinger, a perfect fast one came right through the groove. The Red Sox infield was drawn in close and the ball bounded by Bush into centre, Pick and Killefer scoring. [Tyler's hit provided the winning margin.]

Burt Whitman, *Boston Herald and Journal*

Wagner and Knabe Enliven Game by Coming to Blows

CHICAGO, Sept. 7—Those three tallies in the second inning roused the ire of Coach Heinie Wagner of the Boston troupe. He and Otto Knabe, official barker of the Cubs, had been squawking at each other since the start of the gentle pastime.

At the close of the second round Knabe invited Wagner under the stands. Wagner not only went, he grabbed Otto by the arm and dragged him along through the dugout.

A guy might as well try to wrestle a depth bomb. The chunky Knabe upset Wagner and mopped up considerable dirt with the broad back of the Boston coach. Cub reserves dragged the scrappers apart, just as four or five Red Sox dashed across No Man's Land to the rescue.

The umpires paid no attention to the fracas. Let the boys fight. This is what they've got to do, or work, as soon as the series ends.

Charley Dryden, *Boston American*

Red Sox Make a Stand in the Ninth

In the ninth [with the Red Sox down 3 to 0] Strunk hit a Tyler fast pitch to the far right field corner, away over Flack's head, Amos going into third standing up. Whiteman had a strike to his discredit when he tripled noisily to right centre field to make the score 3 to 1.

The Sox played for the big inning and a sensational victory. Stuffy blazed away at the ball, abhorring the sacrifice, and was tossed out by Tyler, Whiteman being held at third base. Scottie then demonstrated his courage under fire. He had two strikes and a ball to his count, but looked them over, fouled off a few good ones and finally drew a base on balls.

Barrow yanked the weak-hitting Thomas [zero for five in the Series] and inserted a pinch-hitter. Some of the crowd thought this was a made-to-order place for Babe Ruth to bust matters wide apart, even against a southpaw curveballist like Tyler. But Barrow thought differently. He inserted Jean Dubuc [a reserve pitcher] who has always been a good batter against left-hand pitching.

Tyler was putting everything in the world on that old apple and Dubuc seemed a trifle overanxious to hit. Jean fouled the first one, took a ball, had a strike called, and then fouled four times, eventually swinging and missing a low outside slow ball for the second out.

Schang was the last resort. Wallie lined the first pitch and the ball soared high and kerplunked into the eager hands of Charley Hollocher [the Cubs' shortstop], who hot-footed it for his dugout.

Burt Whitman, *Boston Herald and Journal*

Jean Dubuc Goes In as Pinch Hitter with Babe Ruth on the Bench

Sending Jean Dubuc or any other hitter to bat with such a tremendous swatter as Babe Ruth kicking around on the bench is criminal. It was Ed Barrow's hunch and it flivvered.

Yesterday the stage was all set for Babe. Tyler was going badly [in the ninth] and things looked dark for the Cubs. But instead of dispatching Ruth to connect with the needed wallop, Barrow sends Dubuc up in the pinch, a batter almost unheard of, and he gracefully whiffs while the anvil chorus in unison lays on Barrow.

Eddie Hurley, *Boston Record*

[A career .230 hitter, Dubuc had one base hit in 1918.]

World's Series Receipts

For the second game last year, which was also played at Comiskey Park, the attendance was 32,000 and the receipts were $73,152.

Chicago Tribune

[The attendance for Game 2 in 1918 was only 20,040, and the total receipts were $29,997.]

The umpires paid no attention to the fracas.

Let the boys fight. This is what they've got to do,

or work, as soon as the series ends.

Putting the Big Series Back on an Even Keel
Second Game

BOSTON	AB	R	BH	PO	A	CHICAGO	AB	R	BH	PO	A
Hooper, rf	3	0	1	1	0	Flack, rf	4	0	2	4	1
Shean, 2b	4	0	1	5	2	Hollocher, ss	4	0	1	5	4
Strunk, cf	4	1	1	1	2	Mann, lf	4	0	0	0	0
Whiteman, lf	3	0	1	3	0	Paskert, cf	4	0	0	2	0
McInnis, 1b	4	0	1	7	0	Merkle, 1b	2	1	1	6	1
Scott, ss	3	0	0	3	2	Pick, 2b	2	1	1	4	4
Thomas, 3b	2	0	0	1	1	Deal, 3b	2	0	0	1	1
Agnew, c	2	0	0	2	4	Killefer, c	2	1	1	4	2
Schang, c	2	0	1	1	0	Tyler, p	3	0	1	1	2
Bush, p	2	0	0	0	0						
*Dubuc	1	0	0	0	1						
	30	1	6	24	14		27	3	7	27	15

	1	2	3	4	5	6	7	8	9	R	
Boston	0	0	0	0	0	0	0	0	1	-	1
Chicago	0	3	0	0	0	0	0	0	x	-	3

Two-base hit—Killefer. Three-base hits—Hollocher, Strunk, Whiteman. Sacrifice hits—Scott, Deal. Double plays—Killefer to Hollocher; Hollocher to Pick to Merkle. Left on bases—Boston 7, Chicago 4. First base on errors—Chicago 1, Boston 1. First base on balls—off Tyler 4, off Bush 3. Struck out—By Tyler 2. Umpires—Hildebrand at plate, Klem at first, Owens at second, O'Day at third. Time—1 h. 59 m.

[Runs batted in—Killefer, Tyler 2, Whiteman.]

*Batted for Bush in 9th

Boston Herald and Journal

Old Sam Agnew had his throwing wing in fine shape. He chucked out Hollocher, Flack and Pick during the early innings.

Boston Record

Manager Mitchell of the Cubs is now cocksure of victory. The only bird he fears on the Boston team is Babe Ruth.

"When Tyler slipped a bit [in the ninth] I was thinking of changing, but I couldn't. I had to go through with a left hander. A right hander would have had Ruth coming up to hit, and if he got hold of one, good night.

"He is a wonderful natural ball player, and nobody I've ever seen takes the cut at a ball he does. He is liable to knock any kind of a pitch anywhere."

Nick Flatley, *Boston American*

Rival Managers Both Claim They Will Win Today

Ed Barrow

"Today's game was a tough one, especially as we nearly broke it up in the ninth inning," Barrow said. "The Cubs had the better of the breaks, I think, and piled up a lead in the second inning too great for us to overcome. I do not mean to take credit away from Tyler, who pitched great ball and deserved to win. I expect to start Mays tomorrow and hope to make it two and one."

Fred Mitchell

"The task of the Cubs is now easier," said Manager Mitchell of the Chicago club. "We are on even terms with Boston. The Cubs certainly recovered their batting eye and they are confident of retaining it. Tyler pitched a wonderful game and never was in danger except in the ninth, when he grooved them over for Strunk and Whiteman. Those two triples saved Boston from a shutout. I expect to send Hendrix against the Red Sox tomorrow."

Boston Record

World's Series Pickups

Everett Scott met two kids with schoolbooks peeking through a hole in the fence before the battle and paid their way in. Scotty often does things like that. The deacon is some fellow.

Boston Globe

Looking 'Em Over

Rollie Zeider of the Cubs claims he has the only sunfield beak ever seen on a ball field. Rollie at one time was known as Bunions, but the last few seasons he has been called Hook Zeider.

"It all goes to show the wisdom of Providence," says Rollie. "Some folks might think that a nose like mine is a misfortune, but the fact is that it has made me the greatest sunfielder in baseball. All I have to do is turn my head either way, shade one eye with the beak, and catch any fly that was hit."

Harry J. Casey, *Boston Record*

[The thirty-five-year-old veteran infielder was in his last year as a ballplayer, with a weak .223 season in 1918.]

There is plenty of grumbling on the part of the players about the splitting of the series cash. The athletes' money will be passed out individually by the illustrious Commish.

Every eligible player will get an equal share. Thus Pick, who has been a short month with the Cubs, will be paid as well as Hollocher, who didn't miss a game all season.

Pertica [who pitched three innings for the Red Sox during the regular season] is awarded what Babe Ruth, Harry Hooper, et al. collect.

Nick Flatley, *Boston American*

Red Sox Win 3rd Game, 2 to 1

Mays Pins a Defeat on Hippo

CHICAGO, Sept. 7—The vane of world series success swung gloriously back to the champion Red Sox today. They beat the Cubs, 2 to 1, and went away from here with two victories in the old suitcase. They gave James Vaughn one more trimming, though the huge southpaw flung another dandy game of baseball.

The victors collected seven safeties off Hippo Jim and four of the thumps came in the crucial fourth. Apart from that session, he held the A.L. swatters at his mercy.

Blond Carl Mays underhanded his way to triumph and, though in trouble several times, always had the hostiles in control. Mays had one bad inning, the fifth, when a scratchy double and a regular single manufactured the lone Cub tally. He was hit hard enough at other times, but brilliant support pulled him through.

Stuffy McInnis, Wally Schang and Everett Scott were the hitting heroes of the fourth frame batting barrage. After Whiteman was slammed in the ribs with a seagoing curve, Stuffy and Wally made classy wallops, and Scotty perpetrated a perfect squeeze bunt for the victory.

[Winning pitcher, Mays (1–0); losing pitcher, Vaughn (0–2). Boston leads the World Series, two games to one.]

Nick Flatley, *Boston American*

Pick's Desperate Dash Is Futile

Nip and tuck it was all the way, but the grand climax came in the last of the ninth. Two men were out, the Sox had that thin lead of one run, but Pick [the Cubs' second baseman] was on second base, the result of a scratch hit and a steal of second. Mitchell, the gambler, inserted Turner Barber, left hander, to stick for Chuck Deal.

Two strikes and two balls was the count. Then Mays put all his stuff on the next pitch. It was a mite wild and bounced out of the glove of catcher Wallie Schang, a short passed ball. Like the flash of an idea, Charley Pick hot-footed it for third.

Schang moved rapidly and recovered the ball in a twinkling. He plugged the ball to Freddie Thomas, covering third. For a moment it seemed that the throw had retired Pick, but Hildebrand, umpiring at the hot corner, changed his half-made "out" motion and said "safe," just as Pick went into the bag with his body.

Thomas lost the ball and it rolled a mite toward the Cubs' dugout. Instead of getting the ball as quickly as possible, Freddie started to expostulate to Hildebrand, claiming that Pick had intentionally knocked the ball out of his hand.

Quick-on-the-trigger, Mitch [coaching at third] seized the opportunity and waved to Pick to make the dash for the plate. But like a flash, Thomas was over on the errant ball, picked it up and made an unerring, rapid-fire peg to Wally Schang, just in time for that sturdy and positive gent to clamp it madly and soundly into Pick's short ribs for the final put-out.

Bill Klem, the National League umpire behind the plate, gave that sweeping motion of his with the enthusiasm of an Arabian dervish, betoking that Pick had been retired.

A huge groan of disappointment went up from the throng. Pick, Mitch, Rowdy Otto and the other Cubs, disconsolate, trudged to their cave and out of sight.

It was a game of ball, sprinkled with such brilliant plays, that never will be forgotten by those 27,014 who saw it.

Burt Whitman, Boston Herald and Journal

Jim Vaughn Blames Himself for Defeat

The big hurler was peeved and disgusted with himself. "It was my fault. They gave me one run and that should have been enough to win for us.

"Do you remember that one that McInnis hit in that bad inning?" Vaughn asked. [The Red Sox were batting in the top of the fourth in a scoreless tie.] "Well, that was supposed to be a beanball. I got the first two pitches past McInnis for strikes. I wanted to drive him back from the plate, so I intended to shoot the next one close to his bean. My control was bad, and I got it almost over the plate, just where he likes 'em, and he hit it to left field. [McInnis's single sent a base runner to third and kept the rally alive.]

"Schang's hit followed [to drive in the first run of the game], but it might not have done any damage if I had got McInnis out of the way. I think that one pitched ball beat me. If I hadn't messed my aim on that one, they never would have scored, and the one run the boys got for me would have been enough."

Chicago Tribune

One-Run Victories over Vaughn a Sox Specialty

Third Game

BOSTON	AB	R	BH	PO	A		CHICAGO	AB	R	BH	PO	A
Hooper, rf	3	0	1	3	0		Flack, rf	3	0	0	3	1
Shean, 2b	4	0	0	1	2		Hollocher, ss	3	0	0	1	3
Strunk, cf	4	0	0	1	0		Mann, lf	4	0	2	1	0
Whiteman, lf	3	1	1	3	0		Paskert, cf	4	0	1	1	0
McInnis, 1b	4	1	1	12	0		Merkle, 1b	4	0	0	9	2
Schang, c	4	0	2	6	3		Pick, 2b	4	1	2	0	0
Scott, ss	4	0	1	1	5		Deal, 3b	3	0	1	1	1
Thomas, 3b	3	0	1	0	2		Killefer, c	3	0	1	8	0
Mays, p	3	0	0	0	2		Vaughn, p	3	0	0	3	3
							*Barber, ph	0	0	0	0	0
	32	2	7	27	14			31	1	7	27	10

	1	2	3	4	5	6	7	8	9	R
Boston	0	0	0	2	0	0	0	0	0	- 2
Chicago	0	0	0	0	1	0	0	0	0	- 1

Error—Hollocher. Two-base hits—Mann, Pick. Stolen bases—Whiteman, Schang, Pick. Sacrifice hit—Hollocher. Double plays—Hollocher to Merkle; Vaughn to Merkle. Left on base—Boston 5, Chicago 5. Base on balls—Off Mays 1, off Vaughn 1. Hit by pitcher—By Vaughn (Whiteman). Struck out—By Mays 4, by Vaughn 7. Passed ball—Schang. Time—1h. 57 m. Umpires—Klem at plate, Owens at first, O'Day at second, Hildebrand at third.

[Runs batted in—Schang, Scott, Killefer.]

*Batted for Deal in 9th inning.

Boston Herald and Journal

Vaughn is out of luck. He had pitched two really great games [with only one day of rest], holding the opposition to three runs. But his associates have only managed to make one miserable run for him.

Nick Flatley, *Boston American*

[A five-time twenty-game winner, Vaughn was best known for being the losing pitcher in the only double no-hit game in the history of baseball. On May 17, 1917, he was beaten by Fred Toney of Cincinnati, 1 to 0, when he gave up the game's only two hits in the tenth inning.]

Strafing Hippo Vaughn's Swift Slants

One of the big airplanes from the war exposition came down within 100 feet of the top of the grandstand in the sixth and received a tremendous ovation.

Boston Herald and Journal

It was a rather punk afternoon for G. Babe Ruth. Orders to intern him are always given now when a southpaw goes to the hill. Babe is apt to go stale.

Edward F. Martin, *Boston Globe*

[Babe batted only three times in the first three games and had yet to play in the outfield.]

Breaks of Contest against Cub Team

"It was another tough game to lose. We had no luck and no good breaks. All we needed was a little bit to win that one, for it was anybody's ball game clear up to the finish.

"I thought Vaughn would beat them sure," Mitchell said, "but it seems we can't get any runs for him. Of course, we'll have to go some now to win the series, but it is not over, by any means."

Manager Mitchell of the Cubs, quoted in the *Chicago Tribune*

There was a goodly sprinkling of uniforms in the crowd. Numerous sailors and soldiers from nearby training camps devoted their week-end furloughs to watch the last major league baseball in this city until after the war.

Chicago Tribune

While waiting for the show to commence, a flock of dipper girls made the rounds with little baskets collecting for the tobacco fund, to keep our boys in smokes over there.

Charles Dryden, *Boston American*

Pasteboard "Grifters" Got in Their Licks

Ticket scalpers reaped a harvest today for the first time during the series. The reserved seats were snapped up before noon, and when the crowd stormed the park half an hour before the game, the scalpers got as high as $5 for a ticket costing $1.50.

Boston Post

[A series high of 27,054 attended the third game in Chicago.]

Fourteen Years to Glory

The time has arrived to switch a bunch of the limelight on Mr. George Whiteman, the man who had to wait 14 years [in the minors] to show that he had something. In this series he has been one of the big acts.

His catch in the fourth today saved Mays a stack of trouble. Mann had doubled with one out, the first hit of the struggle off Carl. Merkle hit the pill on the seam to left field, but Whitey raced back with the ball, turning, backing against the bleachers and copping it. It was a sweet catch, for the ball stood a fine chance of bounding into the bleachers for a circuit knock. [Balls that bounced over the fence were ruled home runs in 1918.]

Whiteman has been an active bird in the Chicago games. He has accepted 11 out of 12 chances in the left sector; has batted .400, getting four hits, one a triple, in 10 times up; stole the first base of the series; has knocked in a run, drawn a pass and been hit once. There is not a ball player on the Sox fighting harder or showing more gameness and confidence than the Texas hunter.

Edward F. Martin, Boston Globe

CHICAGO, Sept. 7—"When I said that the Red Sox were determined to return to Boston with a two-to-one edge in the series, I was not boasting," said Manager Barrow of the Red Sox tonight.

"We are in the lead and intend to remain there. I think we shall win the series, because we have the better club. I am not ready to say who shall pitch Monday, but it is not unlikely that Ruth will be sent to the mound."

Boston American

Killefer, Betting 10-Cent Cigar on Cubs, Wins $1,000

CHICAGO, Sept. 7—A bet of a 10-cent cigar against $1,000, made as the result of a joke while Chicago was training at Pasadena, Calif., last spring, has been won by catcher Bill Killefer, it was revealed today.

The loser, William Wrigley, one of the Cub stockholders, wagered the $1,000 that the team would not win the National League pennant. Killefer, who accepted the bet in jest, had forgotten about the bet until he was reminded about it by Mr. Wrigley. The sum will be added to Killefer's World's Series share.

Boston Globe

[William Wrigley would buy the Chicago Cubs in 1921 and own them for sixty-five years. Wrigley Field was named after him.]

Commission after Wagner and Knabe

CHICAGO, Sept. 7—The great strategists and wrestlers, Heinie Wagner and Otto Knabe, have come under the frown of the well-known National Commission, the supreme board of baseball.

Heinie and Otto have been ordered by the commish to produce statements in writing not later than Monday morning, explaining the why and the wherefores of their little bout under the grandstand.

Stuffy McInnis was fined $35 by the commission for protesting too much yesterday when Flack was declared safe at first on a close one.

Boston American

World Series Rivals on Their Way Here

CHICAGO, Sept. 7—Smiles wreathed the faces of the victorious Red Sox when they boarded the trains tonight for Boston to engage the Cubs in the fourth game of the series Monday.

The war has eliminated the specials this season. Instead, additional cars were attached to a regular Michigan Central train. The Boston players and Harry Frazee's party occupied two cars, the Chicago club one, the newspaper writers another, and members of the National Baseball Commission and their friends the fifth car.

The players occupied upper and lower berths and no more space was reserved than was absolutely neccessary in order to comply with government orders restricting travel.

Boston Post

Essential!

Ring Lardner Gathers News at Ball Game to Convince Draft Board He's Working

Friend Harvey:

Well, Harvey, this is my swan song for a couple weeks and I know its a bad time to take a vacation because when the draft board says where do you work and I tell them, then they will look on the sptg. page in vain, and then it's good night. But General Crowder says newsgathers was essential, so maybe if I stick some news in this letter they will see it and figure that the strain of gathering it was why I had to lay off a wile. So here is the items I gathered.

           *   *

Harvey, I got some inside baseball news by pumping different athletes. This is about the stragety of the serious. You see Mgr. Mitchell desided to pitch left-handers every day so as Ruth wouldn't play only when he was pitching.

Well, Mitchell wanted to pitch Tyler in the 1st game because he don't need so much rest between games as Vaughn. But Tyler can't hit left-handers, so when Ruth went in the 1st day for Boston, Mitch put Vaughn vs. him, and that was why Wagner or whoever is Boston's brains, pitched Ruth the 1st day so as Mitch wouldn't use Tyler the 1st day and come back with him the 3d day, which would of gave Vaughn 2 days' rest which is what he needs.

           *   *

And also here is the facts about the Wagner-Knabe bout Friday. Heinie was calling Tyler yellow as is the custom, and Knabe yelled at Wagner that he had a fine license to call anybody yellow because he was yellow himself. So Heinie says I'll come down there and show you who is yellow, so Otto says come on and Heinie done so and Otto tackled him by the dogs and thrun him and set on him, but found him harder than the bench, so he got up. And as far as I can see, the argument about who is yellow and vice versa is just where it was before the bloody brawl.

Good-bye, Harvey.

P.S.—Rollie Zeider [the Cubs' reserve infielder] asked me Friday night how Mays hit and I said righthanded. But I was mistaken, Harvey, it's not at all.

Ring W. Lardner, Chicago Tribune

Monday, September 9

THE RED SOX' AND CHIGAGO CUBS' SPECIAL PULLED INTO BOSTON, BETWEEN 10 AND 11 O'CLOCK LAST NIGHT-

Scott, Boston Post

Ruth Crashes into Car Window but Is Not Hurt

Babe Ruth, the mighty left-hand pitcher and slugger of the American League champion Red Sox, and still the team's ace in the hole, narrowly escaped serious injury on the baseball special outside of Springfield [Mass.] last night.

He was standing in the aisle of the Sox car talking to Carl Mays when the train lurched, sending the Colossus aspinning and crashing against a window. The heavy glass was shattered and fell clattering. Babe did not know how seriously he had been injured, but he had the presence of mind not to put out his hands, and was fortunate to escape with only a small cut in his trousers.

Boston Herald and Journal

[The sportwriters glossed over the real story. Ruth had a playful wrestling match with Walt Kinney, a seldom-used left-handed pitcher. Babe took a wild swing at Kinney just as the train lurched, smacking his pitching hand against the steel wall. The middle knuckle of his left hand quickly turned red and swollen, causing Babe considerable pain.

Ed Barrow was furious when he learned of this incident, but Babe assured the skipper that he'd be ready to pitch the next day.]

Players Perturbed Over Share in World's Series

It was not the series or its outcome that occupied the attention of the Red Sox and Cubs on their eastward journey, but the amount of swag they are going to receive for taking part in this classic.

On the way East there were numerous conferences among the players on the matter of World's Series money. Under the present arrangements the athletes declare that the winner's share will only amount to about $900 each man, while the losers will get about $300 less.

Edward F. Martin, *Boston Globe*

Big Fuss Over Cash Split

So lively is the dissatisfaction among the Red Sox that they held a meeting on the train this forenoon and appointed Captain Harry Hooper to enter a vigorous protest to the National Commission.

Paul Shannon, *Boston Post*

[The players were upset with the commission's new policy whereby their series shares would be divided among the top eight teams in the major leagues.]

Bridge Whist vs. Poker

An interesting feature of the trip was the difference in the card games played by the rival teams. In the Red Sox sleepers, bridge whist and hearts predominated, while the Cubs favored poker and the "bones," which entail a more rapid exchange of currency. The game that had the strongest play, however, was the dining car, which had to be changed twice during the trip.

I. E. Sanborn, *Chicago Tribune*

[Playing the "bones" meant shooting dice, or craps.]

Bookmakers are quoting odds of 100 to 40 that Boston will win the series. The Cubs were a 10 to 8 favorite in Chicago before last Thursday's game. The switch in betting has been the result of the surprising strength of the Red Sox against the highly touted left-hand pitchers of the Cubs, who were regarded as unbeatable.

Eddie Hurley, *Boston Record*

First Three Games in Series

BOSTON — BATTING

	AB	R	BH	2B	3B	HR	RBI	BB	SO	SB	AVG
Schang, c	6	0	3	0	0	0	1	0	2	1	.500
Whiteman, lf	10	1	4	0	1	0	1	1	1	1	.400
McInnis, 1b	10	1	3	0	0	0	1	1	1	0	.300
Hooper, rf	10	0	3	0	0	0	0	2	1	0	.300
Shean, 2b	10	1	2	0	0	0	0	2	2	0	.200
Thomas, 3b	8	0	1	0	0	0	0	0	2	0	.125
Strunk, cf	11	1	1	0	1	0	0	0	2	0	.091
Scott, ss	11	0	1	0	0	0	1	1	1	0	.091
Agnew, c	5	0	0	0	0	0	0	0	0	0	.000
Ruth, p	3	0	0	0	0	0	0	0	2	0	.000
Mays, p	3	0	0	0	0	0	0	0	0	0	.000
Bush, p	2	0	0	0	0	0	0	1	0	0	.000
Dubuc, ph	1	0	0	0	0	0	0	0	1	0	.000
	90	4	18	0	2	0	4	8	15	2	.200

BOSTON — PITCHING

	IP	BH	Won	Lost	R	ER	BB	SO	ERA
Ruth	9	6	1	0	0	0	1	4	0.00
Mays	9	7	1	0	1	1	1	4	1.00
Bush	8	7	0	1	3	3	3	0	3.37
	26	20	2	1	4	4	5	8	1.38

CHICAGO — BATTING

	AB	R	BH	2B	3B	HR	RBI	BB	SO	SB	AVG
Pick, 2b	9	2	3	1	0	0	0	1	1	1	.333
Tyler, p	3	0	1	0	0	0	2	0	0	0	.333
Flack, rf	10	0	3	0	0	0	0	1	1	0	.300
Paskert, cf	12	0	3	0	0	0	0	0	2	0	.250
Mann, lf	12	0	3	1	0	0	0	0	0	0	.250
Merkle, 1b	9	1	2	0	0	0	0	2	1	0	.222
Killefer, c	9	1	2	1	0	0	2	1	0	0	.222
Deal, 3b	9	0	2	0	0	0	0	0	0	0	.222
Hollocher, ss	10	0	1	0	1	0	0	0	1	0	.100
Vaughn, p	6	0	0	0	0	0	0	0	2	0	.000
O'Farrell, ph	1	0	0	0	0	0	0	0	0	0	.000
	90	4	20	3	1	0	4	5	8	1	.222

CHICAGO — PITCHING									
	IP	BH	Won	Lost	R	ER	BB	SO	ERA
Tyler	9	6	1	0	1	1	4	2	1.00
Vaughn	18	12	0	2	3	3	4	13	1.50
	27	18	1	2	4	4	8	15	1.33

Baseball Night at the Theatre

The two World's Series teams will attend the Shubert Majestic Theatre tonight to see [the play] "Experience." The players will occupy decorated boxes, and it will be baseball night for "Experience."

Boston Globe

Boston Record

AND THE 4TH GAME OF THE WORLD SERIES WILL BE PLAYED ON THE HOME GROUND-TO-DAY- (IF NOT RAIN)

Scott, *Boston Post*

Babe Ruth's Big Bat Gives Sox Third Win, 3 to 2
Hammers out Long Three-Bagger and Scores Two Men

BOSTON, Sept. 9—Big Babe's mighty bat wrote another page in the annals of World's Series championships yesterday when the Red Sox again downed the Cubs, 3 to 2.

In the fourth inning Ruth came to bat [in a scoreless tie] with two men on base and two men gone. Lefty Tyler, Chicago's most cunning craftsman, was taking no chances. The first two balls served to Ruth were just a trifle wide. Then he slipped one right across the rubber. The next offering missed crossing the pan and Tyler was in the hole. But a second strike cut the plate and now it was up to the Cubs' southpaw to either take a chance or walk the batter.

Tyler tried to slip a fast one past Ruth. A report like a rifle shot rang through the park. Twenty-five thousand people arose as one man, and while the bleachers shrieked in ecstasy, the Cubs right fielder dashed madly for the centre field stands while two red-legged runners scampered about the bases.

The sphere sailed over Flack's head on a line, dropped at the foot of the bleachers, and before the relayed throw was rescued near the Cub dugout two runs had come in for Boston, and the big pitcher was resting on third.

[Winning pitcher, Ruth (2–0); losing pitcher, Douglas (0–1). Save: Bush (1). Boston leads Chicago, three games to one.]

Paul H. Shannon, *Boston Post*

IN THE 4TH INNING
WHEN "BABE" RUTH TRIPLED TO RIGHT
SCORING WHITEMAN AND "STUFFY" McINNIS·

Scott, *Boston Post*

Ruth Hero of Red Sox Win

Fourth Game

CHICAGO	AB	R	BH	PO	A	BOSTON	AB	R	BH	PO	A
Flack, rf	4	0	1	3	0	Hooper, rf	3	0	0	1	0
Hollocher, ss	4	0	0	2	0	Shean, 2b	3	0	1	4	4
Mann, lf	4	0	1	2	0	Strunk, cf	4	0	0	0	0
Paskert, cf	4	0	0	3	0	Whiteman, lf	3	1	0	1	0
Merkle, 1b	3	0	1	9	1	Bush, p	0	0	0	0	0
Pick, 2b	2	0	2	0	2	McInnis,1b	3	1	1	16	1
Zeider, 3b	0	0	0	1	2	Ruth, p, lf	2	0	1	0	4
Deal, 3b	2	0	1	1	3	Scott, ss	3	0	0	3	8
Wortman, 2b	1	0	0	1	0	Thomas, 3b	3	0	0	2	3
Killefer, c	2	1	0	1	0	Agnew, c	2	0	0	0	1
Tyler, p	0	0	0	1	4	Schang, c	1	1	1	0	0
Douglas, p	0	0	0	0	0						
a O'Farrell	1	0	0	0	0						
b Hendrix	1	0	1	0	0						
c McCabe	0	1	0	0	0						
d Barber	1	0	0	0	0						
	29	2	7	24	12		27	3	4	27	21

	1	2	3	4	5	6	7	8	9	R
Chicago	0	0	0	0	0	0	0	2	0	2
Boston	0	0	0	2	0	0	0	1	x	3

Two-base hit—Shean. Three-base hit—Ruth. Stolen base—Shean. Sacrifice hits—Ruth, Hooper. Double plays—Ruth to Scott to McInnis, Scott to Shean to McInnis (2). Error—Douglas. Left on bases—Chicago 6, Boston 4. Bases on balls—Off Tyler 2, off Ruth 6. Hits—Off Tyler 3 in 7 innings, off Douglas 1 in 1, off Ruth 7 in 8, off Bush 0 in 1. Struck out—by Tyler 1, by Ruth 2. Wild pitch—Ruth. Passed balls—Killefer (2). Time—2h. 4m. Umpires—Owens at plate, O'Day at first base, Hildebrand at second base, Klem at third base.

a—Batted for Deal in 7th. b—Batted for Tyler in 8th. c—Ran for Hendrix in 8th. d—Batted for Killefer in 9th.

[Runs batted in—Ruth (2), Hollocher, Mann.]

Boston Post

That Fatal Chuck

Big Phil Douglas, one of the foremost spitballers in the country, was rushed to the firing line in the eighth [with the score tied two apiece].

After Schang had opened up with a beautiful single to centre, Hooper laid down a sacrifice bunt. The ball rolled toward third base and Douglas picked it up. It was a spitter, and when the big twirler hurled it to first base it sailed away over Fred Merkle's head. Schang ran home and the fate of the contest was decided.

Paul H. Shannon, Boston Post

The Cubs rallied gallantly in the ninth [with Boston ahead by one run]. Merkle nestled a single to center and Zeider worked Ruth for his second walk. That ended Babe's work for the day.

Bush took the slab and Wortman laid down a bunt. McInnis dashed in and fired the ball to third in time to force Merkle, killing the sacrifice and Chicago's swell chance to cop the game.

Barber was sent up to bat for Killefer. He slapped a bounder to Scott, who started a lightning double play, and the game was over.

I. E. Sanborn, Chicago Tribune

Babe Wobbles

Had that jam at the Fens terminated differently, G. Babe Ruth would have eliminated yellow from his list of favorite colors.

An iodine-painted finger on his pitching wing, which was bruised during some sugarhouse fun with W. W. Kinney, bothered him constantly, causing the ball to shine and sail. He was ever on the brink of danger, and in the ninth it looked as if he was going to put the combat right into hock.

All the world should know, Babe said, that it was not the finger that was troubling him, but the stuff that was on it, causing him to deadhead six of the Cubs and throw a wild pitch. They may have to change the color of iodine right away if they want Babe to string along with it.

Edward F. Martin, Boston Globe

Ruth Made a Record

By pitching seven [shutout] innings yesterday, Ruth set a record of pitching 29 innings of scoreless ball in World Series games. In 1916, against the Dodgers, he pitched 13 innings without allowing a run in one game. In Chicago this year he shut out the Cubs in nine innings. Then came his seven yesterday before the Chicagoans counted.

Christy Mathewson held the previous record, which was 28 innings, pitching three shutout games in 1905 against the Macks.

Boston Globe

[Ruth's record stood until 1962, when Whitey Ford completed thirty-three consecutive scoreless innings. Babe had an outstanding World Series pitching record, with three wins and no losses and an earned run average of 0.87.]

The playing of McInnis was nothing short of wonderful. The Gloucester boy figured in three double plays and in each instance he brought the fans to their feet. His play on Wortman's tap in front of the plate in the ninth, forcing Merkle at third, was the turning point in the game.

Harry J. Casey, *Boston Record*

Scott Accepts 11 Chances

Everett Scott played sensationally for the Fens gang. The Bluffton Deacon accepted 11 chances and was mixed up in three whopping double plays. He was in on some play in every inning but the sixth. Had he known that time would have been hanging heavy on his hands in that stanza he would have brought his knitting out with him. If he had, there would have been no stitches dropped.

Edward F. Martin, *Boston Globe*

Scott, *Boston Post*

To win now, Chicago must take three straight from the Bostonians, and all of the games must be played at Fenway Park. Truly, a seemingly impossible task for the National League titlists.

Burt Whitman, *Boston Herald and Journal*

Heroes from France Enjoy Sox' Victory

Spick and span uniforms of blue and khaki were plentiful at the game in Fenway Park yesterday, but never has the khaki attracted the attention that it did when the battle-scarred veterans of Château Thierry, the Somme and other fields in France, made their way to the seats in the big grandstand.

Every man in the bunch of more than 50 had faced the Hun amid terrific shell fire, machine gun spray and shrapnel shower, recording the wounds that sent him back to the United States.

They made the most stirring picture Boston has had since the war began. Many of them will never walk again without artificial means. They hobbled on crutches, others had lost an arm or had disabling injuries of various kinds.

Those boys from France were fans of the most rabid kind. Many of them were from the middle and far west and rooted hard for Chicago. There were many others for Boston and they yelled when Babe Ruth put his long drive over in the fourth that sent in two runs.

War appeared to be a forgotten thing. However, one youngster couldn't keep from taking a peek at the sky once in a while to see if a Boche plane was overhead. In France it was not an unusual thing to have a bomb dropped on the field during the game.

Boston Globe

Tessie! Where Was Old 'Gal' at Fenway?

Where was "Tessie?" Forsooth, there wasn't any music at all. President Frazee planned to have music, but so great was the demand for grandstand seats that he was forced to sell the space he had allotted for the band. Curses!

Just the same, it did seem strange to see the gallant Sox in a World's Series game and not hear the happy strains of old "Tessie." She was a good old girl; she put the title over for Jimmy Collins, Jake Stahl and Bill Carrigan.

Yep, "Tessie" was missed.

H. W. Lanigan, *Boston American*

[Collins, Stahl, and Carrigan managed the Red Sox to world championships in 1903, 1912, 1915, and 1916.]

The crowd did not come up to expectations. While there was no material evidence of "Tessie," she must have been there in spirit. It is the first time any Boston club has been in a series that "Tessie" had not been heard from good and proper.

Edward F. Martin, *Boston Globe*

TESSIE

Words and music ©1902 by Will R. Anderson

Piano arrangement ©1998 by Mel Springer

[Boston's Royal Rooters, an all-male fan club led by a bartender known as "Nuf Ced" McGreevey, had entertained World Series crowds since 1903 with "Tessie," a show tune of the era. The song became a battle cry during Red Sox rallies and was sung repeatedly, driving the opposing team crazy.

The first verse of this catchy tune went like this:

Tessie, you make me feel so badly;
   Why don't you turn around?
Tessie, you know I love you madly;
   Babe my heart weighs about a pound.
Don't blame me if I ever doubt you.
   You know I wouldn't live without you.
Tessie, you are the only, only, only.

The Royal Rooters sang "Tessie" at the head of the 1912 victory parade through Boston, following the Red Sox' World Series triumph over the New York Giants. Their most vocal member was John F. (Honey Fitz) Fitzgerald, the former mayor of Boston and the grandfather of President John F. Kennedy.]

Barrow Says "All Over"

"We now have the big edge. The players came through as I have predicted, and when things looked bad they proved themselves a game bunch of men. Sam Jones will pitch the fifth game and I'll have Mays in reserve. We'll finish up the series with the next game."

Boston Herald and Journal

Threats of a strike and refusal to complete the series are mere rumors, as the men realize they could gain nothing by such a move.

Chicago Tribune

Picks Red Sox to Win

Mme. Lora, who is giving a demonstration of mental telepathy at the Bowdoin Square Theatre, and tells the audience all about their business and love affairs, has predicted the results of the four world's series games so far, and today she says Jones will pitch and Boston will win.

Boston Post

Last night Babe was around with a grin as wide as the ocean, for he was satisfied that, at last, he "had caught ahold of one right."

Burt Whitman, *Boston Herald and Journal*

At game time Stuffy McInnis was the only athlete in uniform.

Red Sox and Cubs Strike, Ask More Cash

Victors Want $2,000 and Losers Would Have Purse of $1,400

FENWAY PARK, Sept. 10—A sensation was sprung at Fenway Park when members of the Red Sox and Cubs went on strike. The players of both teams refused to don their baseball uniforms until they were guaranteed that they should receive $2,000 as a winners' end and $1,400 as a losers' end.

With more than 20,000 fans gasping for breath it looked as though baseball had received its final death blow. At game time Stuffy McInnis was the only athlete in uniform. Meanwhile the crowd grew restless and there were repeated cries of "play ball."

Members of the National Commission, Garry Herrmann, chairman; Ban Johnson, president of the American League, and John Heydler, president of the National League, arrived at the ball grounds at 2:22 o'clock and informed President Frazee of the Red Sox and President Weeghman of the Cubs that their players would have to go on the field at once. The club owners carried this message to the players, but the men refused to pay any attention.

Boston Record (Sept. 10 edition)

Scott, *Boston Post*

Strike! Strike! Strike!

A Complete Account of the Funeral Ceremonies of the Once Great Game of Baseball

It is two by the village clock. There are 25,000 fans in the stands at Fenway Park. There are twenty-five players in each dressing room under those stands. They haven't their uniforms on. They are striking. They have asked the National Commission for more money and haven't got any reply.

It is two-thirty by the village clock. There are twenty-five thousand fans out there waiting just the same. There are twenty-five players in each dressing room, and there are a score of scribes without. There aren't supposed to be any scribes there but they get in, even though the magnates and everybody don't want them.

The players have declared that they will not play unless they get a fair piece of the series' receipts. They have told the world and everybody knows it, except the Commish.

The Commish had been told, at 1:10, that there will not be any game. The shock was terrible. The Commish should never be awakened that early.

Byron Bancroft Johnson and Garry Herrmann come into view, just when it is two thirty-five by the village clock. They show the strain of the series, they do.

"If they concede anything to those pups, I'm through with baseball. I'm through, I'm through, I'm through," quoth Byron B., juggling his eyeglasses.

The committee of players enters the umpires' room. The players look serious enough, though they have to grin every now and then when they look around.

"I went to Washington and had the stamp of approval put on the World's Series. I made it possible. I did," said Ban, striking his chest and directing his sobby eloquence right at Harry Hooper.

"I made it possible, Harry," he continued, beating the tattoo on his broad chest. "I had the stamp of approval put on the World's Series, Harry. I did it, Harry," striking his chest. "I did it."

"But, Mr. Johnson," broke in H. Hooper.

"I did it, Harry," interjected Ban. "I had the stamp of approval put on, Harry. I did it."

"Let's arbitrate this matter, Mr. Johnson," declared Garry Herrmann. Then he launched forth into a brilliant exposition of the history of baseball's governing board.

Expert reporters took notes for a while and then quit, befuddled. The umpires and the clubowners retreated.

"Listen," said H. Hooper, in a lull in the terrible babble, "we'll go out and play." They did, and you couldn't blame them.

"By jolly," murmured Ban. "I did it; I did it."

Nick Flatley, *Boston American*

Harry Hooper Saved the Situation

When it seemed as if the players and the representatives of the National Commission, Garry Herrmann and Ban Johnson, were hopelessly deadlocked and the curtailed baseball year would fizzle out in a strike, Harry Hooper, the Red Sox captain, called the turn.

"We will play," he said, acting as spokesman for both teams, "not because we think we are getting a fair deal, because we are not. But we'll play for the sake of the game, for the sake of the public, which has always given us its loyal support, and for the sake of the wounded soldiers and sailors who are in the grandstand waiting for us."

Boston Post

Jim Vaughn, the Hippo of the invaders, stood at the side of Hooper in that conference of umpires, commissioners, players, etc., held in the umpires' room. But during the confab Jim did not say a word. He was saving up his energy for the ball game.

Burt Whitman, *Boston Herald and Journal*

Crowd Begins to Yell

Shortly after 2:30 the crowd began yelling for the appearance of the players. No players showed up, however, but instead four mounted police officers rode on to the playing field.

J. C. O'Leary, *Boston Globe*

Wounded Soldiers Get Great Greeting

The crowd had something to cheer for when a large detachment of wounded soldiers, brought to this country from overseas last Saturday, arrived in the grandstand and took box seats. The entire grandstand and bleachers arose en masse, while the band played "Over There" and gave the heroes three lusty cheers, the loudest and most heartfelt that have yet been given in the series.

Boston Post

While the band was taking a breathing spell the bat boy of the Red Sox voluntarily, or at the suggestion of someone inclined to placate the crowd, appeared in uniform and posted himself on the top rail of the Boston club's dugout. He was the only one in baseball uniform that had been seen by the crowd up to 2:45.

J. C. O'Leary, *Boston Globe*

Called "Bolsheviki" by Fans

By 2:25 the majority of the fans were aware the players were on a strike. They were called "Bolsheviki" and "shameless holdups" and a lot of other names which would not look nice in print.

At 2:50, or 20 minutes after the game should have been started, things remained in status quo. There had been no announcement by the management or any explanation to the people of the cause of the delay or how long it was likely to continue.

The band seated on the green in front of the first-base pavilion was doing heroic work. It played almost constantly, and this seemed to keep the crowd contented and peaceably inclined.

It did look, though, as if there might be a strike of the musicians unless there was some relief for them.

J. C. O'Leary, *Boston Globe*

Hippo Vaughn, Chicago Cubs pitcher

Announcement to Fans

Ex-Mayor Fitzgerald made the announcement of the cause of the delay after the players finally decided to yield. He stated that the Red Sox and Cubs had agreed to compete only for the good of the game and the public.

When the players came on the field an hour late some of the fans started "booing" them, but the majority cheered the athletes and drowned out the "boos."

Chicago Tribune

[The fans cheered and the band played "Sweet Adeline" when "Honey Fitz" finished his stirring speech on behalf of the players.]

Fitzy greased the way for the players when they appeared on the field. Instead of being greeted by groans, etc., the players were heartily cheered, and the crowd of 25,000 seemed to be with them in their demands. There is no doubt the players have been given all the worst of it.

Eddie Hurley, *Boston Record*

Cubs Grab Victory under Shadow of Dollar Sign, 3 to 0
Vaughn Finally Subdues Red Sox with Five Hits

BOSTON, Mass., Sept. 10—Under the sinister shadow of the dollar sign, which would have killed professional baseball in another year if the war had not already done so, Chicago's Cubs defeated Boston's Red Sox today in the fifth game of eternity's last world series by a score of 3 to 0.

The contest was held up for more than an hour by a strike of the players, who demanded more money for their world's series endeavors than the National Commission's rules allotted them.

In spite of the wrangle over the pennies on the corpse's eyes, the two teams went out without preliminary practice and played a whale of a game before a crowd of more than 24,000.

Jim Vaughn finally came into his own by achieving a victory after two previous hard luck defeats. He shut out the Red Sox with only five hits, and one of those would have been an error if the National Commission would appoint an official scorer who knew baseball.

Hollocher led in the swatting with three hits and a walk and registered two of Chicago's three runs. But the two doubles by Mann and Paskert were the real bread winners.

• [Winning pitcher, Vaughn (1–2); losing pitcher, Jones (0–1). Boston leads Chicago, three games to two.]

I. E. Sanborn, Chicago Tribune

AND THE 5TH GAME
ENDED WITH A JOLT
FOR THE RED SOX –

Scott, Boston Post

Laurels for Whiteman

The most brilliant of all Red Sox performers yesterday was the veteran George Whiteman, who saved Sam Jones from destruction in the very first inning.

Jones passed the first man up, and then allowed Hollocher to add a safe hit. A sacrifice by Mann put impending runs on third and second. Mays had been sent to the bullpen in a hurry to warm up.

Dode Paskert, one of the most dangerous hitters on the Chicago team, came through with a sharp line drive that had every earmark of a perfect two-bagger. But Whiteman, tearing in on the run, grasped the ball just before it touched the ground, and, without pausing to set himself, snapped the ball to Dave Shean (at second base) who stood waiting to receive it.

Flack, who had waited on third till the ball was caught, then started for home. But Hollocher, caught between the bases when he figured the drive was a safe one, was doubled by Whiteman before he could get back to second.

Paul H. Shannon, *Boston Post*

Babe Ruth did not get into the game. The nearest he came was to the first base coaching line. The Colossus was missed. His presence in the batting order adds immensely to the punch of the otherwise weak-hitting Hub nine.

Burt Whitman, *Boston Herald and Journal*

In the third round of this splendid battle, Hollocher laid the trail for coming trouble by waiting out the Boston pitcher and drawing his base on four bad balls. Hollocher took plenty of room off the first base bag in the hope of drawing one of Sam Agnew's rapid fire throws. A pitchout was ordered, and when Agnew got the ball well outside the plate he found that Hollocher was fully one-third the distance from first base.

Without pausing an instant, Agnew whipped the ball to McInnis, who turned in his tracks, expecting to touch out Hollocher on the way back to first base.

To McInnis' surprise the runner was not there. He turned toward second and prepared to throw, but found that he was a fraction of a second too late. Hollocher had pulled a delayed steal and gave the Cubs the jump on our expectant title holders. A timely two-bagger by Leslie Mann quickly followed and the run shattered Sam Jones' hopes and redeemed the besmirched pitching reputation of the great Jim Vaughn.

Paul H. Shannon, *Boston Post*

Umpires Will Draw Down More Coin Than Stars

The umpires seem to have the best of this series. These officials drag down 1,000 iron men [dollars] each for their work in the big games. This is more money than such stars as Ruth, Vaughn and Hollocher will get. The umps have no kick coming.

Eddie Hurley, *Boston Record*

Red Sox Helpless before Vaughn

Fifth Game

CHICAGO	AB	R	BH	PO	A		BOSTON	AB	R	BH	PO	A
Flack, rf	2	1	0	1	0		Hooper, rf	4	0	1	1	0
Hollocher, ss	3	2	3	2	5		Shean, 2b	3	0	1	3	2
Mann, lf	3	0	1	2	0		Strunk, cf	4	0	1	4	0
Paskert, cf	3	0	1	3	0		Whiteman, lf	3	0	1	1	2
Merkle, 1b	3	0	1	11	1		McInnis, 1b	3	0	0	9	0
Pick, 2b	4	0	1	4	3		Scott, ss	3	0	0	1	4
Deal, 3b	4	0	0	0	0		Thomas, 3b	3	0	1	1	1
Killefer, c	4	0	0	4	0		Agnew, c	2	0	0	5	1
Vaughn, p	4	0	0	0	3		Schang, c	1	0	0	1	0
							Jones, p	1	0	0	1	3
							*Miller	1	0	0	0	0
	30	3	7	27	12			28	0	5	27	13

	1	2	3	4	5	6	7	8	9	R
Chicago	0	0	1	0	0	0	0	2	0	- 3
Boston	0	0	0	0	0	0	0	0	0	- 0

Errors—None. Two base hits—Mann, Paskert, Strunk. Stolen base—Hollocher. Sacrifice hits—Mann, Shean. Double plays—Merkle to Hollocher, Hollocher to Pick to Merkle (2), Whiteman to Shean. Left on bases—Chicago 6, Boston 3. Base on balls—Off Vaughn 1, off Jones 5. Struck out—By Vaughn 4, by Jones 5. Time of game—1 hr. 42 m. Umpires—O'Day behind the plate, Hildebrand at first, Klem at second, and Owens at third base.

[Runs batted in—Mann, Paskert (2).]

* Batted for Jones in the ninth.

Boston Post

The Sox did not give up easily. In the ninth inning they made a gallant stand. Miller drove a ball to the left field bank and only the "Goddess of Luck" prevented him from making a two-bagger. Mann fell going up the bank and caught the ball in his hip pocket. Then Hollocher scooted to left field and made a sensational catch of Hooper's Texas Leaguer. The Cubs earned yesterday's win.

Eddie Hurley, *Boston Record*

After the game Hooper said that he was sure the game of the next day would be played. The commission indicated that the players' shares would go to the Red Cross if they did not play out the string.

Burt Whitman, *Boston Herald and Journal*

MR· MILLER TRIED TO START A RALLY IN THE NINTH BUT—!

Wallace Goldsmith, *Boston Globe*

Heinie Wagner of the Red Sox wants to know how the National Commission expects a fellow to live on the share he will get out of the world's series when they charge 20 cents for a 5-cent mushmelon in a hotel.

You're wrong, Heinie. They charge 20 cents for half of it.

Arthur Duffey, *Boston Post*

There will not be a repetition of yesterday's strike. The players have promised to finish the series for the paltry share of the coin which is theirs. According to official figures the players of the winning club will get less than $900.

Eddie Hurley, *Boston Record*

Red Sox Are Again World's Champions

Mays Holds Cubs in Check—Whiteman's Wonderful Work Mainly Responsible for 2 to 1 Victory

BOSTON, Sept. 11—Again the Boston Red Sox are champions of the world.

At exactly five minutes past three o'clock yesterday afternoon, even before the wires began to tell the country that Barrow's men had won the deciding contest, a carrier pigeon, released from the press stand by exultant soldiers, started on its long flight to Camp Devens with the news of the fatal third inning and the downfall of the Chicago Cubs.

* [Winning pitcher, Mays (2–0), losing pitcher, Tyler (1–1). Boston defeats Chicago, four games to two.]

Paul H. Shannon, *Boston Post*

George Tyler came back with only one day's rest and pitched a game that ought to have been crowned with glory. He would have shut out the

Hubites but for a muffed fly ball by Flack which gave them their two runs in the third inning.

I. E. Sanborn, Chicago Tribune

Whiteman Hero of Sox Victory

Two bases on balls in the third inning—one to Mays, the other to Shean—had put two men on the sacks, and they were at third and second when Whitey came to bat with two men out. A consultation followed and for a moment it looked as though Chicago would pass him and take a chance on the even more dangerous McInnis. Finally the Cub board of strategy decided to make the batter hit.

With one ball and one strike the count, Whitey got hold of a ball and drove it with the speed of a bullet into right field. Flack, who was playing well out, tore in to catch the liner. He reached it by a desperate sprint, but the ball had been driven with such force that it tore his hands apart and dropped to the ground while Shean followed Mays across the plate. The crestfallen Flack made a futile throw home, but there was no play. Chicago's hopes of wresting the championship from the Boston team died at the same time.

Paul H. Shannon, Boston Post

15,238 at Final Game

Cold weather influenced many people not to attend the final game, but what probably kept many fans away was the hour's delay before Tuesday's game, while the players and the commission tossed out ultimatums at each other.

Boston Globe

Deal Cuts Off More Runs

The Cubs made a sensational defense in the last half of the fourth, and Charley Deal [the third baseman] stopped at least two runs by a sterling play. Scott led off with a single and was sacrificed ahead by Thomas. Schang drew a pass and Mays caught the Cubs flatfooted with a bunt toward third which he beat out. That filled the bases with one down. [Boston was ahead 2 to 1 at this point.]

Tyler was not fussed a bit, but pitched coolly to Hooper. Harry could only rap an easy bounder to Merkle [at first base], who forced Scott at the plate. Shean was next and pulled a vicious bounder over third base. Deal barely reached it with one hand, but knocked the ball down a few feet behind the bag. Anchoring his spikes to third base, Deal threw himself flat on the ground and picked up the ball in time to force Mays for the third out. If Deal had tried to recover the ball and then touch third base, Mays would have beaten it and Schang would have scored.

I. E. Sanborn, Chicago Tribune

Whiteman Makes Great Catch

In the eighth frame Barber led off as a pinch hitter for the Cubs. He hit the ball squarely on the trade mark and lined it into short left field.

Tearing in at breakneck speed, Whiteman made a shoestring catch, grabbing the ball just before it reached the ground, and turned a complete somersault after making the catch. The achievement completely stopped the opposition, and gave the stands a chance to cheer and shriek for three full minutes.

In accomplishing this feat, however, Whiteman badly wrenched the muscles of his neck. Compelled to leave the game a minute later after courageously trying to resume play, he was given a tremendous tribute as he passed into the dugout. Manager Mitchell, in warmly commending this man's work during all six games, said that the catch was one of the most spectacular he had ever witnessed in a post-season battle.

Paul H. Shannon, *Boston Post*

George Whiteman, Red Sox left fielder

The last play of the final professional combat went from Shean to McInnis, Stuffy holding up the ball as the fleet Les Mann was running it out for all he was worth. Then Hooper, Ruth, Mays, Shean, Schang, Scott and others did a fadeout. Down came the curtain and from out of the stillness that swept over the battleground came a lone voice, piping up, "Those Red Sox always were a lucky bunch."

Edward F. Martin, *Boston Globe*

Defeat of Cubs Gives the Red Sox Fifth World's Series Title

WHITEMAN'S CLOUT WAS CALLED BY THE OFFICIAL SCORER A FLACK ERROR BUT IT SCORED 2 RUNS -

Scott, *Boston Post*

IN THE 7TH, THOMAS GOT A BARE HAND CATCH OF MERKLE'S CLOUT AND A THROW TO 1ST BASE—2ND OUT—

ARMY PIGEONS CARRIED THE SCORES TO CAMP DEVENS.

WHEE!

270TH WIN WORLD CHAMPIONS RED SOX

IN THE 8TH WHITEMAN SPRINTED IN AND DIVED, CATCHING BARBER'S FLY, TURNED A SOMERSAULT AND SAT UP WITH THE BALL IN HIS MIT—

AND 2 MORE CUB PINCH HITTERS WERE OUT IN A ROW—

FINISH—

Scott, *Boston Post*

The Final Blow That Caused Hubbub in Hub

Sixth Game

CHICAGO	AB	R	BH	PO	A		BOSTON	AB	R	BH	PO	A
Flack, rf	3	1	1	2	0		Hooper, rf	3	0	0	1	0
Hollocher, ss	4	0	0	0	4		Shean, 2b	3	1	0	2	4
Mann, lf	3	0	0	2	0		Strunk, cf	4	0	2	0	0
Paskert, cf	2	0	0	5	0		Whiteman, lf	4	0	0	2	0
Merkle, 1b	3	0	1	8	2		Ruth, lf	0	0	0	1	0
Pick, 2b	3	0	1	3	1		McInnis, 1b	4	0	1	16	1
Deal, 3b	2	0	0	2	1		Scott, ss	4	0	1	3	3
Zeider, 3b	0	0	0	0	0		Thomas, 3b	2	0	0	1	2
Killefer, c	2	0	0	2	2		Schang, c	1	0	0	1	2
O'Farrell, c	1	0	0	0	0		Mays, p	2	1	1	0	6
Tyler, p	2	0	0	0	3							
Hendrix, p	0	0	0	0	0							
*Barber	1	0	0	0	0							
**McCabe	1	0	0	0	0							
Totals	27	1	3	24	13			27	2	5	27	18

	1	2	3	4	5	6	7	8	9		R
Chicago	0	0	0	1	0	0	0	0	0	-	1
Boston	0	0	2	0	0	0	0	0	x	-	2

Errors—Flack, Tyler. Stolen base—Flack. Sacrifice hits—Hooper, Thomas. Bases on balls—Off Tyler 5, off Mays 2. Hits—Off Tyler, 5 in 7 innings, off Hendrix, none in one inning, off Mays, 3 in 9 innings. Hit by pitcher—By Mays (Mann). Struck out—by Tyler 1, by Mays 1. Time of game—1h. 46m. Umpires—Hildebrand at plate, Klem at first, Owens at second and O'Day at third.

*Batted for Deal in 8th
**Batted for Tyler in 8th
[Run batted in—Merkle.]

Boston Herald and Journal

Whiteman Was Performer to Smear Dope

Boston Red Sox are champions of the world and the dope is smeared all over the baseball map.

The man who smeared the dope was Whiteman. Eleven years ago this fellow and Tris Speaker came into baseball from Texas, and Whiteman was adjudged a failure. He has been in and out, up and down, in baseball.

I have no desire to bunk the fans of Peoria, Toronto, or other way-points, but Whiteman, in this series, was greater than Cobb and luckier than C. Webb Murphy.

He was active in all four of the Red Sox victories; got on base more times and in more ways than any other player; made the decisive plays, and yesterday he capped the climax.

His line smash, made after two strikes were called, with two out and two on base, was muffed by Flack and sent home Boston's two runs. Then, in the eighth, when Mitchell was rushing up his reserves, Whiteman made the most spectacular play of the series and saved at least a tie.

Barber was hitting and mauled a vicious line drive to left. Whiteman came tearing forward, dived at the ball, clutched it, turned a somersault and rolled to his feet with the ball still clutched in his fingers.

The hit seemed a certain triple, and the catch stopped the last rally of the Cubs, who were fighting desperately under the nearly perfect pitching by Mays.

Hugh S. Fullerton, *Boston American*

Hippo Vaughn and Lefty Tyler will be heroes till the end of time. Each southpaw hurled three shows. Each game was a masterpiece of the pitching art. With even an ordinary break all those six games would have been Chicago shutouts.

They lost, but they won undying fame, and deserve just as much credit as do Carl Mays and Battering Babe Ruth, each of whom grabbed off a couple of series pastimes.

Nick Flatley, *Boston American*

[Vaughn won 1 and lost 2, with an earned run average of 1.00, allowing 3 earned runs in 27 innings. Tyler won 1 and lost 1 with an earned run average of 1.17, allowing 3 earned runs in 23 innings.]

The Last Say

BOSTON, Mass., Sept. 11—At the conclusion of the game deciding the world's championship the rival managers gave out statements. Here they are:

Manager Barrow—"It was a wonderful series. The Red Sox played machine-like baseball and presented a defence the Cubs could not break down. The Cubs gave us a great battle. No two gamer teams ever fought for the championship. I wish to congratulate the Cubs for the fight they made.

Manager Mitchell—"All the glory belongs to Boston. I congratulate the Red Sox club. It was a contest between two teams playing tight baseball. The pitching was the best in world series games for years. It was a tough series to lose.

Chicago Tribune

Frazee Pleased

"Boston clubs have never lost in a World Series," said Pres. Frazee, "and the championship deserves to remain here until the war is won. Manager Barrow deserves great credit for the victory. The players are to be complimented for their success and the fans for the liberal support accorded wartime baseball at Fenway Park this year."

Boston Globe

Carrier pigeons were released at the end of each inning, the birds taking to Camp Devens [thirty miles west of Boston] a progressive report of the contest.

The one that was released at the end of the fifth inning evidently did not have its mind on its work, for it started downtown, but must have realized that it was in the Army now, for it turned about suddenly and decided to go back to Devens.

Edward F. Martin, *Boston Globe*

The spectacle of Ban Johnson with his arm around Harry Hooper and sobbing: "You know I love you, Harry," and then declaring that he was the man who saved baseball and he alone, and calling upon Harry to witness that he was the big man of baseball, was certainly a fine sight on Tuesday.

Here was Hooper, calm and dignified, presenting his case in an impressive way, while the American League head was spilling tears all over the floor. No wonder Hooper became disgusted and offered to play the game for nothing.

Arthur Duffey, *Boston Post*

Ring Down the Curtain

Gene Ahern, *Boston Record*

Friday, September 13

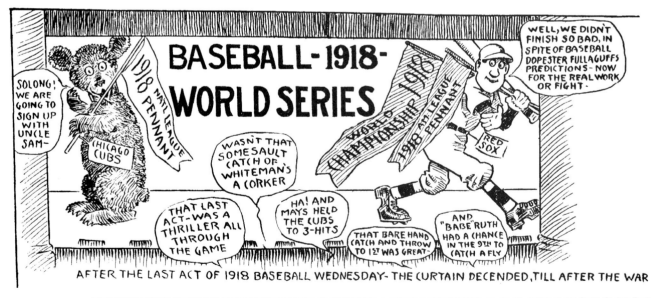

Scott, *Boston Post*

The Year the Red Sox Won the Series

Final World Series Averages

BOSTON — BATTING

	AB	R	BH	2B	3B	HR	RBI	BB	SO	SB	AVG
Schang, c	9	1	4	0	0	0	1	2	3	1	.444
Whiteman, lf . .	20	2	5	0	1	0	1	2	1	1	.250
McInnis, 1b . .	20	2	5	0	0	0	1	1	1	0	.250
Shean, 2b . . .	19	2	4	1	0	0	0	4	3	1	.211
Hooper, rf . . .	20	0	4	0	0	0	0	2	2	0	.200
Ruth, p, lf	5	0	1	0	1	0	2	0	2	0	.200
Mays, p	5	1	1	0	0	0	0	1	0	0	.200
Strunk, cf . . .	23	1	4	1	1	0	0	0	5	0	.174
Thomas, 3b . .	16	0	2	0	0	0	0	1	2	0	.125
Scott, ss	21	0	2	0	0	0	1	1	1	0	.095
Agnew, c	9	0	0	0	0	0	0	0	0	0	.000
Bush, p	2	0	0	0	0	0	0	1	0	0	.000
Miller, ph	1	0	0	0	0	0	0	0	0	0	.000
Dubuc, ph . . .	1	0	0	0	0	0	0	0	1	0	.000
Jones, p	1	0	0	0	0	0	0	1	0	0	.000
	172	9	32	2	3	0	6	16	21	3	.186

BOSTON — PITCHING

	IP	BH	Won	Lost	R	ER	BB	SO	ERA
Carl Mays	18	10	2	0	2	2	3	5	1.00
Babe Ruth	17	13	2	0	2	2	7	4	1.06
Joe Bush	9	7	0	1	3	3	3	0	3.00
Sam Jones	9	7	0	1	3	3	5	5	3.00
	53	37	4	2	10	10	18	14	1.70

CHICAGO — BATTING

	AB	R	BH	2B	3B	HR	RBI	BB	SO	SB	AVG
Hendrix, p . . .	1	0	1	0	0	0	0	0	0	0	1.000
Pick, 2b	18	2	7	1	0	0	0	1	1	1	.389
Merkle, 1b . . .	18	1	5	0	0	0	1	4	3	0	.278
Flack, rf	19	2	5	0	0	0	0	4	1	1	.263
Mann, lf	22	0	5	2	0	0	2	0	0	0	.227
Tyler, p	5	0	1	0	0	0	2	2	0	0	.200
Paskert, cf . .	21	0	4	1	0	0	2	2	2	0	.190
Hollocher, ss . .	21	2	4	0	1	0	1	1	1	1	.190
Deal, 3b	17	0	3	0	0	0	0	0	1	0	.176
Killefer, c	17	2	2	1	0	0	2	2	0	0	.118
Vaughn, p . . .	10	0	0	0	0	0	0	0	5	0	.000
O'Farrell, c . . .	3	0	0	0	0	0	0	0	0	0	.000
Barber, ph	2	0	0	0	0	0	0	0	0	0	.000
McCabe, ph . .	1	1	0	0	0	0	0	0	0	0	.000
Wortman, 2b . .	1	0	0	0	0	0	0	0	0	0	.000
Zeider, 3b . . .	0	0	0	0	0	0	0	2	0	0	.000
	176	10	37	5	1	0	10	18	14	3	.210

CHICAGO — PITCHING

	IP	BH	WON	LOST	R	ER	BB	SO	ERA
Phil Douglas	1	1	0	1	1	0	0	0	0.00
Claude Hendrix	1	0	0	0	0	0	0	0	0.00
Hippo Vaughn	27	17	1	2	3	3	5	17	1.00
Lefty Tyler	23	14	1	1	5	3	11	4	1.17
	52	32	2	4	9	6	16	21	1.04

Each Sox Regular Receives $1,108.45

Money talked at Fenway Park yesterday and had the floor all day. After splitting up the winners' share of the series money, $20,837.45, some of the World Champion Red Sox started for home and essential occupations. The rest of them will be on their way soon.

At a meeting of the regulars in Manager Barrow's office, shares amounting to $1,108.45 each were awarded to Manager Barrow, Capt. Hooper, Strunk, Whiteman, McInnis, Shean, Scott, Agnew, Mayer, Bush, Schang, Jones, Mays, Ruth and Wagner; $750 was given to Fred Thomas; $500 to Trainer Martin Lawlor; $300 each to Sec. Larry Graver, players

Pertica, Kinney, Miller, Dubuc, and Cochran, who joined the team late in the season; Dick Hoblitzell, who was captain when he departed to accept an Army commission, and Dutch Leonard.

Groundkeeper Jerome Kelley received $100, the clubhouse boy and mascot $25 each and the veteran groundkeeper, John Haggerty, long a familiar figure about Boston ball parks, $117.45.

Edward F. Martin, *Boston Globe*

[The Red Sox opposed the National Commission's edict by refusing to split the money equally. Fifteen players got full shares and eight players received lesser amounts.]

The quince is divided, and the lock has been snapped on home plate. It's all over.

Eddie Hurley, *Boston Record*

NO DOUBT IT WILL BE LIKE THIS
NOW THAT THE WORLD SERIES IS CASHED IN

Scott, *Boston Post*

War Gives Whiteman His Opportunity, Jumps from Obscurity to Series Hero

When courageous, little George Whiteman, after completing the greatest play in the World's Series last Wednesday, was compelled to leave the game by an injury sustained in spearing that sharp line drive of Barber's, he was accorded the greatest tribute ever paid to a player.

Rising as one, many with their hats removed, the fans cheered the game veteran to the echo as he limped painfully from the field and entered the shadow of the Boston dugout. It was probably the last tribute that the Texan will ever receive from such an aggregation.

Seldom in a world's series do stars come through in the way expected, and Whiteman played far more brilliantly than Cobb, Speaker or Honus Wagner ever showed.

According to Harry Hooper, Whiteman acquitted himself as no National or American league star ever did before. It is almost pathetic to think that big league baseball will probably know him no more.

Paul H. Shannon, *Boston Post*

George Whiteman carried home the big black bat that broke up the world's series. It's made of Cuban wood and George would not part with it. He used this bat when he hit the ball that Max Flack dropped and Whitey claims it's lucky.

Babe Ruth tried to win the bat from Whiteman before the latter started for Texas, but there was nothing doing. Whiteman and Ruth used this bat most of the season and it was considered the luckiest piece of wood in the bat pile.

Eddie Hurley, *Boston Record*

The World Champions of 1918

Fred G. Lieb of the New York Sun says:

"The World Series between the Red Sox and the Cubs was the finest exhibition of baseball yet seen in the classic. It was the best played series in the 15 year history of the event.

"For the first time a team fielded its way into the world's championship. One misjudged fly ball, which Whiteman lost in the sun, was the only mistake charged against the Red Sox.

"It was against this stone wall defense that Chicago was obliged to hammer. The Red Sox never provided the Cubs with any breaks."

Harry J. Casey, Boston Record

POSTSCRIPT

Boston Red Sox

After a fast start in 1919, the Red Sox slipped out of the first division in late May. They struggled for the rest of the year and finished in sixth place, twenty and a half games behind the Chicago White Sox. Boston's 66–71 record was their worst since 1907. The Red Sox didn't post another winning season until 1935, finishing last nine times during that period.

Carl Mays

Carl had a frustrating start in 1919, winning 5 games and losing 11, despite a team-leading 2.48 earned run average. He was losing to the White Sox 4–0 on July 13 when a throw by catcher Wally Schang clipped him on the side of the head during a steal attempt. Disgusted by his terrible support, Mays stormed off the mound, slammed down his glove, and blew into the clubhouse.

Mays never played another game for the Red Sox. President Frazee traded him to the New York Yankees a few weeks later; there he finished the year winning 9 games while losing only 3, with a dazzling 1.65 earned run average.

Carl went 26–11 in 1920 and then led the Yankees to their first pennant in 1921, with a 27–9 record. Although he finished his career with 207 victories against only 126 defeats, he will always be remembered as the pitcher who killed Ray Chapman with a beanball in 1920.

Joe Bush

Joe missed almost the entire 1919 season because of a sore arm, pitching only 9 innings without earning a victory. He recovered from his arm miseries and won 31 games over the next two seasons with the Red Sox.

Bush was sent to the New York Yankees in 1922 and led them to the American League pennant, winning 26 games while losing only 7. He went on to win 19 games in 1923 to help the Yankees win their first World Series. Joe finished his career with 195 wins, only 46 of them with the Red Sox.

Dutch Leonard

Dutch was traded to the Yankees following the 1918 season, but he refused to report to them. He was sent on to Detroit, where he won 14 games in 1919. Leonard pitched for the Tigers through 1924 and finished his career with 139 wins.

Sam Jones

Sam had a tired arm in 1919 and was a 20-game loser for the Red Sox. After another poor season, he bounced back with 23 wins in 1921. He was rewarded with a trade to the New York Yankees, leading the Bronx Bombers to their first world championship in 1923 with 21 wins and only 8 defeats. Jones finished his stellar career in 1935 with 229 victories, only 64 of those wins with the Red Sox.

Harry Hooper

Harry was stricken with Spanish influenza at the start of the 1919 season and struggled the entire year, finishing with a .267 batting average. He rebounded in 1920 with a solid .312 season. But when he sought a salary raise, Harry was traded to the Chicago White Sox in 1921.

Hooper went on to play five seasons with the White Sox, batting over .300 three more times. The greatest right fielder in Red Sox history was elected to the Hall of Fame in 1971.

Stuffy McInnis

Stuffy batted .305 in 1919 but scored only 32 runs, with just one home run. After two more solid seasons with Boston he was sent to Cleveland in 1922. McInnis finished his nineteen-year career in 1926 with 2,406 base hits and a lifetime average of .308.

Dave Shean

The veteran second baseman batted a paltry .140 in 1919, with only 14 hits. His career was over.

Fred Thomas

Fred never played another game for Boston. After the World Series he was sent to the Philadelphia Athletics, where he became the starting third baseman in 1919. Thomas's career was over after 1920, with just three years in the big leagues. His lifetime batting average was only .225.

Amos Strunk

The fleet center fielder was hitting a solid .272 midway through the 1919 season when the Red Sox sent him back to Connie Mack's Philadelphia Athletics. He played until 1924 with both the A's and the White Sox, batting .332 for Chicago in 1921. Strunk spent only one and a half years in Boston; his career spanned seventeen years, with a lifetime .283 average.

Wally Schang

Wally batted .306 in 1919 and .305 in 1920. His reward was being traded to the New York Yankees the next year.

The veteran catcher helped the Yankees win the pennant in 1921 with a great .316 season. Schang caught for New York during three straight pennants and their first world championship in 1923. He finished his career in 1931 with six .300 seasons and a lifetime .284 batting average.

Everett Scott

The brilliant shortstop was at the top of his game in 1919, batting .278 and fielding superbly. After two more solid seasons with Boston he was traded to the Yankees in 1922, anchoring their infield for the next three years.

Scott was one of the premiere shortstops of his era and played in 1,307 consecutive games, a record that was broken eventually by Lou Gehrig.

Babe Ruth

Babe became the greatest slugger in baseball in 1919, shattering the major league record with 29 home runs. He also led the American League with 103 runs and 114 runs batted in. However, his career as a pitcher was winding down, as he won only 9 games while losing 5.

The Colossus was sold to the New York Yankees on January 5, 1920. Bostonians reeled in shock as FOR SALE signs were exhibited at Faneuil Hall, the Boston Public Library, and the Boston Common.

Babe went on to crush 54 home runs while batting .376 in 1920 for the Yankees. He finished his career with 714 home runs, but only 49 were hit with Boston. Ruth was elected to the Hall of Fame in 1936.

Since Boston sold Babe Ruth to New York, the Yankees have won twenty-four world championships. The Red Sox have not won since 1918.

George Whiteman

The star of the 1918 World Series never played another game in the major leagues. The Red Sox sold him back to the minors in March 1919. He continued playing until 1929, retiring at the age of forty-seven. Whiteman set a minor league record with 3,282 games played and had 3,388 base hits.

Edward Barrow

Barrow managed in Boston through 1920, leading the Red Sox to two second-division finishes. He became the general manager of the New York Yankees in 1921, helping them win eleven pennants and eight world championships. Barrow was president of the Yankees from 1939 to 1945 and was elected to the Hall of Fame in 1953.

Harry Frazee

President Frazee sold or traded eleven players from the 1918 Red Sox during the three years following their World Series victory, most of them going to the New York Yankees. He desperately needed cash to support his Broadway plays, his ex-wife's alimony payments, and his creditors. Frazee finally sold the last-place Boston Red Sox on July 11, 1923, for $1,250,000.

A Letter by Harry Hooper*

SANTA CRUZ, CAL.
May 10, 1973

Bowie Kuhn
Commissioner of Baseball
New York, N.Y.

My Dear Commissioner:

Last August at Cooperstown I gave you a verbal account of the 1918 World Series. You said you would investigate the matter. I have been hoping for a letter from you.

In his book *The Boston Red Sox*, Fred Lieb claims to have been one of the newspapermen who were in the crowded umpires' room in the Red Sox ball park. Lieb gives a fairly accurate account of the meeting.

He wrote, "In high humor and about three sheets [to] the wind, Ban [Johnson] reached the park about five minutes before game time to learn that the entire park was waiting for him."

[Commissioner] Herrmann was the first to talk, but after a short oration on his accomplishments and what he had done for baseball, he was pushed aside by Ban Johnson, who started to talk in his bombastic way. Then he stopped, broke down, and started to cry. He came over and put his arm around my neck and cried on my shoulder. "Go out and play, Harry. I love you Harry, so go out and play." He kept repeating, "I love you Harry, go out and play. For the honor and glory of the American League, go out and play."

No one else had a chance to talk. I looked at Les Mann [Chicago's outfielder and captain], pushed Johnson away, and, addressing the newspapermen, said, "It is apparent that we have no one to talk to. Please excuse us and we will go back and talk to the players."

Les and I went back and explained that the commissioners were drunk and in no condition to talk. There were 24,000-plus fans waiting to watch the game. After discussing the matter we finally decided that we had no chance of getting them to split the gate as it always had been. Not wanting to punish the fans, we decided to play the game.

Les and myself went back to the umpires' room. Addressing the commissioners and the newspapermen, I said, "The members of both teams, not wishing to disappoint the crowd, decided to finish out the series on one condition, that no action will be taken by the commission against either club or members of the clubs."

Ban Johnson shouted, "Go out and play, everything will be all right. No action will be taken. Just go out and play."

With that the meeting broke up in confusion. We had made one mistake; we didn't get the members of the commission to sign the agreement that no action would be taken.

Shortly before Christmas each member of the Red Sox champions received a letter from [Commissioner] Heydler which stated, "Owing to the disgraceful actions of the players in the strike during the Series, each member of the team is fined the Series emblems and none would be given."

You are probably thinking that it's been so long ago I do not remember. But this matter has been kept fresh in my memory by my repeated attempts to get the players' emblems that they won in a hotly contested series.

---

*Edited with permission from John Hooper, Harry's son.

Many regulars' [positions] were filled by minor leaguers: Dave Shean, Geo. Whiteman, who was the fielding star of the series, and Fred Thomas. These men had their first and only opportunity to participate in a World Series. They probably would have been glad to get only their emblem. They are all gone so far as I know, but their next of kin could receive the pins and emblems.

The only thing the ballplayers were asking for was that the division of the first four games be made in the usual manner. We had heard rumors that the purse was to be divided among the players of the first four teams [in each league]. We were never consulted and didn't know the commissioners were going to divide it four ways until after we had played the first two games.

There was actually no strike. The game was delayed over an hour because two commissioners showed up drunk. Heydler, the chairman, never spoke one word at the meeting at the ball park. I could never figure whether he was stoned or dead sober.

I was playing in a golf game with Landis [baseball commissioner from 1920 to 1944] when I told him about the so-called strike and being fined our emblems. He said, "That's the first time I heard about this. I want you to write me a report and I will look into it."

I wrote a detailed account in longhand covering several long sheets of paper. I never ever received a reply. I took it up with more commissioners afterwards but never heard from them.

A number of times I have been interviewed about the so-called strike. But in almost every case the interviewer would twist the story so there were a number of different accounts of the event attributed to me.

I have a letter from Mr. Spink, the owner of the *Sporting News*, dated Nov. 1, 1951.

> I don't believe you will ever forget that day that Ban Johnson made his famous speech at Fenway Park. That was quite an incident, wasn't it? It would have been considerably more than an incident if you and Les Mann had not shown the consideration you did.
>
> With all good wishes and kindest regards.
>
> Charles G. Spink and Son

Another letter [by Mr. Spink] dated May 17, 1961, recalled the incident.

> I will never forget the meeting in the umpires room at Fenway Park, when you and Les Mann were waiting the arrival of Ban Johnson to discuss a bigger cut from the series. It was a war year. The game had been held up. Mr. Johnson (slightly under the weather) put his arm around you and told you to go out and play for the honor of the American League. You went.

I didn't intend to write so long and I hope you don't have too much trouble reading it.

What I had hoped you would do, and still hope, is that you will research the Boston papers printed the day after and following that game, September 10, 1918.

I hope this finds you and yours in good health. I am feeling OK. Bothered by arthritis. Also slipped off a step and sprained my achilles tendon. I was on crutches for five weeks. Still not walking too good, but am able to drive my car.

Appreciating a reply.

Most sincerely yours,

Harry Hooper

AFTERWORD

Just before Christmas, 1918, John Heydler, chairman of baseball's National Commission, wrote a letter to every member of the world champion Boston Red Sox team. It read, "Owing to the disgraceful actions of the players in the strike during the Series, each member of the team is fined the Series emblems and none would be given."

Infuriated over this decision, Red Sox president Harry Frazee announced, "The team that won the world's championship in the concluding year of the world's greatest war deserves a suitable memento. The men will get them."

It didn't happen. The commissioners, including President Ban Johnson, never gave the players their due reward. Harry Hooper, as captain of the team, appealed to every baseball commissioner until his death in 1974. His quest for justice was repeatedly ignored.

Following his father's death John Hooper took up the cause. But another twenty years went by without any response from Major League Baseball. The 1918 team became a forgotten footnote in baseball history. Hooper, Mays, Ruth, and Barrow went to their graves without receiving a series pin, pennant, emblem, or any official award.

In 1993 a glimmer of hope appeared when Glenn Stout wrote an article in *New England Sport*, the journal of the New England Sports Museum. Entitled "The Last Champions," Stout revealed Ban Johnson's vendetta against Harry Frazee and the 1918 Boston Red Sox, which led to the denial of their awards.

Stout and his editor, Fred Kirsch, collected several thousand petitions outside Fenway Park and asked both the Red Sox management and Major League Baseball to grant the World Series emblems to the 1918 champions.

The Boston Red Sox responded by organizing a special ceremony for the descendants of the 1918 world champions. Babe Ruth's daughter, Harry Hooper's son, Fred Thomas's wife, and Harry Frazee's great-grandson were among the small group of relatives who belatedly received the 1918 championship emblems at Fenway Park on September 4, 1993.

"I want to thank the Boston Red Sox for taking this step," said John Hooper. "All through the years my Dad, Harry Hooper, made requests to every baseball commissioner to get medals awarded the players, realizing that many of them would have no further chance to get such an award. When my Dad died I continued the quest. Now the Boston Red Sox have shown courage and consideration to see that the medals are awarded."[*]

More than 31,000 fans endured a chilly New England rain to view the unique awards ceremony, while family members stepped on the field to receive a stick-pin similar to the award that should have been given in 1918. It read, "WORLD'S CHAMPIONS—1918—BOSTON RED SOX."

The Boston Red Sox and Major League Baseball gave a wonderful tribute to the 1918 team. On the eve of the seventy-fifth anniversary of Babe Ruth's 1–0 shutout against the Chicago Cubs, the 1918 world championship pennant was slowly raised above the center field bleachers, while the fans rose to honor those long-deceased players with a standing ovation.

---

[*]Boston Red Sox press release, "1918 Red Sox Champions Finally Awarded," August 26, 1993.

Justice has now been served to Harry Hooper, Dave Shean, George Whiteman, and the rest of the 1918 Boston Red Sox players. It is time to move on and overcome the so-called curse that has been hanging over the Red Sox for the past eighty years. Perhaps this will be the year the Red Sox finally win another World Series.

Ty Waterman and Mel Springer

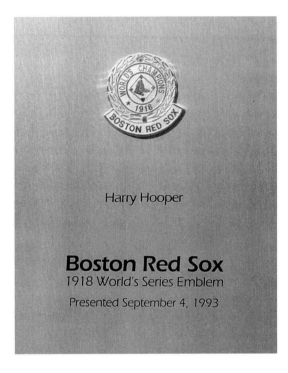

GLOSSARY

agate	baseball	keystone	second base
apple	baseball	lammed	hit soundly
barker	coach	marker	run
big show	world war	mooched	ambled, wandered
bingle	base hit	onion	baseball
bludgeon	bat	orchard	ball park
box	pitching mound	pan	home plate
boxmen	pitchers	pill	baseball
bunting	pennant	pill server	pitcher
buzzer	fastball	pillows	bases
canto	run	portsider	left-hander
counting station	home plate	sacks crushed	bases loaded
crepe hanger	agent of gloom	shine ball	illegal pitch
cripple	3 and 0 pitch	slabmen	pitchers
cushion	base	soaked the apple	hit the ball hard
deadhead	give a walk	spangles	baseball uniform
domestics	home team	spheroid	baseball
dope	inside information	station	base
flail	bat	swag	profits, money
fliverred	failed, flopped	whale	smash the ball
foozle	error	whanged	whacked the ball hard
frank	base on balls	willow	bat
garden	outfield		
gonfalon	flag or pennant		
hassock	base		
the Hub	Boston		
kalsomine brush	shutout		

THE SPORTSWRITERS

The real authors of *The Year the Red Sox Won the Series* are the sportswriters. They traveled with the teams, were frequently paid room and board by the ball clubs, and wrote with a colorful, partisan style that portrayed their deep love of the game. We owe a debt of gratitude to them for this book.

Harry J. Casey—*Boston Record*
(1886–1918)

Harry Casey had been the sports editor of the *Boston Record* for three years when he contracted the Spanish influenza and died in December 1918. His death came as a shock to his colleagues and friends. During his short career Casey also wrote for the *Boston Herald*, the *Boston Traveler*, and the *Worcester Telegram*.

James Crusinberry—*Chicago Tribune*
(1879–1960)

James Crusinberry had a long and distinguished career as a sportswriter for five Chicago papers, including the *Chicago Tribune* (1911–1921). In 1910 Crusinberry founded the "Pink Sheet," a baseball news publication covering the Chicago White Sox and Chicago Cubs.

Crusinberry was the first sports editor for the *New York Daily News* (1921–1924) and a radio sports commentator for CBS until his retirement in 1948.

A charter member of the Baseball Writer's Association and the president of the BBWAA in 1929–1930, Crusinberry was best known for helping reveal the story of the 1919 Chicago Black Sox scandal. He was honored in 1958 by being asked to throw out the first ball of the World Series in Milwaukee.

L. C. Davis—*St. Louis Post-Dispatch*
(1865–1940)

Lynn Carlisle Davis began his literary career by sending anonymous jingles about sports events and personalities to the *St. Louis Post-Dispatch*. The editor was impressed and printed a public appeal in the sports section asking L. C. to call him.

Davis left his clerical position and wrote a column known as "Sports Salad" from 1912 until his death. His gentle, humorous prose and poems were printed on the *Post-Dispatch's* comic page under the title "The Man on the Sandbox."

A dignified, quiet gentleman, Davis brought joy to his readers throughout his long career. Several of his poems, including "Ty Cobb vs. Germany," appear in this book.

Charles Dryden—Syndicated Columnist
(1869–1931)

Reporting for newspapers in San Francisco, New York City, Philadelphia, and Chicago, Charley Dryden coined many famous baseball phrases. His assessment of the pitiful Senators, "Washington: first in war, first in peace, and last in the American League," became a classic. Dryden was the first writer to call a baseball park a "ball yard" and to use the term "pitcher's mound."

Owing to his candid style of reporting, Dryden was barred by the New York Giants' owner from entering the Polo Grounds in 1906. He climbed a telephone pole outside the ballpark and wrote his stories while perched on the crossbar.

One of baseball's wittiest writers, Charley Dryden received the J. G. Taylor Spink Award at the Hall of Fame induction ceremony in 1965.

Arthur Duffey—*Boston Post*
(1879–1955)

"Duff" was once considered the fastest human being in the world. A sprinter in the 1900 Paris Olympics, he set the world record for the 100-yard dash in 1902, with a mark of 9.6 seconds. An international celebrity, Duffey's mailing address was "Nine and Three-Fifths."

Duffey joined the *Boston Post* staff in 1908 and wrote a popular column called "Answers to Queries," which resolved many a sports argument throughout Boston.

Bob Dunbar—*Boston Herald and Journal*

Dunbar was a fictitious name. Articles in the column "Sporting Comment" with his byline were ghostwritten by anonymous writers.

James V. Fitzgerald—*Washington Post*
(1889–1976)

Fitzgerald was the sports editor, city editor, and editorial writer for the *Washington Post* from 1917 to 1925. He later authored five books, served as an assistant to President Truman, and was the Director of Information for the Labor Department.

Nick Flatley—*Boston Evening American*
(1886–1930)

Flatley served as baseball editor for several Boston papers and wrote for the *Evening American* beginning in 1913. His strong advocacy helped lift the ban on Sunday professional and amateur athletics in Massachusetts in 1929. A very colorful writer, Flatley's article "Strike! Strike! Strike!" was a classic tale of the 1918 World Series.

Hugh S. Fullerton—Syndicated Columnist
(1873–1945)

Fullerton was the writer who first broke the story of the 1919 Black Sox scandal. A nationally renowned columnist, he wrote for the *Cincinnati Enquirer* in the 1890s, Chicago's *Tribune*, *American*, and *Record*, the *New York World*, and several other papers.

One of the original organizers of the Baseball Writer's Association, Fullerton specialized in forecasting the exact number of hits, runs, and errors that teams would make in the World Series. Considered one of the great writers of the early twentieth century, Fullerton coined the word "dope," meaning inside information.

He received the J. G. Taylor Spink Award at the Hall of Fame induction ceremony in 1964.

Eddie Hurley—*Boston Record*
(1889–1938)

A hard-working columnist, Hurley was an all-round expert on sports. He covered horse racing, football, baseball, and boxing throughout his career with the *Boston Traveler*, *Lynn News*, and *Boston Record*. Hurley's stories are tinged with humor; they include pieces about Joe Bush's vocal cords and Connie Mack's watch fob.

Ring Lardner—*Chicago Tribune*
(1885–1933)

Lardner wrote more than 4,500 articles for numerous papers, including the *Chicago Tribune*, the *Sporting News*, and the *Saturday Evening Post*. His nationally syndicated column appeared in more than a hundred newspapers.

Lardner's special humor and slang made him one of the top writers of the early twentieth century. His "You Know Me, Al" stories, about an eccentric baseball rookie, which were based on Lardner's experiences covering the White Sox and Cubs, helped thrust him into national prominence.

A devoted baseball fan, Lardner suspected the White Sox of throwing the 1919 World Series. On a train ride to Chicago during the series, Lardner walked through the White Sox car singing, "I'm forever blowing ball games." He was so disenchanted by the scandal that he eventually stopped reporting baseball and going to games.

Ring Lardner received the J. G. Taylor Spink Award in 1963 at the Hall of Fame induction ceremony.

Edward F. Martin—*Boston Globe*
(1884–1918)

The witty, popular baseball writer for the *Boston Globe* died a few weeks after the season ended. Martin was stricken during the terrible 1918 flu epidemic, dying one day after his wife.

A *Boston Globe* employee from 1900, Martin was the police and fire headquarters reporter before replacing the late Tim Murnane as the American League baseball reporter.

James C. O'Leary—*Boston Globe*
(1862–1948)

"Uncle Jim" was the dean of American baseball writers at the time of his death. He started in 1889 as a telegrapher and eventually became the *Globe*'s baseball editor for three decades. O'Leary was identified by the bow ties and felt sombreros he had worn since he was a correspondent in the Spanish-American War.

An intimate with hundreds of ball players, "Uncle Jim" O'Leary was everybody's friend, except when playing bridge or poker.

Robert L. Ripley—*Boston Globe*
(1894–1949)

A world-famous cartoonist, Ripley made a fortune with his "Believe It or Not" cartoons that were syndicated in three hundred newspapers. He was a radio and TV entertainer, an author, and a star of movie shorts, and he had exhibits in both the Chicago and New York World's Fairs.

Ripley's career began in 1910, when the *San Francisco Bulletin* hired him to draw sports cartoons. He arrived in New York in 1913 as a cartoonist for the *New York Globe* and drew two or three cartoons a week in 1918 for the *Boston Globe*.

Irving E. Sanborn—*Chicago Tribune*
(Birth and death dates unavailable)

Sy Sanborn went to the *Chicago Tribune* in 1900 after nine years as the sports editor of the *Springfield* (Mass.) *Union*. He was an early confidant of Ban Johnson and Charles Comiskey during the formation of the American League.

A charter member of the Baseball Writer's Association, Sanborn served as its president for three years. He retired in 1921 after reporting almost 3,000 games.

Morris Scott—*Boston Post*
(1880–1922)

Morris Scott was a cartoonist and sketch writer for the *Boston Post* for fifteen years. His daily cartoon strip was a regular feature of the sports page. Scott was also the illustrator for the *Bingville Bugle*, the *Sunday Post*'s special supplement, after which Bing Crosby was named.

Scott was highly respected in newspaper circles; he was a very private man, devoted principally to his craft and his family.

Paul Shannon—*Boston Post*
(1876–1939)

The *Boston Post* sports editor for thirty-two years, Paul Shannon covered thirty-two consecutive World Series, a record that no other reporter in the country could match.

He was a practical joker, loved to play bridge, and read a book a day. As a charter member of the Baseball Writer's Association he carried card number two. Shannon was the president of the BBWAA when he died in a drowning accident in Florida.

Frank "Burt" Whitman—*Boston Herald and Journal*
(1887–1949)

Burt Whitman had been the sports editor of the *Boston Herald* for thirty-two years when he collapsed during a Red Sox–Browns game in St. Louis. A former president of the Baseball Writer's Association, Whitman was almost elected the National League president in 1934.

Admired by peers and players alike, Whitman had a special relationship with Ted Williams, whom he counseled during some rough moments in Williams's career.

A gentleman of high integrity, Whitman wrote the lead stories in this book for the first two games of the 1918 World Series.

We offer our gratitude to the rest of the sportwriters and cartoonists in our book.

Henry Daily, Francis Eaton, H. W. Lanigan, and T. E. Powers of the *Boston American;*

Bugs Baer, Wallace Goldsmith, Rex Prouty, and Melville Webb of the *Boston Globe;*

John J. Hallahan of the *Boston Herald and Journal;*

Billy Evans of the *Boston Post;*

Arthur Sears Henning and M. F. Murphy of the *Chicago Tribune;*

"Wampus" of the *Cleveland Press;*

Tom Powers of the *Detroit News;*

Berndt of the *New York Journal;*

W. J. Macbeth of the *New York Tribune;*

Milton Bronner of *Stars and Stripes.*

BIBLIOGRAPHY

Books

Boswell, John, and David Fisher. *Fenway Park*. Boston: Little, Brown, 1992.

Creamer, Robert W. *Babe*. New York: Simon and Schuster, 1974.

Golenbock, Peter. *Fenway*. New York: G. P. Putnam's Sons, 1992.

Lieb, Fred. *The Boston Red Sox*. New York: G. P. Putnam's Sons, 1947.

Ruth, Babe, and Bob Considine. *The Babe Ruth Story*. New York: Penguin Books, 1948.

Shaughnessy, Dan. *The Curse of the Bambino*. New York: Dutton, 1990.

Sowell, Mike. *The Pitch That Killed*. New York: Macmillan, 1989.

Thorn, John, and Pete Palmer. *Total Baseball*. New York: Warner Books, 1989.

Wagenheim, John. *Babe Ruth: His Life and Legend*. New York: Henry Holt, 1974.

Zingg, Paul J. *Harry Hooper: An American Baseball Life*. Urbana and Chicago: University of Illinois Press, 1993.

Newspapers

Boston American, 1917–18; October 14, 1930.

Boston Globe, 1917–18; March 18, 1948; March 29, 1949.

Boston Herald and Journal, 1917–18; May 9, 1949.

Boston Post, 1917–18; December 5, 1922; January 21, 1939; January 25, 1955.

Boston Record, 1917–18; July 5, 1938.

Chicago Daily Tribune, 1918.

Cleveland Press, 1918.

Detroit News, 1918.

New York Journal, 1918.

New York Times, 1918; February 13, 1931; December 28, 1945; July 2, 1960.

Philadelphia Evening-Bulletin, 1918.

St. Louis Post-Dispatch, 1918; March 8, 1940.

Washington Post, 1918; August 26, 1976.

INDEX

Illustrations are indicated by italic page numbers. Page numbers on which newspaper names are given as sources of articles or cartoons are not listed here.

The Year the Red Sox Won the Series